THE CHARGE OF BRIT BRIGADE

Tales from Post-Socialist Prague

JO WEAVER

Book design by creationbooth.com

DISCLAIMER
Most names and identifying features of the people who appear in this memoir have been changed to protect anonymity. In addition, some of the plots and quite a lot of the timeline have been altered, often for similar reasons.

Dedication

To Mum. You always said you were "small but perfectly formed".
You had the biggest brain and the kindest heart and always
encouraged me to take risks and "go for it". Without you, I would
never have done any of the things I ended up doing, good or bad.
I hope you are somewhere up there getting ready to read this.

"Pleased to meet you," I responded.
"I'm Joanna. Well, everyone calls me 'Jo'.
I suppose you know that."

What a Godforsaken Place!

"GOOD EVENING, LADIES and gentlemen. This is your captain speaking. We have just landed in Prague, where the temperature outside is minus 20 degrees."

What did he say? Minus 20 degrees? Does that mean we can't get off the plane? Is it dangerous? As if being delayed three hours on our flight from Paris to Prague wasn't enough. I looked around at the handful of equally weary passengers and wondered if they were all as depressed as I was to be landing in such a godforsaken place. Difficult to say. But after a long day of travelling, I wasn't going to hang about and, as we pulled up at the somewhat ramshackle stand, I grabbed my handbag and was first down the steps and onto the narrow path that had been shovelled through the snow to enable us to make our way into what appeared to be an aircraft hanger, nearly falling arse-over-tit as my smart black court shoes skidded on sheet ice.

It was just before midnight on the first of December 1990. Just over a year since the 'Velvet Revolution' that saw the then Czechoslovakia escape from the claws of communism and head towards being a 'normal' Western country. At that time, only three flights a week flew from London to Prague and one of those was via Paris – the one I was on – such was the demand (or lack thereof). The arrivals hall, if you could call it that, had just a handful of customs officers hanging around and looking as if they were from a Second World War movie, and all were looking suspiciously at us strange foreigners as we made our way inside, hanging onto their machine guns as if they might pull the trigger at any minute.

And then, after standing shivering at the one carousel that was bringing in our bags for about half an hour, I found that it wasn't actually bringing mine, and so had the challenge of finding someone – anyone – that could help me to make sure that my luggage did, eventually, turn up. Somehow, I managed to find the one member of staff that wasn't a police officer and who was still working and, even more surprisingly, managed to explain what I needed by way of a bit of German, a bit of English and a lot of hand-waving. Whether that had worked, I wasn't sure, but by the time I had signed the completely illegible forms and walked outside, all the taxis had gone home and the airport was shutting up for the night. And there I was, standing alone in the cold wondering what on earth I should do, and, being a bit of a catastrophist, imagining myself left stranded and freezing to death fairly soon, with no-one around who would know who I was when they found my body.

Luckily, and it really was a life-saver since there were no such things as mobile phones – or any sort of phone at all at that time – just as I was imagining the worst, a lone old Skoda rattled up and a slightly dodgy-looking and elderly driver leant out and asked me if I needed a taxi. Or at least, I assumed that was what he said, since it was all in a completely unrecognisable language. But, since there were no other options as far as I could see, I leapt in anyway, and we coughed and spluttered our way into the city centre.

It was difficult to tell what Prague really looked like on that first journey. It was so cold, the air was full of snow and smog, and the old boy driving had to keep wiping at the windscreen to clear a hole in the fug that covered most of it, while holding the wheel with one hand. Since there was so little lighting along the streets and few other cars, it was difficult to know how many times we might or might not have had a collision. But somehow, within about 40 minutes, we were pulling up in front of the communist-style monstrosity known as the Continental Hotel, which was to be my home for the three weeks I was in Prague to work.

The hotel was one of just a handful that had permission from the former communist regime to open in the 60s and was, I soon found out, the workplace for most of Prague's prostitutes, as well as the scene for many a shoot-out between rival mafia groups. It wasn't that surprising – in retrospect, it was at the time! – that the first thing I noticed as I walked towards the entrance was a big picture of a gun stuck to the glass, with a red line through it and the words 'no guns' underneath. Well, thank God I had forgotten mine.

I felt a bit like I imagined my dad must have felt when he arrived in London just before the war. His Austrian Jewish parents had sent him as a little kid on one of the 'Kinder trains' and he had ended up being transported to work on a farm in Somerset. According to Mum, the only good thing that could be said about his time there was that he learned to speak English fluently. He was not just any old kid either, he came from a very grand family who were direct descendants of a famous composer. Most of his grandness was knocked out of him while he was in the UK and then on his return to Austria in 1946, when he found out that all of his family had perished in Auschwitz. He then met my mum in Vienna where she had been sent by the British Foreign Office, having worked as a codebreaker during the war and, soon after meeting, they got married and moved back to the UK a few years later.

It was due to my Central European roots that the HR woman in the London-based merchant bank I had just started working for had suggested I do a stint in Czechoslovakia since, as was the case with so many English people in those days, she didn't really understand that there was any real difference between the different European countries. Many still don't!

Anyway, there I was, in a dark and hostile town where I knew no-one, couldn't speak the language, and had no idea what was going to happen next. Plus, I had absolutely no luggage, although that did turn up miraculously three days later and, since the bank demanded that us ladies only wear skirts to work, and as I had gone straight to the airport from the office in a fairly lightweight dress and coat, I was completely under-dressed for the freezing weather conditions.

The morning after I arrived, I was met in the hotel reception by a tall and willowy Czech girl called Monika, who I had been told to look out for and who wasn't immediately obvious, since the whole place was full of tall and willowy Czech girls. Then I spotted her, pretty in a blond and pale-eyed sort of way, but also extremely unfriendly – which I soon found out to be the norm. After a brief greeting in broken English, she headed off out of the hotel ahead of me and down a rather grand snow-covered and deserted avenue, barely saying a word, until the road opened up into a huge and imposing square.

"Hang on, hang on," I said, as she marched along with her nose in the air. "What on earth is this? It's gorgeous!"

"It's Staroměstské náměsti, the Old Town Square. 14th Century. "What is this 'gorgeous' word?"

"Well, you know, it means lovely, beautiful."

I should just say here that it was absolutely bloody freezing, and I was slithering about all over the place in my court shoes as we tottered through the thick blanket of snow on the ground. Despite that, I had to stop and look around, much to Monika's annoyance. Encircled by the ever-present smog, the towers of the magnificent white cathedral on the corner disappeared up into the clouds, while, diagonally opposite, the whole square was overlooked by two towering and blackened gothic structures I later found out were the spires of the Týn Church, a landmark that could be seen from every viewpoint in the city.

I felt as if I had just walked onto a film set for a Victorian fairy-tale, or similar. There were horses and carriages lined up in front of the beautiful astronomical clock, the horses blowing out steam while the drivers huddled together, puffing on cigarettes, and looking around hopefully for any stray tourist daft enough to venture out in such weather. And, along each side of the square, rows of terraced houses painted in blue, green, pink and yellow pastels, which made the whole place look like some sort of glorified chocolate box. Who knew this was what a former Eastern Bloc country could look like? Certainly not me.

We made it to the office without exchanging another word, and since nothing, so far, had been anything like I had expected, I wasn't that surprised to find that my base for the next three weeks was just one of the two very small rooms the bank was subletting from a Czech law firm for the immediate future. Our office was situated on the fourth floor of a tall and narrow building just a few minutes' walk from the Old Town Square and we entered through a kind of reception area, where an enormous bald and elderly man (I later found out he was the somewhat notorious senior partner of the law firm) was standing talking to a young and dark-haired girl dressed in what appeared to be a large tissue and thigh-length boots. Both of them completely ignored Monika and me. We then walked across to a set of double doors which led into the bank's section, where, sitting in the first room was a rather unsavoury looking young guy that Monika, for some weird reason, appeared to have taken a shine to.

"Hi," he said, in a posh English voice, looking up from the papers he had scattered all over the large and rather nice old desk he was sitting at. He had a pair of glasses perched on his spotty nose and a strand of blond greasy hair sweeping across his forehead, which gave him a grubby look.

"I'm Michael. I've been here for two months, heading up the operations." That was surprising, since he looked about 25.

"Pleased to meet you," I responded. "I'm Joanna. Well, everyone calls me 'Jo'. I suppose you know that. I'm only here for three weeks, but I am ready to do whatever is necessary."

"Well, welcome to Prague then Joanna. Let's put you to work."

"You know, darling, that snake should never have been allowed to come to Prague."

Three Weeks is a Very Long Time

WITHIN A SHORT time of arriving in Prague, I was counting the days until I could return to London, since the whole Czech experience was so miserable. Mind you, as I was completely broke at the time, I was also counting the money I was saving since all my expenses were being paid for by the firm and there was absolutely nothing for me to buy. That was actually a good thing, since I am always partial to a bit of comfort spending.

Michael had proven to be completely obnoxious, which made each day quite difficult since we were sharing an office and, for the first week, it was just the two of us, with the occasional appearance of Monika, who tended to pitch up first thing and leave soon after to 'go to the bank' or somewhere, only arriving back much later in the day. One afternoon, when she wandered in at about 3.00 pm, I asked her rather apologetically, "Where exactly have you been all day?"

"What do you mean? I told you I went to the bank."

"But that was at 9.00 am. Surely you weren't there all morning!"

"Well, I was for most of it. I always have to queue for ages, and then today I met one of my friends who had also been queuing and she invited me for coffee. When I left her it was lunch time and I had to go and buy something to eat. I just got back now. Is that okay?"

Ah, I thought. *Of course. Silly of me to ask!* I later learned that during communism, when everyone was given a job and there was no real motivation to work hard or otherwise, people would literally clock in then go off and do what they wanted before arriving back to clock out at the end of their afternoon. Which was often at about 3.00 pm. No-one cared. Hence why Monika saw nothing wrong in spending most of her day out socialising.

Michael had no interest in what Monika was up to as long as she paid attention to him, since he clearly fancied the pants off her and she played up to him at every opportunity. In the meantime, I was rattling away on the old typewriter for hours on end, having admitted to being able to type on my first day in the office, and was now being treated as if I was there to be Michael's personal PA. To say I was aggrieved would be an understatement but since no-one else was giving me any guidance as to what I actually *should* be doing, I couldn't really complain.

Things improved marginally when a larger-than-life red-headed Czech woman called Eva pitched up in the office a few days after my arrival. As an 18-year-old troublemaker she had escaped the communist regime in the 70s by being smuggled from Czechoslovakia to London in an arranged marriage and shortly after arriving spent her time working as a waitress in a Tyrolean restaurant as she spoke fluent German and suited a *dirndl*, being, as she put it herself, rather rotund with large boobs. Somehow, and it was beyond everyone's imagination as to how she did it, she had learned English, studied in between waitressing, and managed to get a law degree before she joined the bank. According to her, although it was later disputed, when the 'Wall' came down in 1989, she had marched into the London boss' office and demanded they opened an office in her former home town since, 'it will be the next big place to do business,' and, as soon as the powers that be followed her advice, she spent two or three days a week in the newly opened Prague office, causing havoc.

Eva wasn't everyone's cup of tea, and I wasn't completely sure about her at first. She seemed to have pretty much every trait I disliked; she was loud, shrieked at everyone in her 'Greta Garbo' voice, called everyone 'darling' (bosses, clients, ministers), laughed way too loudly, was incapable of being anywhere less than an hour or so late and bitched about whoever crossed her path behind their back. She also smoked about 100 cigarettes a day and drank like a trooper. The only good thing I could see on her arrival was that she disliked Michael even more than I did, so the two of us kind of ganged up on him, often filling the room with so much smoke – I was already up to about 40 a day by then – that he had to leave and go for a walk to get some air.

I understood from Eva that she and I were supposed to be in charge of drumming up business for the bank, and, since Eva knew just about everyone in senior positions in the Czech political and business worlds – most of them having been former dissidents like her – she was very good at getting paths smoothed for existing clients and opening doors for us to pitch for business. Soon after she arrived, she told Michael to stop treating me like a secretary and dragged me out to help her with the various meetings she had set up, usually while flying in and out of Prague. This could be quite stressful since she was always hours late for everything, could never remember people's names and tended to forget what it was, exactly, that we were meeting them to discuss. Plus, most of the meetings we went to were primarily in Czech, which I barely understood a word of as yet. Eva, though, would rush about everywhere, her scarves flying behind her, perfume wafting about her head in a cloud, shrieking 'darling' this and 'darling' that and then we would sit down and start our pitch to whoever we were meeting, which, surprisingly to me, was usually successful.

One day we met with one of the Czech ministers up in the Prague Castle, (which is not actually a Castle in the traditional sense of the word, but is the huge expanse of buildings that tower over the city and that house many of the government offices), who Eva of course knew well, and, even though it was only about 10.00 am, he was thrilled to see her.

"Evička [an affectionate way of saying her name, meaning 'little Eva'], it has been so long since we last saw each other. Shall we have a small shot, yes?" He then produced a bottle of vintage whisky which the two of them proceeded to drink their way through while Eva flirted outrageously with him. Eventually, after we had been there for about an hour and I might as well have been invisible, the Minister agreed, without really knowing what we were there to persuade him to do for us, to do anything 'Evička' wanted him to do.

"Darling," she answered. "You have always been such a poppet, thank you." And then she flourished the paperwork we had prepared earlier, and he signed where he was told. Soon after, we tottered out and Eva roared with laughter. "Stupid old bugger, he has no idea what he has just signed! He always was an idiot."

Another advantage of Eva being in the office was that even though we worked long hours, she never wanted to go straight home at the end of the day since she stayed with her parents whenever she was in Prague and would persuade me, as if I needed persuading, to go with her to one of the two Czech restaurants she knew that had passable food. After a week of eating hot dogs from a kiosk on the Old Town Square, and then spending the rest of the evening in my hotel room, going out to a restaurant was the ultimate treat, even though it could be exhausting. Once there we would eat and drink way too much, puff our way through numerous cigarettes, and then she would hold forth about everything and anything, although most conversations ended up, eventually, with her talking about her dislike of the boss of the office, Clive. I was yet to meet him.

"You know, darling, that snake should never have been allowed to come to Prague," she would say, puffing away on her hundredth cigarette of the day. "He has no idea what he is doing and all the Czechs hate him. I should be the boss. It was my idea to open this office. But he is out to stop me. You'll see."

I let her rant, all the time thinking I had no intention of seeing anything much, since I would soon be leaving Prague and was definitely not planning on coming back. I was intrigued, nonetheless, to meet the famous Clive who, I had been told, was due to arrive the Monday of my final week.

That morning, I arrived in the office even earlier than usual and was surprised to see both Michael and Monika already at their desks, awaiting Clive's arrival. After everything I had heard from Eva, I wasn't really sure what to expect, but it definitely wasn't the rather glamorous and fair-haired 'British businessman' that burst through the doors halfway through the morning. He turned the air blue with his swearing about the taxi that had brought him in from the airport, patted Monika on the bottom (that was sort of allowed in those days) as he passed her heading out to make him coffee and then looked me up and down in a slightly lecherous way.

"You look like a good strong girl," were his first words. "Jo, isn't it? Short for Josephine?" He giggled to himself.

"Well, no," I responded. "It's Joanna actually. But everyone calls me 'Jo'."

"Bugger that. I will call you Josefina. Suits you better."

I realised straightaway that not only was Clive completely brilliant, he was also barking mad, having spent most of his professional life in Iraq and then Beijing. Whether he was mad before he went there, or he became so from being there wasn't clear, but the stories he could and did tell on a regular basis definitely cheered me up. Also, since he was staying in the same hotel as me and always wanted to go out to eat, we had two ridiculous nights out before he headed back to London. I honestly can't remember ever laughing as much.

He was what I would call a typical 'London banker' to look at. He was of a medium height and size, had fair hair that was slightly receding and the habit of rolling his eyes and wrinkling his nose every time he was warming up to tell a dirty story, which was most of the time. But God, he worked us hard. In between doing all the typing (I was still the only one that could), fighting with the telephone and fax machine (both of which rarely worked), running about to meetings with Eva, and trying to find new employees, which was more or less impossible, the days went on forever. And all the while, I counted my hours until it was time to leave, only feeling slightly sad I wouldn't see Eva and Clive again, but not in the least bit worried about missing the others.

"There are only two dishes here.
Both are vile."

16

The Dog & Duck

By the time I got back to London, it was nearly Christmas and all of my friends had been enjoying the party season and getting well and truly into the Christmas spirit. I, though, had gotten so down from the cold and grey of Prague that by the time I got off the plane, just three weeks after I had left, all I was interested in was sleeping a lot, eating some good food and having a rest. And by New Year, I was determined that I would never go back. Then, in early January, I was sitting minding my own business in my tiny little office in the City of London with nothing much to do when the same HR woman appeared at my door again.

"Hi, Joanna," she said with a nice bright smile on her face that didn't bode well. "You made such an impression in the Prague office they would like you to go back again. This time for six months. What do you say?"

"Prague? You've got to be joking!"

"Well, no," she answered. "I'm not, actually. They need someone like you and really there is not a lot work for you here in London." That sounded a little bit like a threat, but honestly, I couldn't think of anything I would want to do less and turned the opportunity flat down. Until, that is, my then boss called me in and advised that it wasn't really a good idea to say no, since, at that time, there was a good chance that a lot of us corporate finance people might soon be getting one of those 'letters left on our desks', which was the way that people were made redundant in those days. To cut a long story short, and much against my will, I agreed to return.

I had been back in Prague for a couple of weeks, and nothing had really changed, although it was possibly even colder and snowier than before Christmas. Michael was as annoying as ever, Monika was even lazier, and there was no sign yet of Eva or Clive after the Christmas break. I was back to staying in the Continental Hotel, where I had already heard of two different shoot-outs in the bar between rival gangs regarding some dodgy dealings by the sex

17

workers and pimps that hung around all day and night looking for punters. Despite that, I had managed to get a bit friendly with a few of the girls that worked the bar as I had made it a habit to sit downstairs some evenings just to avoid another long night in my room, even if I had to duck the bullets.

What *was* different, though, was that part of the new deal I had struck with the bank was that they would pay for me to fly back to London every other weekend. And on my return from my first return trip, early one Monday morning, I made a friend. While I was standing by the luggage carousel waiting to see if my luggage would arrive this time, I was hailed by a very good-looking, tall, dark and clearly dangerous English guy. I could spot the type from a hundred metres away.

"Excuse me, darling," he said in a very sexy voice, edging around the carousel to where I was standing. "We haven't met before. I'm Simon Sharp." He paused, piercing blue eyes giving me the once over. Clearly, I was supposed to know his name.

"I'm Joanna. Or Jo as most people call me," I replied, not giving very much away. "So, what are you doing here, Simon Sharp?"

"I run a real estate company with my partner Jonathan Fox. We specialise in looking for apartments for expats moving to Prague. Maybe you need one?"

"That would be great," I replied. "But I'm not sure if my company will fund an apartment just for me. How does it work?"

"I'll explain it all to you tonight. I'll be out with Jonathan, so join us and I can introduce you to a couple of other expats that we have already found flats for. Where are you staying? I'll pick you up at about 8.00 pm."

Well, why not, I thought. Even if they can't find me a flat, at least I can meet some new people. So, at 8.00 pm that evening, I came down to the hotel reception and found Simon pacing around, puffing on his cigarette and looking shifty.

"Ah, there you are," he said, with a quick glance over at two of the working girls sitting at the bar. "Let's get out of here. Too many people I know." And with that, we swept out of the hotel and marched off to the Old Town Square where we headed for a door hidden between two dark and abandoned-looking shops on the corner of the square.

"Where are we?" I asked as he pushed the door open for me to walk ahead of him.

"Welcome to The Dog & Duck," he responded.

The Dog & Duck was actually just one big room in the basement of what was a completely dilapidated old building and was nothing like an English pub, which one would have expected in view of its name, but then it wasn't really called The Dog & Duck. Simon and the others I met that night just called it that to make them feel at home. As we walked down the stairs and entered the main bar area you could barely see through the smoke that hung in the air since everyone at that time was puffing away on vile-smelling Czech cigarettes, and the only drinks on offer were the famous Czech beers that the boys were all – I soon found out – addicted to, or the most disgusting local wine imaginable.

"Come and join us," said a very plummy voice coming from the one long table that ran down the centre of the room where a group of young, obviously English guys were all sitting. It felt as if I had entered a boys' public-school canteen.

"You must be Joanna. Simon has told us all about you." The owner of the voice, I soon saw, was the dark and very glamorous looking guy sitting at the head of the table who proceeded to look me up and down and then say, "Come and sit here. I'm Jonathan." He patted the corner of the bench to his left.

Jonathan Fox, I later found out, was the son of one of the richest men in England and he had brought Simon to Prague with him when he had turned up just after the Revolution with a bucketload of his dad's money and a determination to build an empire. I was immediately in awe of him. He was striking looking, with almost-black hair and beautiful but cold grey eyes and a voice you could cut crystal on. Mum would love him, I thought, since she was a terrible snob when it came to the way people spoke.

Simon had been to the bar and ordered more beers for everyone around the table but, on my request, got me a red wine, as beer is not my thing. The wine was terrible and tasted a bit like a cross between vinegar and something a lot worse, but it got better as the evening went on and, with all the banter going around the table, I soon forgot about just how rude the barmen were and how hard and horribly uncomfortable chairs the chairs were, and started to enjoy myself.

"There are only two dishes here," said Jonathan while everyone was discussing ordering some food. "Both are vile. But don't worry, you will soon get a taste for them. Personally, I would recommend the goulash. It's made with chunks of fatty meat cooked in a weird creamy sauce full of capers and chopped red peppers that give the whole thing a nasty bitter taste, but it's a lot better than the Viennese schnitzel, which is so tasteless we think it may well be made out of dog."

Everyone collapsed with laughter at the description, having, presumably, heard it all before, and soon we were all tucking into enormous plate loads of food that looked exactly as described. I must say, I struggled to do more than just push it around my plate and take a few bites here and there.

Not that it mattered, though. Being in the company of other English people, laughing at their humour, and knowing that being 'accepted' by Jonathan and Simon meant I was now part of the 'in' crowd would, I knew, make a huge difference to my life in Prague. For the first time since I arrived, I headed back to the hotel that evening almost looking forward to the following day.

Working days followed a very similar pattern. Each morning I would leave the hotel at the crack of dawn, walk along Pařížská Street, which is known today as the 'Bond Street' of Prague and is a beautiful tree-lined avenue full of top designer boutiques, and peer into the dirty windows of the few shops that were open, only to see dusty and empty shelves with an occasional display of Coke cans, grimy looking underwear, and little else. Sometimes, I would smile at someone I recognised as being a regular on my route and they would look away and pretend they hadn't noticed me (one friend that I knew later on made it a mission to get at least one person to smile at her by the end of each day; she often failed). Then I would cross the Old Town Square and marvel at just how beautiful it was, before heading down Celetná to our offices. Just a short walk later I would arrive to find that, as usual, the lift wasn't working, or the security guard that saw me every single day asked for my identity, or our new receptionist was running late, yet again, and there was no-one there to open the door. Then I'd go into battle. First with Michael, who continued to drive me mad, then with Monika, who I once told was a 'walking miracle' as she had never, to my knowledge, worked a full week, but always took at least one, if not two days off sick (that, again, was a hangover from communism, when it was perfectly normal to be 'ill' a lot of the time and not then go to work). And then the endless problems we had with getting any work done at all.

There was only one telephone line in our office and that continually broke down as there were just a handful of international phone lines throughout the whole country, with the result that they were always being used; we would spend half of the day picking up the phone, dialling the number, hearing the engaged tone and then putting it down again. Then we'd do the same over and over again until we got a line. The fax machine (remember those?) was the only way to communicate with the outside world on paper but, since it shared the phone line, we could only really get it to work late at night, which meant one or other of us returning at midnight, or pitching up at the crack of dawn, to send out whatever had accrued during the day.

Then we had just an old typewriter and a new Wang computer that no-one knew how to use. Since I had been nominated to do all of the typing, it quickly became apparent that it was also my job to fix the computer when it broke down from overuse. One evening, just as we were finalising some documents for an important meeting the next day, it completely gave up the ghost, resulting in my needing to call the London office for help. After a few attempts, I got through to a guy on the bank's help desk, who helpfully said, "I think the only option you have is to go to an IBM store in the morning and order a new part."

To which I responded, "Are you joking? We barely have shops that sell normal food here, let alone a bloody IBM store! You're going to have to tell me how to fix it somehow."

Which, to be fair, he did. And it worked!

The only break from the drudgery of it all was at lunchtime when we would go downstairs to the awful restaurant under our office. Clive would be dressed in his tan, British city overcoat, with a velvet collar, which made him stand out like a sore thumb, and he would lead the way into the restaurant, where the same waiter every day would greet us.

"Can I help you?" No smile and absolutely no sign that he had ever seen us before.

"Yes," said Clive. "We would like a table for six."

The waiter would look around the empty restaurant, debate whether he could tell us it was full, and then lead us to the table the furthest from the door, which we sat at every day, five days a week. And then disappear.

Eventually, he would appear again and reluctantly discuss the lunch menu, which was always the same. We would order and then would wait as long as it took before Clive got up, stormed through the swing doors that led into the kitchen and demanded some service, in a mixture of English, German and Czech. Eventually, we would be handed a bowl of fatty goulash, or some dodgy looking chicken with chips, and then we would leave, returning to do exactly the same again the following day. An unfortunate consequence of that, though, was that I ate more each day than I would usually eat in a week and, in the space of just a few months, I put on about 10 kilos, plus I drank and smoked until I was more or less blue in the face.

By the time we had finished work for the day, and that was never much before about 9.00 pm, there was only one thing to do, at least in my case, and that was to head to The Dog & Duck and drink as much as humanely possible. The only exception to that being when Clive was in town and wanted us all to dine together and that, as you will hear later, was an experience quite unlike any other.

This is Where you Hear it First!

WITH SO MUCH work during the day and then boozing every evening, my weekends were mostly spent sleeping, with the occasional foray out to walk around the town and get to know all of the main sights. If I stopped to think about it, which I often did, I was quite lonely. That started to change though after I had found a very nice flat for myself right in the centre of town, much to the chagrin of Simon, who had been trying to find me something suitable ever since I had met him.

The flat came about from my having sat next to one of the administrators of a very famous client of the bank on the plane back to London one Friday evening. I already knew him a bit as we had been involved in the case in the early days when the client had 'gone missing' and his extensive list of assets was being tracked down. It was a coincidence that we were sat next to each another and I was trying to ignore him, but the more the champagne flowed – those were the days when BA plied its business-class passengers with booze pretty much non-stop – the more he was trying to catch my eye in order to start a discussion. Eventually, after about the third bottle, I gave in and asked him how the tracking down of the client's assets was going.

"It's going well, but it's very slow," he said. "We have, though, found one thing that I rather fancy trying to keep for myself: a lovely flat right in the centre of town. Would make a change to stay there rather than one of the ghastly hotels that I keep on being put into."

My ears pricked up. "Maybe you could rent it out while you decide what to do with it?" I suggested, smiling encouragingly at him.

"Well, there's an idea. Are you looking for somewhere? Perhaps we could rent it to you and I could stay there when I am visiting?"

I wasn't sure if he was being completely serious, but, you know, I had already realised that just about every man that flew into the city turned into a sex maniac within just a few hours of landing.

23

"You never know, maybe I could take a look at it anyway and then we could discuss?" I answered.

I could see he was weighing up the idea. Meanwhile, the champagne continued to flow, and since I was used to huge amounts of booze by that time and he clearly wasn't, by the time we left the plane he could barely walk. I ended up having to wheel him out on a trolley from the luggage area to the Arrivals Hall where his rather stern-looking wife was waiting to collect him. I think his embarrassment once he sobered up ensured that he sorted out the flat for my use soon after and, once the keys had been handed over, I never actually saw him again. Thankfully.

The flat itself was much nicer than anyone else's, even though everyone that passed through suspected it had cameras hidden all over the place and that there were, potentially, spies in the neighbouring flats. This meant that whenever anyone came out from the UK office, I was expected to have them staying with me. Note, I had two bedrooms, so it wasn't quite as bizarre a requirement as it might sound. It did mean, though, that I would often meet a senior partner or some other heavyweight coming out of the bathroom in the morning scantily dressed, and they would then join me for breakfast. Most of the time, though, I lived there alone and without a TV or working telephone. It could be very solitary, but that was how it was for most of us, hence why so many of us preferred to spend our evenings in The Dog & Duck and, soon after, the new places that were springing up all over town.

The difference for me, though, was that, as far as I knew, I was the only female expat at that time, and that wasn't always easy. While I was good friends with the ever-increasing group of guys in our 'Dog & Duck' group, Prague in those days was something like Willy Wonka's Chocolate Factory for men, which made it a nightmare for any expat woman that passed through, since we became more or less invisible.

Everywhere we turned there was a pretty young predator on the look-out for a supposedly wealthy expat man who they believed would take them back to the UK or the US to live in a castle. Of course, it was fun to watch the boys 'at work', especially as Simon liked to give tips to the new arrivals and had taught most of them the phrase '*Dobrý den, kozy ven*', which they would all say proudly to whichever girl approached and which means 'Good day, show us your tits'. Sadly, if you were a supposedly rich foreign guy, you could get away with saying such a thing and most of the time, it actually worked. While I was generally happy to be one of the lads, I missed having girlfriends, and even though I wasn't particularly looking for a relationship, since I really didn't want to stay working in Prague indefinitely, I could see I would never be able to meet a nice bloke who would be interested in me while I lived this kind of life.

The stories I could tell about that time – okay, I'm going to tell some of them now –   might get me lynched, since many of our original group are now 'serious businessmen' in Prague and no-one meeting them nowadays would dream that they could have behaved as they did. But, at the time, their antics became very well-known, due in no small part to my having started to write a daily 'news bulletin' which talked about whatever or whoever I had seen the night before. It was called *This is Where you Hear it First* and I faxed it out anonymously to every fax number that we had on the company mailing list every morning: clients, friends, people we had met on the plane, and so on, and which generally sent the boys into a frenzy; to the point they would all go out of their way to behave as badly as possible and do even crazier things that evening in the hope that they would get a mention in the bulletin the following day.

I got the idea for *This is Where you Hear it First* from observing how all the expat guys behaved when they first arrived in Prague (and how many of them carried on behaving!). For some reason they seemed to get on the plane in London, or wherever their home was, as normal, professional young men, often with long-term girlfriends or wives back home. But then, somewhere on the flight over, they turned into sex-crazed lunatics and once they spotted all the pretty Czech girls looking for a western boyfriend their previously relatively well-behaved selves went out the window.

In some cases, their behaviour wasn't that surprising. Simon, I soon realised, was a total nutcase. I'm sure he would have behaved the same wherever he had been living. I had known guys that drank too much before, those that gambled or took drugs, or were hopeless womanisers. But I'd never met one that did all of those things together and more.

Simon had already been through a divorce and a bankruptcy in London before coming to Prague and it would be hard to imagine a worse place for someone like him to pitch up in. During the day, he and Jonathan worked really hard. Come the night, though, and Simon would be off, often with the rest of us in tow, at least for the early part. First to The Dog & Duck, and then to one awful nightclub after another. There was one, the name of which I can't now remember, which we had to drive out to as it was in a huge stand-alone house somewhere on the outskirts of the city. We would park outside and then walk through the gates where there were guards standing waiting to search everyone for guns – of course – and, rather bizarrely, a large grizzly bear in a cage. Then we entered an 80s style disco, complete with a glitter ball, where a few of the less adventurous of our gang, me included, would drink and jig about among the (pretty scary) crowd gathered there. Meanwhile, the naughtier ones, led by Simon, would head downstairs to all sorts of activities I wouldn't even dream of mentioning here. Suffice to say, it involved girls, the exchange of large amounts of money and a lot of serious gangsters hanging around. I also remember that on a Thursday night there was a live lesbian show that drew in a much bigger crowd than usual.

Anyway, once he had had enough of whichever club we had pitched up in, Simon would usually move on, having collected a couple of girls to accompany him, and try his hand at the nearest casino in order to impress them. Unfortunately for him, though, the evening usually ended soon after since he would quickly gamble away whatever money he had managed to lay his hands on, and the girls would then move on to new conquests.

That was Simon and, as he boasted when *This is Where you Hear it First* came out each day, he was always in the lead over everyone else when it came to the amount of mentions he had from his activities the night before. In just the first few weeks of my sending out the bulletin, I had already included him being chased down the road by a two-metre-tall transvestite after we had pitched up at the 'tranny bar' that we often frequented due to it being a lot nicer than any of the others, and then failing to pay his bar bill. Then there were the nights he turned up at one of our flats asking for a loan, or to be hidden away from whoever was on his tail. Plus, he was often, sometimes unbelievably due to the state of him, the winner of the 'who can be the first to get a girl to go home with them tonight' competition that took place most evenings. Even when he was the worse for wear, from drugs, booze or both, he still had a wicked charm about him.

A lot of the guys that hung out with our gang were desperate to get into the bulletin, but they couldn't compete with Simon; I would only mention them occasionally to keep them happy. The ones I really liked to write about anyway were those that had appeared at The Dog & Duck shortly after their arrival in Prague and who had been very serious about the job that they were there to do. Many of those would turn up spouting off about how we should all be patient with the locals, promising that they were going to take Czech lessons straightaway and keen to learn about Prague. And then, a few weeks later, they would be off, just like everyone else.

I remember one of the early arrivals, a very 'normal' guy called Rory Jones who had been sent out to head up the first major advertising agency to open up in the city. He came from London, was passionate about football, had a serious girlfriend at home and voted Labour. He was also a bit older and a bit shorter than the rest of us. We could imagine him back in his flat in Sidcup, or wherever it was, coming in from a day in the city, putting on his slippers and settling down to watch *Match of the Day*, or something similarly boring. The first night he arrived at The Dog & Duck he was wearing a very smart red blazer which, he said, he always wore when he was going out somewhere new. He sat himself down at the end of the table and proceeded to lecture us all about the rude way in which we were talking about the locals, insisting that we should make much more of an effort to blend in with them.

"You need to remember what the Czechs have been through over the past 50 years or so of communism and be more patient with them," he told us. "And these poor girls, you can't blame them for wanting to have a foreign boyfriend and better their lives. The way you talk about them you make them sound no better than prostitutes."

"Yeah, yeah, yeah," we said. "Let's see if you are still talking such a good game in six months' time." And, of course, he wasn't.

Soon after that first meeting with him, I was walking across the Old Town Square and who should be walking just ahead of me but Rory. How could I miss the bright red jacket? He was hand in hand with a very pretty and very young girl who, I later found out from one of the others, was the receptionist in his new office. Needless to say he got a nice mention in the following morning's bulletin and was chuffed to bits that he had made it in there so quickly, even though I hadn't actually mentioned his name, just the red jacket.

Most evenings, I would observe what was going on around me and then would get into the office early the next day and rattle off my thoughts from the evening before on the typewriter, before faxing it out to everyone on our growing contact list and then sit and wait for the calls to come in. At first, no-one knew where it was coming from, and when they were all discussing it later that evening I would act innocent, but eventually they worked it out. And then behaved even worse because of it.

One morning, Clive called me into his office to say that he had had a complaint from a client who suspected that the bulletin was coming from our fax machine. I expected that this may well be the end of my stint in Prague. Nothing of the sort. Clive had simply told the client that he knew absolutely nothing about it and assured him that he would try to find out where it was coming from and deal with it accordingly. And then told me that as a punishment, I would have to discuss what I was going to write each morning with him first, since he thought it could be even spicier. I actually did do that, but he always got completely carried away with his suggestions, to the point that I had to calm him down each day, otherwise God knows what the repercussions could have been!

Uncle Clive

THE FACT THAT Clive was in charge of the Prague office was one of the main reasons I continued to work in Prague. He was a very tough boss and a real stickler for 'attention to detail' (words I still use to annoy my own staff on a daily basis) but everyone knew he was completely brilliant. We were his 'chickens', as he liked to call us, and he was the 'old cockerel'. I learned so much from him: how to charm difficult clients, how to look at a problem from lots of different perspectives, how to work *hard* ! He never got tired, so we couldn't either. He was always the first person in the office and the last to leave. He was just so different to the bankers I had worked for in London; they would see a problem and often that would be the end of the deal. Clive, though, would see a problem before it existed and have a solution up his sleeve before anyone else even noticed it. He could also be a complete bastard. But then, just as we all started to hate him, he would turn into a 'total pussycat', as Eva would say. Plus, what we 'chickens' all knew, and the clients generally didn't, was that outside of work, he was a raving lunatic. I liked that.

On the nights when Clive was in Prague, he would usually take us all out for dinner and regale us with the most hilarious stories of business from his previous life. These would be accompanied by a lot of eye rolling, puffed up cheeks and filthy jokes, while he worked his way through numerous bottles of wine, packets of cigarettes (even though he said he didn't smoke) and bucket loads of ice cream, since no meal in his view was complete without a load of ice cream *'mit Schlagsahne'* (German for 'whipped cream'), as he would say to the waiters with a cackle.

Often, after dinner, we would head off to one of the dodgy nightclubs – the dodgier the better in his view - to see what the various stars of *This is Where you Hear it First* were up to. Clive would sit himself down at a table on the side of the dancefloor with whoever else was still with him, which usually meant me and Eva, if she was out from London, whichever clients we were wining and dining that evening, and then Simon and/ or Jonathan, if they were around, often with a girl or two in their group. In those days, they would introduce whichever lovely was with them as someone that 'had been for an interview' with their company that day. Clive would chortle away, always asking whether 'they got the job' and, if so, why, before the night was out. Clive had always liked Jonathan, probably because he had been to the same public school, albeit at a different time, and he always called him 'the Silver Fox', which was rather appropriate. Plus, like me, he was always on the look-out for anything scandalous that could be included in the following morning's bulletin. In the early days, I couldn't not be with him since he stayed in my flat – at least that was the story – but we both knew that while he used to come back with me at the end of an evening, once I was off to bed he would sneak out to God knows where, arriving back before I got up. Most mornings I would meet him in the kitchen, both of us pretending that he had been there all night, and then we would have a chat about nothing before heading off to the office.

One evening, as we all headed home, Clive announced he was going back to the office with Eva, apparently to do some last bits of work but, in fact, to drink huge amounts of the vile local liquor, known as *Becherovka*. When I arrived in the office the following morning, I found him lying fast asleep and naked in the bath in the cloakroom, covered only by the bathmat – thank God – and with the curtains from the windows in the main office crumpled all over the floor. Apparently, he had been demonstrating to Eva – and some other randoms who had joined them – how to absail, using the curtains to hold onto while he jumped off the desk. Eva turned up some hours later and never did explain what exactly had gone on that night, but whatever it was, they both took a good few days to recover.

Clive had names for everyone and made-up words that we all learned and continued to use. At least, I still do. He would rush into the office some mornings and say, "Right chickens, we've got a load of big potatoes pitching up today, so look lively!" and the Czechs would look at us in bewilderment, until they understood that in his world 'big potatoes' meant important clients. Then, when the pressure was on, which was most of the time, he would run into our room asking if we were about to go 'legs up', in other words, fall over backwards and collapse. Or, if we had a hangover, which was most of the time, he would ask us whether we had 'the black dog on our shoulders'. And each time he would giggle away to himself and bring out another wild story about a similar situation with an Iraqi gangster or some Sheikh, which may or may not have been true.

In the early days we had an important French client who always brought his assistant Sylvia to the office. Clive was sure they were having an affair. Well, they probably were. Everyone was in those days. Every evening, Clive would regale us with lewd and presumably made-up stories about the client and 'Mademoiselle Sylvie', which he would pronounce in a French accent, while twiddling an invisible moustache and rolling his eyes. He was so embroiled in his stories that some days he called Sylvia 'Mademoiselle Sylvie' to her face, before flirting outrageously with her in a way she seemed to enjoy and that caused us all to have to leave the room and collapse into giggles.

We had another client at that time, a metal trader Clive believed was an arms dealer, and who he called 'The Butcher of Košice'. He may well have been right. One morning I turned up to the office to be met by two large thugs outside the front door, both armed to the teeth. I had just opened the door when Clive rushed at me.

"Josefina, I've got The Butcher in the office and he is in a bad mood. He keeps brandishing his pistol about and making threats to the other side. Can you make him a cuppa with a good slug of jigger in it to calm him down? Sharpish?"

There was one thing though that was guaranteed to whip Clive into a filthy mood and that was the Czech taxi drivers. At that time, they were notorious, and, once tourists started to arrive in Prague on a regular basis, there were endless stories about them in the international press. Clive, however, took it on himself to single-handedly try to get them cleaned up. Whenever we got into one and before we even got started, he would ask the driver if he had a metre and gesture for him to turn it on (the law required they have them, but they never wanted to use them). And then he would sit in the front seat glaring at the meter until he was sure it was fixed to run much faster than it should – another of the taxi drivers' tricks. At which point he would shout at the driver to 'stop the car' and then yell at whoever else was with him to 'get out and run', which we all then did. One time we got out and the taxi driver leapt out after us waving a gun, but Clive just urged us to run faster. And then, once we had got away, he collapsed into hysteria, shrieking, "Did you see the bugger's face? Ha! That will show him." And off we went back to the office for a slug of whatever was on offer.

By the time I'd been in Prague a full year, I was starting to wonder if I would ever be able to go back to London and, even though I loved Clive and Eva and some of my new friends, I had come to realise that the corporate finance world wasn't really for me. Slowly, though, I was hatching a plan. Every night I was out with the boys at The Dog & Duck we would discuss how Prague lacked so many things; shops that sold nice vegetables and fruit, or shampoo and deodorant, or pretty much any of the regular products that we Brits required on a daily basis but were impossible to find. The result was that all of us brought back as much stuff as we could from the UK, or wherever we came from, every time we travelled home. My suitcase was always full of cosmetics and food (cheese, bacon and hot cross buns, to name a few). Some of my new friends even started doing a bit of a trade in sausages and shampoo. We even discussed trying to get an M&S franchise, or similar, to set up shop in Prague.

Then all of us grumbled about the impossibility of finding good people and considered opening an employment agency or starting a restaurant, or a courier service, or opening a sandwich shop, or a coffee bar or a gym; the possibilities seemed endless. Somewhere along the line though, and despite being pretty much broke, I was shaping the idea of offering a kind of 'one-stop-shop' for companies entering the still very tricky Czech market, since it seemed to me that so many of them had very little idea of what doing business in Czechoslovakia was really all about. Whereas I, of course, knew it all…

One day I was out for lunch with one of our regular clients, a very dodgy-looking Swede called Bjørn. Clive absolutely loved him. Bjørn was short and dumpy, with big, blue-framed glasses and thick blonde hair. He had a twinkle about him, even though he was far from being an oil painting. Despite never being exactly sure what Bjørn was up to, Clive was happy to keep on advising him on various different business deals, none of which ever came to fruition, nor did he ever pay.

"Sometimes," Clive would say to me when we heard that Bjørn had just arrived, "you have to think long term. We need to look after the acorns, as one day one of them might grow into a socking great oak tree."

I often thought about that once I was out on my own and doing a similar thing. But anyway, over lunch I mentioned to Bjørn my rough business idea and he listened but didn't seem particularly enthusiastic. Then, later in the afternoon, Clive called me into his office.

"Josefina, I hear you are leaving," he said, pacing up and down the room, rolling his eyes and muttering to himself under his breath. To which I responded by saying that I didn't know what he was talking about.

"Bjørn told me about your idea," he said, "I think you should give it a go. You'll never get a chance to do something like this again and, if it fails, you can just go back to London. In fact, I won't let you not do it."

And so, it began. Rory, of the red jacket and advertising expert fame, advised me that the name of the company should sound like what it was selling and suggested 'Jo Weaver & Associates', on the basis that I was kind of selling myself (or at least, my know-how on the market). I initially laughed at that, imaging other people answering the phone and having to say such a mouthful. But then I thought it could work if we shortened it to JWA, even though it was a bit meaningless. And that's what I settled on. Clive had Michael set up the company (that put him in his place), adding a 'Prague' to the 'JWA' when he found out that a JWA already existed. All I then needed was an assistant and a few bits of office equipment and I would be ready to go. Without really trying too hard, JWA Prague was born to a 26-year-old single woman with a chequered career history, very little money and who was living in a country that she didn't really like. Was I a bit crazy? Probably. But then, what was there to lose?

Going it Alone

NOWADAYS, I GET people coming to me to seek my advice and to ask me to have a look at their business plans. Of course, they nearly always show a huge profit within a very short timescale, which immediately puts me right off, and I invariably tell them that they should forget going it alone and find a job. Actually, when I started, it didn't even occur to me to draw up a business plan. I was just sure that there was a demand for what I was offering and, if I was the only one supplying it, then I should be able to monetise it! At that time, I definitely didn't have much money. In my first year in Prague, I had earned a lot, but most of it went on paying my debts in the UK and buying clothes. I think I managed to save about £1,000 during that whole time.

My own 'plan', as far as it went, was based on how much money I needed just to survive. Forget about any sort of profit. And that meant, first and foremost, to pay the rent on my new flat. Once I left the bank, I had to move from my relatively lovely, company-owned luxury apartment into a grotty little 'two-plus-one', as these things are called here in Prague. That meant one bedroom for me and a sitting room which became the office. Then, I needed to cover the bills, buy at least one flight a month back to the UK to see my mum, buy necessities and occasionally eat. Oh, and buy lots of cigarettes too, as smoking was one of my main vices. Of course, I figured I would still be out and about every evening, but the cost of alcohol and clubbing was minimal and, besides, the boys would probably pay for me. On the other hand, I knew I would need an assistant/ translator, since my Czech at that time was virtually non-existent. I would also have to buy a few bits and pieces to stock the office. All in all, I reckoned I could get by on about 30,000 Kč a month, which, at that time, equated to about £600. And I figured that if I couldn't earn that, then I really would have to regard myself as a failure.

My first challenge was to find an assistant. The average salary at that time was about 12,000 Kč a month, which was equivalent to about £250. Visitors were astounded when they found out how little people earned, but you had to think about it in the context of life in the Czech Republic, which cost so little. Public transport was more or less free of charge and most families lived in state-owned apartments, for which they paid a tiny amount of rent, and heating, electricity and so on were very cheap. I thought, therefore, that if I paid a bit over the going rate – and, bearing in mind that by that time I had a lot of 'connections' – I could find someone pretty good.

As soon as I sent out word I was looking for an assistant – one of the benefits of keeping *This is Where you Hear it First* going was my ability to spread information easily – I heard from one of the guys about a young Czech girl that had just arrived back in Prague after a stint of modelling in Milan, Lucie.

What he actually said was, "She is probably pretty useless, but she looks fantastic so everyone will want to shag her, and for sure you can get her very cheap!"

I asked him to see if he could hook us up, and shortly before I left my old job, Lucie arrived at the office for an interview.

Needless to say, Clive was completely over-excited about her and had been out to have a peep as she arrived, after which he said, "You've got a good, strong girl waiting for you out in reception," which, in Clive speak, meant 'a bit of alright'.

In she walked, tall and very skinny with long, straight black hair and slanted blue eyes in a beautiful face, looking about 15 years old and close to tears.

"So, tell me, what you have been doing since you got back to Prague?" I asked, innocently.

"I've been in a drying-out clinic." Blimey, I didn't expect that! "Honestly, you don't want to employ me. I'm unable to do anything," she was looking down at the floor, twisting a handful of hair around her fingers. Her nails were chewed down to the quick.

"Well," I said, "I'm sure you're able to do quite a lot, especially after everything you've achieved already. Living in Milan and away from your family when you were so young must have been very tough. And, you know, I'm a bit of a nutcase myself." I laughed ruefully. "I actually think we might work very well together. Why don't we just give it a try and see what happens?" And just like that, I had found myself an assistant. Stunning looking, very good English, and ready to work for peanuts. What could be better?

To start off with, we had just one second-hand computer, which we shared for typing documents and faxes – yes, we had started having computers by then – and a manual typewriter that Clive had let me have as a 'leaving present'. We also had a telephone/ fax machine attached to the single phone line that only worked sporadically; websites, emails and so on were still light years away. However, the work started to come in almost immediately, mainly from my group of friends, since all being boys, they needed help with just about everything, from buying furniture, typing documents and looking for staff, to preparing brochures and other more superior marketing materials. They then spread the word as and when they met newcomers, especially if they were British. Plus, Clive kept us busy with various random things, at least until he found my replacement.

Since advertising possibilities were limited, if not non-existent, all of us, even the big companies that were gradually opening up in Prague, relied mostly on word of mouth to 'spread the news'. Even now, many people still believe that the only marketing they need to do is to be 'out there', as Prague is such a small town and, in time, everyone got to know everyone else. But, in those days, we built our contacts through frequenting one of just two pubs that we felt comfortable in. The Dog & Duck, for the Europeans, and a newly opened bar called Joe's Bar, which attracted the Americans due to its American owner (not Joe!).

If companies had the budget, however, a good way to announce their arrival in town was through the organisation of some sort of event, and it was event management that we soon became known for, even though it wasn't really what we had planned on doing, nor was it as easy as my friends thought. Simon, for example, would start most of his more or less hourly calls each day with, "Am I interrupting you from blowing up balloons?" which started to become not very funny quite soon. Even though Prague is full of beautiful ballrooms and other amazing places to hold a party, at that time the suppliers we needed to put on a show were in very short supply. For example, there was only one catering company who, first of all, produced pretty awful food and second, had such a monopoly that they charged huge sums for the pleasure of eating it. Companies that could provide everything else that we needed to produce a western-standard event were, as far as we could see, non-existent.

One of our first events was for a well-known accounting firm that wanted to announce its arrival in Prague. We agreed that a party for all the great and good would be the best way to do it. We had taken the UK-based boss, a woman, to see a few different venues and she had decided on one of the many amazing rooms in the Prague Castle. Prague Castle is not actually a castle as such, but a whole area of the city with some parts dating back as early as the 12th century. It houses many famous landmarks, including the incredible St Vitus Cathedral, which has one of the tallest spires in the world and can be seen from all over the city. It also has several different presidential and governmental offices and some individual palaces, many of which have baroque or similar grand rooms available for rent, which are guaranteed to knock the socks off foreign visitors. One of these was our chosen venue.

One of the many problems with this room, though, was that it was way too big for the number of people attending the event. Our client suggested that the way we could deal with that was to fill it with lots of big plants and flower arrangements and 'small it down'. Of course, we agreed, since we always agreed; the client is always right, and all that. But the minute we got back to the office we freaked out. How to find a florist? And how to find a florist that could provide huge plants and flower arrangements?

We decided that Lucie would write a note saying that if so and so was interested in working with us on a big event and could supply a lot of plants and flowers, they should call us. Then, one evening we walked around the centre of town together, looking for the very few flower shops that existed in the city, and sticking the note through their doors in the hope that one or other would respond. Within a few days we had calls from seven different companies, who we agreed to meet outside the chosen room in the castle the following Monday. Together, we would see the space and discuss what they could do.

Sure enough, Monday morning saw a motley crew of florists, all men, gathering outside the huge black gates that led through to the venue. Most of them seemed to know each other and stood in a group looking very unfriendly and incredibly scruffy in their jeans and big overcoats, puffing away on vile-smelling Czech cigarettes.

Lucie led the way. "Good morning, everyone, and thank you for coming to meet us. I am Lucie, and this is our company's managing director, Jo Weaver." Then she gave a huge smile that usually would be guaranteed to melt all normal men's hearts. Not this lot though.

No sooner had she made the introduction than one of the older and more unpleasant looking men who appeared to be the ringleader, responded, "Where's she from then? Doesn't she speak Czech?" and they all sniggered.

"Mrs Weaver is English," replied Lucie. Faced with such a hostile looking group, Lucie felt the need to flip my name to the formal word for a grown-up female, that being the equivalent of 'Mrs', even though, at that time, I wasn't actually a 'Mrs' at all. Far from it! She looked ready to burst into tears.

They continued to mutter between themselves. The ringleader said something else that I couldn't understand, took his cigarette out of his mouth, chucked it on the floor and ground it into the cobbles.

I turned to my assistant. "What did he say?" I asked.

Lucie looked embarrassed. "They don't want to work for us. They're saying that you're a foreigner and they don't trust you to pay them, so they are going to leave. They're saying that we have wasted their time."

"Okay," I said. "Fine. Tell them to leave."

And they left, all except one young guy who stood there looking embarrassed. "I'll do it," he said. "Show me what you want."

Mr Dvořák was a bit underwhelming looking, but then weren't they all. He was pasty-faced and had mousy hair, which had already started to recede, and didn't exactly fill us with a sense of confidence.

But beggars can't be choosers. Incidentally, I should just say here that in more than thirty years of working with him, I never did find out what his first name was. The Czechs are very formal and the older/ senior-positioned/ better looking/ person in a conversation has to offer to the younger/ lower positioned/ uglier one that they can speak 'informally' together before first names or less polite wording can be used. Since neither of us could work out who was younger or the most senior positioned (although the 'uglier' point was clear), we always stayed formal!

The catering, then, was straightforward, seeing as in most of the big venues there was an unbreakable contract in place, which meant that if you booked that venue you had to use their caterers. And since there were no other caterers anyway, the point was moot. But we did work hard to persuade them that these clients and their guests would be mostly foreign and, as such, they required a different offer to what they might usually provide for the locals. This meant that there didn't need to be so much food, but there had to be a lot of booze, and the wine, in particular, had to be imported from elsewhere in Europe, since Czech wine, at that time, was nearly undrinkable.

That was one rule that I learned very early on, as all events at that time followed a fairly clear process. If the majority of the guests were foreign, having enough booze was the main priority. That meant imported wine, plenty of Czech beer – Pilsner Urquell and Staropramen being regarded as some of the best beers in the world – and plenty of soft drinks, such as Coke, and water for the drivers. Unlike the locals, those driving would probably not drink alcohol (and it is worth noting here that Czechs don't generally regard beer as alcohol, despite the fact that Czech beer has a far higher alcohol content than most). Food, then, could be very simple and light, ideally with an emphasis on salads, cheeses, hams and so on, and steering clear of anything too heavy and creamy. And they wouldn't care too much about the entertainment, as long as they were given plenty of time to chat to one another; a bit of classical music or a jazz singer in the background was all that was really needed.

If, however, the guests were mostly Czech, the opposite in all cases applied. There needed to be a ton of food, with the focus very clearly on meat, cream, more meat, more cream, and desserts with, yes, lots of cream. It was a bit tricky if you were a vegetarian, although, in those days, that was still a bit of a rarity. If you were, then you might have been lucky enough to be offered a bit of unidentifiable greenery and perhaps an omelette with ham to go with, since, at that time, ham fell under the 'vegetarian' umbrella. It generally didn't matter what the quality of the food was or how it looked, but there needed to be bucketloads for everyone, and it had to be served early on. Czechs like to sit down and eat, not around a table so that they can talk – as they don't chat much when they are eating, or actually like talking to each other much anyway. Instead they prefer to sit in rows of chairs, with or without a table in front of them. And then, once they have eaten everything in sight, they will drink copious amounts of whatever is available, irrespective of the quality, and then either slump in their chair for the rest of the evening, fall over in a heap, or jig about and maul each others' partners.

Czechs also like to give and receive speeches, and these can go on forever. At Czech events there will often be a Master of Ceremonies, who might be a somewhat well-known TV personality or similar, and who will usually stand on some sort of stage and speak very earnestly about the host and, possibly, the reason for the event, for way too long. And then, at various points through the evening, the MC will introduce one or other of the hosts or guests, who will then make their way, often very unsteadily, to the stage, and continue with a bit of earnest rambling about nothing in particular until the next person is ready to take over. In the meantime, everyone will sit quietly and continue to eat and drink until they are told otherwise. Of course, if you then factor in the need to have these speeches translated (in the case of a mixed audience), then some of the guests may well lose the will to live. In short, whenever a client mentioned 'speeches', we always tried to rein them in.

Not that we ever had very much luck in that department. The Czechs do like to talk.

There was, however, one thing that the Czechs liked more than drinking and eating and that was sex. Prague is often known as the 'European Capital of Sex', a name which it totally deserves. I'm afraid this subject did come up a lot in our discussions and often features in the organisation of events and, of course, it is a constant feature of *This is Where you Hear it First.* One story I particularly liked in my early days was told to me by an American friend, who, having met the girl of his dreams, was invited to a party in her hometown out in the country to celebrate her parents' wedding anniversary.

The party started as usual. Everyone filed into what he described as a kind of old-fashioned 'schoolhouse', all dressed in their finery, and made their way to the buffet tables, which were loaded with the standard meat, cream and dumpling type of food, as expected. And then they sat down in the rows of chairs that lined the walls and ate as much as they possibly could. At about 9.00 pm, the lights were dimmed, the doors opened, and out walked a young lady dressed in old jeans, a white T-shirt and plimsolls, who then walked into the middle of the room and slowly removed all her clothes. Meanwhile, the guests looked on, forks raised, nonchalantly chewing until she was completely naked. She then picked everything up from the floor and made her exit to quiet applause. Then the drinking continued as if nothing had happened.

We never suggested that we organise a striptease, nor a pole on the stage for a pole dancer – although we were asked a few times – but most clients would get a bit 'edgy' with us when we were planning an event. Bear in mind we were two young ladies at this time, and our (usually male) clients felt awkward discussing such things! Often, the client would say something like, "We were thinking that it might be nice to have a bit of additional entertainment."

At which point, I'd swallow a little too obviously and stutter innocently, "Yes, that's a good idea. What sort of thing were you thinking?"

"Something that would be typical of the Czech Republic? You know, we have noticed that there are a lot of very pretty girls around. Could we maybe hire a few models or hostesses to come along?"

"Oh yes, sure," I'd continue. "What would you like them to do exactly?"

"Well, maybe they could be there to greet everyone? Or just walk about and break things up a bit? You know, we will be mostly men." Then they would pause and look at me. "What do you suggest?"

Continuing my innocent act, I would usually answer something like, "Yes, of course, we can hire some girls and you can decide what you would like them to do on the night." Lucie and I would giggle about it later on and wonder how long it would be before they would say what they really meant.

But back to the event in the castle; we had the florist lined up, the caterers had been beaten into submission (almost) and the castle was going to supply us with screens, microphones and so on. Our guests were all RSVPing and keen to come, and the clients were happy with how everything was progressing. Lucie and I were aiming to be at the venue just after lunch to make sure that everything was being set up as planned, and then we would get changed in a cupboard, or whatever was available, so that we 'looked the part' when the guests arrived at 7.00 pm.

So, there we were on the day of the party. Everything was in place and we were feeling as confident as we ever could in those circumstances. At 3.00 pm, the caterers were putting out the tables, the stage was being set up, and the room looked spectacular, with all the white and gold tablecloths and candles setting off the beautiful frescos on the walls and ceiling, which themselves were lit up by the spotlights around the room and already in place on the stage. All we needed was the florist to turn up and then we were done. But then, 4.00 pm came and we had no florist. 5.00 pm and no florist. By 5.30 pm, I was starting to sweat. Lucie was getting hysterical.

"Can we call him somehow?" I asked.

"He doesn't have a phone," said Lucie. "Not at home and not in the shop."

By this time, the head of the catering company, a short and stocky middle-aged Czech guy with black hair combed over his bald patch and a small moustache that made him look vaguely familiar, had marched over to us for about the hundredth time to demand that we deliver the flowers and plants straightaway since, he said, "The tables don't look nice without any flower arrangements. And the room is much too big with so few tables."

"I know," I responded, wondering whether he was expecting us to suddenly produce all the plants and flowers out of a hat. I turned to Lucie, "Let's get out of here. I can't stand him any longer. I know a 'watched pot doesn't boil' and all that, but at least we will be ready as and when bloody Dvořák does turn up!"

We stood outside the gates leading into the building and paced. By about 6.00 pm we debated running away. And then, about 20 minutes before the guests were due to arrive, a white van appeared.

"I am so sorry, my van broke down and I had to go and borrow a friend's," he said, leaping from the cab and throwing open the doors, where all our huge plants and flower arrangements were waiting to be unloaded. At which point, Lucie grabbed two of the soldiers that were marching outside, much to their delight, and persuaded them, obviously very easily, to come and help us, while I ran inside shouting at everyone I passed to come and help. Out came the caterers, the manager of the building, the ladies from the cloakroom and we all rushed everything into the room – all set, one minute before the CEO pulled up with his entourage and swept in.

"Well," said our client when she followed a few minutes behind him. "This all looks lovely. I can't believe how easy it has all been. Well done."

Pardubice

I GREW UP in a very posh country town called Royal Tunbridge Wells, which is in the southeast of England, where my mum moved us from London shortly after my dad died when I was just three years old. She had been left with three kids and no money, so had sold our house in London and moved us to Tunbridge Wells, where she took in Nigerian medical students as a way of making money. You can imagine the horror of the 'disgusted of Tunbridge Wells brigade', having such a deformed family and its lodgers move in. Especially when she sat us all by the garden fence to have breakfast in the summer or took us out shopping; Tunbridge Wells being a town that has still barely ever seen a foreigner, let alone a black one. Mum, having been a codebreaker in the war, and who had travelled on her own to Nigeria to be by my dad's side when he was dying and then found that she had been left without any money soon after returning, didn't really care what people said, and neither did I, nor my older brother and sister. They had inherited Mum's fearsome brain and went onto great things, while I apparently took after my dad in being sports-mad, driving everyone crazy by wanting to spend all my time either riding horses – always other people's since we couldn't afford our own – playing tennis, or doing any other sport that was on offer. That carried on right through school. Mind you, I didn't often show up to school and, if I did, it was mostly to disrupt the class by being naughty. Eventually, however, the reality of being relatively poor, plus the fact that I wasn't really one of those girls whose sole aim was to find a husband and settle down with kids – which was still the norm in England, even then – made me realise I needed to think about a career.

At that time though there was no such thing as 'careers guidance' for girls so, if I couldn't be a showjumper, tennis player or anything else related to sport, I was clueless as to what to do. But, since my brother had studied economics, and I was good at maths, I decided I would follow in his footsteps. That didn't help too much in my career strategy so, cutting an enormously long story short, I had ended up in the mergers and acquisitions department of the bank from which I was picked and sent out to Prague. From day one, I mostly hated it but realised that if I managed to hang in there, I might just earn enough money to eventually buy my own horses or play in a posh tennis club or do pretty much any of the things I had yearned for when I was young but which we could never, ever afford.

As far back as I could remember, though, my real passion had always been horse-racing, particularly National Hunt, which, for the uninitiated, means racing over fences. One of the very first things that we in the UK knew about Czechoslovakia during Communism – or, at least, those of us that were interested in such things – was the televising of an annual horse-race called the *Velká Pardubická* that took place every year in Pardubice, a town in the east of the country. Every so often there would be grainy black and white footage of the race on *Grandstand*, the Saturday afternoon sports programme at that time, showing horses racing over enormous fences and through heavily ploughed fields. Sadly, many of them fell and were killed or injured along the way. There was a lot of publicity when some mad amateur English jockey decided to travel over with his horse and give the locals a run for their money. Unfortunately, that didn't happen (I think he fell halfway around) but it certainly brought a lot of attention to the race.

Shortly before leaving the bank and going out on my own, I met one of the main people involved in the Pardubice racecourse and, not only that, he invited me to come and take a look at it. For various reasons, not least the actual setting up of the company, I didn't get around to taking up the invitation until much later but, eventually, Lucie and I took to the road to pay them all a visit.

At this point, I should just mention I didn't have a car, and Pardubice is a longish way from Prague. As you know, when I first arrived, I had no plans to stay and even when I realised I was there for the long-haul, I couldn't see the need to have a car nor, I felt, would I ever have the nerve to actually drive around Prague. The roads were – still are – a nightmare with all the cobbled and narrow streets, signposting only in Czech and with roadworks a permanent feature. In those days you could rarely venture down the street without seeing a car crash. Then there were the trams, which have right-of-way and their own completely indistinguishable road signs and that rattle about all over the place with bad-tempered drivers ringing the bell at any car that looks as if it might get in the way. Most drivers, whether car or tram, were appalling. I used to say that the Czechs drive as they are as people: they only ever see as far as the end of their nose, never anticipate anything, never give way, believe that they are the best and think that someone else's misfortune was/is a cause for celebration. There, that should have lost me a few friends!

For our 'big trip' to Pardubice, I borrowed a car from Simon. When I say a car, it was actually a little green van which was probably not the kind of vehicle the goons in Pardubice expected us to turn up in since the Czechs believe that having a flashy car is imperative if you are someone 'important'. I didn't let on to Simon that I had never driven in Prague or ever actually been outside the city at all, nor that I had only driven on the 'other' side of the road a few times some years before. But I was a good driver and fairly confident about the trip until Lucie, who was coming with me to navigate and translate started to freak out at pretty much every turn. That wasn't helped by the fact that she had never read a map before in her life – the maps anyway weren't very accurate – and, as you have probably realised by now, she was generally stressed about just about everything anyway. So, not only did we arrive at the racecourse an hour late, but both of us were nervous wrecks; her from doubting my driving (she was grabbing hold of the dashboard every five minutes and muttering '*ty vole*' under her breath, an untranslatable rude Czech phrase) and me from having heart failure each time she grabbed something, squeaked, or made some other frightened noise along the way.

We eventually arrived in Pardubice in one piece but were very, very late. That said, the people we were there to meet, being Czech, were not particularly bothered, as being horribly late is kind of the norm over here. They were a motley group. Tomaš, the main guy, who I went on to call 'Big Tomaš', was the owner of more than half the shares in the racecourse and was clearly a local mafiosi – tall, big, chubby, dark haired and bearded – and everyone was terrified of him. He took some delight in telling us, after I explained that our drive down had been a bit fraught, that he had written off at least three different Mercedes over the past year during his regular travels between Pardubice and Prague, where I later found out he had a live-in mistress, of course, while in Pardubice he had a wife. I remember making a 'note to self' at that point never ever to get into a car with him. Then there was the racecourse manager, also called Tomaš (who obviously became 'Little Tomaš'), and who was also chubby, dark haired and bearded, but smaller. And then Mirek, who was gnome-like and blond and didn't say much, but from his bowlegs and general attire, he was clearly the 'horsey' one; in fact, we soon found out that he was the local racing trainer and was based on the racecourse itself.

Even though they didn't mind us being late, they were definitely put out by the fact that we were women and quite young – or very young, in Lucie's case. And since they had been told that 'Joanna' was a horse racing expert from England, they had obviously expected someone older and, of course, male. Plus, somewhere along the line, the story of my horse riding/ racing prowess had grown into my being a successful Olympian, if not a world champion. Since they soon realised that that had been an exaggeration, they were a bit doubtful as to how useful I could actually be. And if I couldn't be useful, then why was I there?

To be fair, once they got over their initial prejudice, they did behave very hospitably towards us and, as is standard in Czech business meetings, once we had all sat down they offered us a shot of *slivovice* (the local plum brandy) as a 'welcome'. I said no, but Lucie kicked me under the table then told me in English that it would be rude to decline and that even she, a recovering alcoholic, would have one in order not to offend them. So, a couple of shots of what, in my then limited experience, is one of the vilest and strongest alcohols ever to be invented, were duly slammed down by all of us, before Big Tomaš explained why we had been invited.

"We hear that you know all about horse racing," he said in strongly accented English and with a bit of a sneer on his face.

"Hmm, well, not *all* about," I said nervously. "But I did grow up amongst horses and I did a lot of *parkur* (I thought they would be impressed if I used the local word for showjumping) when I was a teenager. And I know a lot of racing people in the UK."

"Well, so we are hoping that you can find us some sponsors," Big Tomaš continued, "as well as sell some of the tickets to the main races. We know how much you English like this sport!"

"We can certainly try on both counts," I responded. "Let's take a look around and then we can see what we can do."

It was clear right from the beginning they needed a lot of help, as the racecourse was near bankruptcy. Part of the reason for that was the trouble they had been having with the local animal rights activists who regularly turned up and disrupted the race, which, for obvious reasons, scared off any potential sponsors. Without sponsors for the races, even breaking even each race-day would be a challenge, unless they increased the cost of the tickets significantly, but that would put off the locals. I could see that this could be a pretty big challenge. But there we were, and I wasn't going to give up the opportunity of at least taking a good look around in a hurry. First off, I suggested we take a look at the course so we could at least get a feel for it all. And that, I have to say, was pretty damned exciting as it looked exactly as it had on the TV.

Set in what is really a huge and very pretty park, the racecourse itself wasn't that different to those in the UK, but the fences were designed to be dangerous rather than particularly difficult, and the ground, in a good part of the course, was ploughed (instead of the usual velvety green grass), and which added a lot to the horses' exhaustion when they galloped through it. My first thought, therefore, was that the course could be made a great deal safer quite easily, and then the animal rights people would shut up. And if they could be shut up, getting sponsors should be a great deal easier.

After walking around the course, we stopped in front of the main stand to discuss how we could help to sell tickets. The main problem on that front was that there was just the one viewing stand, and while it was five floors high, each floor was just open space, with row after row of wooden benches and just a few loos near the entrance to each floor. Oh, and a café on the ground level. And since the locals wouldn't pay much in the way of entry fees, the Tomašes had the idea that if they reconstructed the first two floors in order to offer private 'boxes', then tickets for those floors could be sold for a great deal more than usual, especially to foreigners since, according to them, they had more money than Czechs. Much, they said, as happened at Ascot or Cheltenham. In their dreams!

"Maybe," I said, "that is where we can help the most at this point. I'm sure that a lot of my friends could bring clients down for a day's racing. But we would need to offer them catering, have tables and chairs in each box and so on."

"That's exactly what we plan," said Big Tomaš. "If you can bring us the people, we will give you the boxes."

"And then, who knows, if you are up for making a few changes to the course as well, we might just get a sponsor," I said out loud to the world in general.

Fantastic. My first 'sports marketing' project, something I had already tried to get into before ending up at the bank in London, and in horse racing of all things. What could possibly go wrong?

Growing the Business

WHAT WITH OUR regular 'projects', which generally meant anything my friends couldn't or wouldn't do – but *we* would if they paid – and then 'winning' the work for Pardubice, a couple of things started to become clear to me. First, I would soon need to consider taking on another person. If I had to take Lucie to meetings, in particular to Pardubice, which we now planned to visit once a week, we would have to leave our office unstaffed for an awful lot of time. Second, if I took on another employee, we would soon be very short of space, since the room in my flat was too small to house more than the two of us.

When discussing this with the gang in The Dog & Duck one evening, a newly arrived real estate guy I hadn't written about yet – I was still doing the *This is Where you Hear it First* bulletin and had an ever-increasing amount of material to work with, but nothing as yet about him – mentioned a very cheap property that he had just been offered to market. It was cheap because, as he said, "It won't be for everyone." I didn't care about that, so quickly agreed to go and see it the next day.

U Obecního dvora – I know, don't even worry about what that means – had a huge wooden door set into a row of 16th century apartment buildings on one of the narrow and cobbled back streets near Prague's beautiful Old Town Square. Like so many of these old buildings, once you entered through the main door you were faced with a large and pretty courtyard first and then, in this case, a path that led across to what appeared to be a tiny little cottage. The cottage had its own front door that opened-up into a small hall, with a door to the right that led into one good-sized room that looked out onto the pathway, and through that a smaller room facing out onto what appeared to be a secret garden. Immediately opposite the entrance was a flight of stairs that led to the first floor, and then another flight of stairs up to who knew what. The door to the right on this floor opened into a narrow corridor with a bathroom and small kitchen on the left, a tiny room to the right – that was just

51

about big enough to swing the proverbial cat in – and then a big airy room at the back with French doors that opened onto a small terrace overlooking the garden. As far as I was concerned, it was love at first sight.

The price to rent it was a little bit more than my flat, but the location was much better. I figured that the downstairs main room would easily accommodate four desks in the future, while the back room could have a meeting room table, and then the first floor would become a flat for me. The agent's 'not for everyone' comment wasn't really clear, but once we had moved in, we quickly found out why he had said that. First, the landlord's son lived on the second floor, and he was very odd looking, with spiky red hair, a nose-ring and bad skin, plus he wore very strange clothes that made him look like something from a Dickensian novel. It was a bit odd to hear him arriving home late at night and walking past the door to my 'flat' before heading up the next flight of stairs. But I got used to it and, anyway, despite appearances, he seemed harmless enough.

The other problem was that the elderly neighbours in the historic buildings either side of the entrance didn't like our landlord – although we only found that out much later – and they definitely didn't like foreigners; I found that out straight away. They also didn't like us having our office there, since, as they told Lucie on one of their many visits, we had way too many people visiting us, they were often noisy, and some, God forbid, were young foreign men, which led them to believe that we would soon be having riotous parties and all sorts of other goings on. If only! The consequence of all of *that* was that they installed a huge bolt on the main doors and put up a notice that said the doors must be kept locked at all times.

The problem for us was that every time someone came to visit, they would buzz the doorbell and then one of us had to go out and unlock the door, let them in, lock the door again and then go through the same process when they left. And since we had, as they had expected, a *lot* of visitors, that became a drag. We stopped locking it at one point and all-out war broke out between us. At that time, most Czechs were paranoid about security, which was funny really since there was so little crime, other than the fights that broke out between rival mafia gangs, and the ongoing problem with taxi drivers. As far as I could tell, for regular people, Prague was completely safe.

The reason we had so many visitors once we moved into our cottage was not so much that we had a lot of business, although, I have to say, the work continued to come in and never really slowed down. It was more because we were very close to the Old Town and, soon after we moved in, an Irish pub called The James Joyce opened not so far away, and that meant that Simon, Jonathan and the others often used to pop in on their way to the pub each afternoon/ evening/ whenever to try and persuade us to join them. Incredibly, sometime after we had settled into Obecního Dvora, another Irish Pub opened immediately opposite us, bringing yet more visitors each afternoon, and, if it was late enough in the day, work soon continued in the bar, rather than in the office.

By that time the city was changing every single day. Newly reconstructed apartments were coming on the market all the time, western-standard offices (albeit still without telephone lines), were being built and opened, and new shops and restaurants were appearing on every street corner. Most exciting of all, in my book at least, was the opening of a new nightclub, *Lávka* ('small footbridge'), which was in an amazing location right next to the famous Charles Bridge, and since it had a huge terrace at the back that stretched out over the water, most of us would end up sitting out there at the end of most evenings as it was the coolest – in every sense of the word – place to be. It is worth noting that in the first year, most of my friends back home – and probably me too, before I got to Prague – thought that all the ex-Eastern Bloc countries were freezing cold, with tons of snow on the ground all the year around. Not a bit of it. Summers in Prague are mostly boiling hot, something that has always cheered me up no end.

Another thing that helped change our lives was the opening of the first decent restaurant in the city. Called *Vinárna v Zátiší* (literally, 'wine restaurant in a quiet area') it soon became the only place to go to eat for those that could afford it (unfortunately not me very often at that time!). The owner was a young Indian guy, Kumar, who, while he eventually became a good friend, was more on the periphery of our group as I think we were all a bit in awe of him. We all loved Zátiší though as the food was as good as anything we could have found in our own respective countries, and some of the richer boys would have competitions to see who could spend the most evenings in a row there, the winner having done about three weeks without a break. Of course, the opening of these western pubs, restaurants and clubs was driven, in the main, by the huge number of foreign companies that were rushing to enter what was seen as a market with huge opportunities. That meant that more and more expats were turning up and finding their way to either The Dog & Duck or, soon after, The Joyce. And with that came more and more work for companies like mine.

With all the new people arriving, so my group of friends expanded. Simon was still a very big part of my life but somewhere along the line – I cannot really remember exactly when – he met a former model (another one), Francesca, who he soon announced he would marry. It was hard to believe that anyone would be mad enough to take on Simon, but Francesca was living a tough life as a single mother and we all kind of felt there was a bit of a deal made between them, although we never actually voiced that.

I was of course sad about the likelihood of seeing less of Simon, since barely an hour went by each day without us speaking to each other or him turning up at the office. But, by that time, my group of friends had expanded considerably. I wasn't as close to Jonathan as I was to Simon, but I still regarded him as a close friend, especially once I met and became friends with his wife, Annabel, which meant that we often ended up going out together as a group. Annabel was also a former model (for God's sake, the place was full of them!), English, and stunning. She was blonde, blue-eyed, had an amazing figure and was very clever. She was a bit intimidating, to say the least, but it was just so nice for me to have an English female friend that I put up with feeling a bit like the poor relation. I have to say, though, it came as a bit of a shock when Annabel first pitched up since, until then, I had assumed that Jonathan was single, being almost as much of a player as Simon, and often making the *This is Where you Hear it First* newsletter. Once I realised that he had a wife, I thought that I should probably stop mentioning him, much to his annoyance.

Jonathan was one of the first people in Prague to be able to buy a building since, at that time, it was more or less impossible to find anything for sale. That building was soon reconstructed and turned into very nice flats, which were quickly rented out to other expats even before the paint had dried. I can remember, a bit remorsefully, sitting in The Dog & Duck one evening and Jonathan mentioning that he was paying a couple of people to hunt down buildings that could be bought relatively easily. He had suggested that if we all put, say, £10,000 into a pot, he could probably buy something decent for all of us *and* reconstruct it. And we all said, "That sounds great, Jonathan, but we don't have £10,000!" Imagine where we would be now if we had have done. But I digress.

Another newcomer that had joined our group was Katy. She arrived shortly after I went out on my own and soon became a very good friend. When I first met her, I thought she was such a sweetheart, both in looks – she was small and petite with a pixie face and closely cropped brown hair that made her blue eyes stand out – and manner, since she was always so nice to everyone and seemed completely out of place among all of the tearaways. I don't think I ever saw Katy in trousers; she lived in pretty floral dresses and soft ballet-pump-type shoes, even when it was freezing cold outside, when she would turn up and spend a good few minutes peeling off layer after layer of colourful sweaters. But then I found out that she was the youngest ever partner in one of the big accounting firms that had opened up early on and heard from one of her colleagues that she was as tough as old boots and that most of the other partners were terrified of her. It was funny, really; I doubted that I would ever have been friends with someone like Katy if we had met in London; she was so not 'my type'. A bit too serious for me, too intellectual and too 'girly'. Plus she chewed her nails down to the quick, which I hated. And was a terrible time-keeper. Same comment. But being an expat, as I have reflected on numerous occasions over the years, throws you together with lots of very different people, and often the thing that brings you together is that you are all going through the same issues – living abroad, battling with the language, being homesick, and so on. This was the case with the two of us, since we both missed having English-speaking female company. And now we had found each other.

Katy, Annabel and I often went out for a 'girls' night', which meant a few drinks in the pub first and then off to a casino, before joining up with the boys at Lávka at the end of the night. Those evenings we would get togged up as if we were going to a casino in London, rather than a complete and utter dive full of Vietnamese gangsters and small-time Czech crooks. Katy and I would do our best, but sadly, our best was never quite as glam as Annabel, who would turn up in designer dresses dripping with real diamonds looking completely gorgeous.

Another new arrival who became a best friend – albeit male – was Ewan, who was one of the funniest and possibly craziest guys I had ever met. Ewan arrived in Prague to set up the local offices of an international real estate agency, having just qualified in London, but it was clear, even then, that his heart wasn't completely in it. What his heart *was* in, though, was making as many people laugh as possible, something he was very successful at. From the minute I met him, barely a day went by where I didn't speak to and/ or see him, especially once Simon became the happy husband. He was dark, short, good-looking and very fit, having been a serious rugby player. And he could sing like an angel – he was Welsh, after all – aren't they all good at rugby and singing? It was funny that he quickly became such a good friend as my mum always used to say, 'never trust a Welsh person' and 'never trust a short man'. Ewan ticked both boxes. Needless to say, when Mum actually did meet him, they hit it off like a house on fire.

Speaking of which. The first time I met Ewan was in The James Joyce, when it had only been open a few weeks. I had gone there with Lucie after we had both been working late and he was among a group of boys, all of whom had been in the pub for a few hours and were clearly the worse for wear. Ewan had been describing a party trick that he and his friends used to do back home, and the other boys hadn't believed him, so he had just asked one of the Irish barmen to bring him a glass of sambuca to demonstrate as we walked in.

"What you do," he said, "is you drop your trousers, pour the glass of sambuca over your arse, and then set fire to it." He promptly did just that.

As we walked through the door, therefore, we were met with a short Welshman running around the pub with his trousers around his knees and his arse on fire. Painless, apparently, but no-one else wanted to try. I think Lucie never really forgot her first encounter with him. But the boys brought him into their group with open arms, as did I, and it wasn't long before he was the new 'leader' in the *This is Where you Hear it First* charts, in place of Simon.

Within a few weeks of its opening, The James Joyce, or 'The Joyce' as we called it, had become the place to go, and pretty much every evening, I and most of the others would end up there at the end of our working day. Not only did we meet and do business there, but we found staff, made new friends and – in the boys' case – picked up young Czech girls who had very quickly realised that this was the place to meet the rich foreign boys before they headed off to one club or another. The Joyce even cooked up a really good Sunday lunch, which meant that just about everyone I knew would gather there at the weekend too. And it was in The Joyce that I first met the clients that changed the course of my business. They were from one of the UK's biggest companies at the time, Bass Brewers, and were in Prague to buy the near bankrupt and run-down brewery, the home of the famous Czech beer Staropramen.

"He hasn't been out today," he said,
"so he might be a little bit lively.
We saved him especially for you."

Bass Brewers

SOON AFTER LUCIE and I had moved into our cottage and got into the routine of driving in the borrowed van to Pardubice each week, we were joined by Jana, a Czech girl that I had noticed in The Joyce one evening. She caught my attention partly as her English was so good and partly as she was short, dark and hugely overweight, rather than the usual stamp of a Czech girl; tall, blonde and skinny. Plus, there was something a bit sad about her but, after we chatted a bit, I could tell she was very smart. She spoke about five different languages fluently, had lived for six months in the UK as a nanny, and was looking for a job. Jana, I felt, could be the ideal third member to our team and when I suggested she come and join us she accepted suspiciously enthusiastically – I later found out that that was due to her having been dismissed from various different jobs over the past few months due to her being impossible to work with, but taking references and doing any other checks were way into the future.

By this time, we had a lot of regular work and were starting to make a reasonable profit. As usual, in addition to the various events we were getting involved in, my friends were keeping us busy with the preparation of various marketing materials for them: brochures, leaflets, billboards and that kind of thing. I realise that anyone reading this under the age of 30 probably doesn't know what I mean by such things, but you can look them up if you type 'pre-historic marketing activities' or something similar into Google. Plus, Simon had asked me if we could organise his wedding, which was turning into a major project in and of itself. Then we had Pardubice, which was almost a full-time job all on its own.

During our first few trips we mostly discussed improvements to the course and then started working with the Tomašes to put together a package for sponsorship. Once we had found a sponsor, we felt we could concentrate on selling the private boxes. But, while construction hadn't yet started, we were already talking to various people who were all keen to buy one. I hadn't yet worked up the courage to discuss payment with the Tomašes as, at every meeting, they would talk about how broke they were. I wasn't too worried. If we could find a sponsor and/ or sell the boxes, then the money would be rolling in. That just shows how naïve I was in those days.

We had a kind of 'love/ hate' relationship with the Tomašes. On the one hand they obviously had high hopes we would be able to help them with their various issues but, on the other, it clearly irked them to be in a position where they had to listen to what a relatively young English woman had to say, and I was never sure I could really trust them. We worked the most with Little Tomaš, who I didn't really like as it seemed to me that he took quite a lot of pleasure in causing trouble. Sometimes, having told him that we would arrive at the racecourse at a certain time we would get there to find the office closed and no-one around and then we would have to wait for an age for him to turn up. Other times, he would take great delight in telling us that, while he believed we were doing a good job, Big Tomaš was very unhappy with us for various reasons that he couldn't really explain. Sadly, this was, as I gradually realised, standard Czech backbiting.

Then Mirek, the trainer, was a bit of a dark horse, if you pardon the pun. I was never quite sure if he liked us or not. On one of our visits, he asked if I would like to ride one of his horses the next time I visited which, I felt, was a real 'hand of friendship'. Plus, of course, it was way too tempting to say no to, even though, at that time, I hadn't ridden for about five years. On our next trip, therefore, I turned up with my jodhpurs, boots and helmet, which I had brought to Prague, just in case, some time ago. I spent the whole drive down trying to calm Lucie who was having complete kittens as, while she had seen a lot of horses in the distance before, she had never been up close and personal with them. Out came Mirek, leading a nice-looking chestnut horse, saddled up and ready to go.

"He hasn't been out today," he said, "so he might be a little bit lively. We saved him especially for you."

"Okay. But you know I haven't ridden for a few years?" I responded through Lucie, who was translating from some distance away, "I hope he will be nice to me."

"Don't worry," said Mirek, "he has a good nature." He then he offered me his hand to give me a leg-up into the saddle.

Thankfully, my body remembered what I was supposed to do and once I was onboard with my feet in the stirrups, I gathered up the reins and asked the horse to walk on through the gate that led towards the racecourse, smiling smugly to myself.

"You look like something from *Black Beauty*," said Lucie. I felt she was alluding to my looking rather like a blonde version of Elizabeth Taylor, rather than anything to do with the horse itself, and sat up a bit straighter, with a smile on my face.

That smugness didn't last long. With the Tomašes and Mirek gathered at the gate to watch, the so called 'good natured' horse decided to put on a show as we hit the turf and, accompanied by a string of almighty farts, he jumped about fifty metres to the right, stuck his head in the air and charged onto the racecourse proper as if we were getting ready to take part in the Velká Pardubická itself. I – thank God – managed to stay on board and, not wanting to give the Tomašes or Mirek any sort of satisfaction, tried to appear as if that had been my plan all along. Then, once I got behind the stands and away from all the watching eyes, I managed to yank the bloody animal round in a circle and give him a good talking-to. From then on, I was more or less in control, but after about half an hour or so of cantering about a bit aimlessly, I'd had enough. Nearly two years of debauchery and not much exercise had taken its toll on my muscles!

Once I had deposited the horse back with his stable lad and joined Lucie, she informed me that the Tomašes and Mirek had been chuckling away to each other when I first got into the saddle as, she said, they had clearly set me up and were expecting some fireworks. So much for the 'hand of friendship'. Poor Lucie, she had such a nervous disposition and admitted to having been basically sick when the horse bolted out onto the racecourse. Mainly, she said, as she was worried how she would get back to Prague if something happened to me and vowed never to go near a horse again! Thanks for the concern.

One day, I was sitting in the office and the phone rang. We still only had the one phone line, of course, and whoever was nearest would just pick it up and answer. On that day it was me, answering in my poshest 'receptionist-style' voice, I heard a British male voice with a northern accent asking if they could speak to 'Mrs Weaver'. I debated saying, 'Please hold on while I go and get her,' but didn't think I could carry it off, so simply said, "This is me. Can I help you?"

"Well, I hope so," the voice said. "My name is Maurice Potter. I'm in charge of marketing for Bass Brewers. I'm not sure if you know about it, but we have just bought the Staropramen brewery in Prague."

"Yes, of course," I said, nearly fainting on the floor, since Bass Brewers at that time was one of the biggest companies in the UK and the boss was a household name who was on the front of the newspapers all the time.

"We are looking for an agency to work for us in Prague and we got your name. Could we meet in the next couple of days? Maybe in The James Joyce?"

"Sure, that would be great," I said. "We look forward to it."

The following afternoon, I made my way to The Joyce, with Lucie in tow, to meet Maurice. He was sitting at a table with two other middle-aged guys; they looked relatively friendly, but he was positively terrifying: quite handsome in a '*Kojak*' kind of way but not in the least bit cuddly. And, unusually, he showed not a flicker of interest in Lucie, or me (although I never really expected anyone to notice me when she was around anyway). I later found out that he had a completely gorgeous wife, who had travelled to Prague as well, and who was even more terrifying than him, hence why he was so unfriendly. Maurice did most of the talking, explaining that the purchase of the brewery was a huge deal for them and, while many companies treated Prague as just a small market, for them it was a very big expansion and they would be pouring a lot of money into their marketing. Which meant, therefore, that they needed an agency on the ground to help. *Gulp.*

Bass had some very detailed plans for their arrival on the market, which they explained while we listened intently. Lucie later said that she hadn't understood a word of what had been said, since their northern accents were quite strong but, thankfully, she was sensible enough to keep quiet. One of the things they mentioned and that made us sit up was that the plans included involvement in some form of sponsorship as soon as possible, since Bass, traditionally, liked sports sponsorship, especially football and horse racing.

"Aha," I said. "I have just the thing."

So began our long relationship with Bass. The amount of work that was required was huge, even without the soon-agreed sponsorship of the Velká Pardubická. It transpired that the Managing Director of the Prague office was a horse-racing fan and loved the idea of getting involved, even though Maurice was a bit reluctant, and was happy to pay quite a lot of money for the sponsorship. On one hand, that was very exciting but, on the other, I was permanently stressed as to whether we could pull off such a big deal, especially as so much depended on the Tomašes in Pardubice actually performing. That was the bit that worried me the most.

"Imagine being Mr Short when
you were about two metres tall!
No wonder he was a bit odd."

Where's all the Money Gone?

WITH THE ONGOING changes that were being made to the racecourse and the sponsor in the bag, plus the amount of general work we had to get through on a daily basis, we soon decided we would have to reduce our visits to the racecourse for a while and instead focus on the sale of tickets/ boxes for the main race day in October, the Velká Pardubická.

We had discussed with the Tomašes the idea of having ten boxes built on the two first floors of the main (and only) stand and that each box would hold about 25 people. When I said 'boxes' what I had in mind was that each of the two floors that presently just consisted of rows of benches would be divided by partitions into five separate room-type spaces. And that each room or box would be carpeted, fitted out with a few tables and chairs, maybe have a TV screen in the corner and, ideally, have its own cloakroom too. As far as I could tell, I thought we were all on the same page with that. Bass, being the main sponsor, would have three boxes as part of their sponsorship and we aimed to sell the rest of them for DM 2,000 each, a price that would include entry tickets for 25 people, a free bar in each box and a buffet lunch. To make things easy for everyone, the racecourse would invoice each company for their box and then pay us a 15% commission for each payment received. *Simple.*

During the summer we remained very busy, partly with our regular work and the preparations for Simon's wedding, and the rest of the time with the sale of the boxes at the races and the work for Staropramen, more generally. At this early stage, the wedding planning mostly involved looking for a suitable venue and, as mentioned previously, Prague has a lot of those, which meant lots of visits and then lots of discussions, and then making endless lists of what else we would need to organise and what the priority of each thing should be. This changed most days, since Simon and Francesca could barely agree on anything, from the religion the service was to be conducted in and, therefore, the venue, to the type of food, the music, the timing of the event and who should attend (which didn't bode well for their future, in my view). Added to that, Simon was planning for most of his large North London Jewish family to fly over, which meant a lot of people for us to transport from the airport and around town, as well as finding a hotel that they could all stay in (good hotels were still thin on the ground in those days). Thankfully, most of Francesca's family lived in the US and wouldn't be attending, but her large group of friends would. Well, not all of them, as Simon wasn't keen. And so it went on.

In the meanwhile, as I had expected and hoped, the boxes in Pardubice were selling quickly, but even that wasn't as straightforward as it sounded. Jonathan had been a sure bet and had booked two boxes, one for his team and one for his most important clients. He then introduced me to another of his old friends who had just arrived in Prague, an immensely tall stockbroker called Thomas Short, who also booked a box the minute we met. Imagine being Mr Short when you were about two metres tall! No wonder he was a bit odd.

Thomas had to have his box next to Jonathan's, while Jonathan didn't want him anywhere near, since Thomas's wife was an old friend of Annabel's, and since Annabel wouldn't be attending, Jonathan had 'plans'. Are you with me so far? Thomas had arrived in Prague to open his own stockbroking firm and saw the idea of having a box at the races as the ideal way to wine and dine his potential clients and really announce his arrival. I remember having a conversation with him as we got nearer the date of the races in which he wanted to know whether the box would be soundproofed as there would be a lot of very confidential conversations going on. He also requested that we had the menu sent to him so that he could check that the wines would be of the quality expected, which, bearing in mind our budget and the location, was about as likely as an elephant turning up and winning the big race itself.

Anyway, once the word got out that Jonathan and various others had bought boxes the others sold very quickly and, as we got closer to race-day, everything began to take a reasonable shape. I had even sent our invoice off to the racecourse for our percentage commission. The Tomašes continually assured me that the changes to the course had been finalised and, to date, there was no sign of any interest from the animal rights people, so that was good. Then we had a press conference at the beginning of July to discuss the sponsorship and just about every journalist in town turned up to find out more and wrote about it in a relatively positive light, at least compared to when Bass first turned up in Prague and the headlines in all the papers said 'Bass steals the family silver' (thank God that had nothing to do with us, but still, we were nervous as to how they might treat the sponsorship of the horse race). I even began to feel a bit more relaxed…

Shortly after the press conference, though, when Maurice had given me a long list of things to check at the racecourse in regard to their sponsorship, we decided that we really needed to go there one more time to see how everything was and to get answers to our last remaining questions.

The first thing that struck us, as we made our way up the long drive to the racecourse entrance, was how everything looked very much the same as usual, except that the track and the parkland where the actual racing took place were very brown and parched looking; summer in Pardubice had been even hotter than in Prague that year. Indeed, that was one of the things that surprised me when we first got involved with the racecourse, the fact that their 'steeplechasing season' took place in the summer, as opposed to the winter, as it did elsewhere in Europe, and which was obviously due to the winters in the Czech Republic being freezing cold and with a lot of snow. That said, rattling about on hard ground takes an awful toll on horses' legs, let alone any jockeys' bodies if they fall onto it.

Worryingly, as we neared the office and, more importantly, the stand, we could see that nothing there looked to have changed a lot either and, as we made our way inside and found only Little Tomaš waiting to meet us, I started to have a bit of a sinking feeling about it all.

"Just you today?" I asked him, noting that he was already looking even shiftier than usual.

"Yes, the others are on holiday, as is usual during July and August, so it's just me," he responded.

"Ah, okay. So, what shall we do first? Discuss the requirements for Bass, or go out and see the boxes in the stands?" I was already sensing that all was not as it should have been, when Little Tomaš started to squirm.

"Well, about the boxes," he said, looking anywhere other than at me or Lucie. "I'm afraid we haven't been able to build them as we had originally planned as we ran out of money."

"But you had the money from the people that booked them!" I said, my voice rising slightly hysterically. "Plus, most of the sponsorship money must have been paid by now?"

"Yes," he replied. "But unfortunately, we had to use that for other things and then we ran out of cash altogether."

"So, what shall we do?"

He didn't answer, just shrugged his shoulders and looked sulkily at both of us as if it had nothing to do with him. I felt sick. Lucie looked as if she would actually *be* sick at any moment. I thought about all those people that had paid money for the boxes and had even worried about sound-proofing and the quality of the wines. I would have to go back to Prague and tell them that there were no boxes and, not only that, that the money had gone. That would pretty well finish us off before we had really started.

We left as soon as I could face the drive. There was no point in sitting talking to Little Tomaš, who I quite happily could have punched in the face. It didn't seem worth trying to discuss the requirements of Bass at that point as I doubted the Tomašes would be able to organise any of the many things that the contract that we had signed required them to do. It was a disaster.

On the drive back, Lucie was near to tears as she always took everything to heart and worried that anything that went wrong was her fault, either for not translating something correctly or misunderstanding what had been agreed. But, of course, it didn't have anything to do with her and, judging by Little Tomaš' behaviour, I was pretty sure they had just taken the money and used it for whatever they fancied. Or, more likely, they had used it to line their pockets, leaving me to take the rap for it all. They would lose nothing.

To make matters worse, Lucie decided to use the drive back to Prague to tell me about all the problems she was having with Jana who, she said, was sweet and nice when I was around but a complete cow when I wasn't. I can't say I was completely surprised as I had already found her to be very argumentative. She was also a 'blamer', as I called it. A rather unsavoury trait of the older Czechs, who would always say that it was someone or something else's fault every time there was a problem, never theirs. And in our office that meant that poor old Lucie was, according to Jana, responsible for just about everything that went wrong. What I hadn't realised though was that part of the reason for Jana's excessive moodiness, another trait I had noticed and as Lucie was now telling me, was that she had been shagging 'one of our clients' but she wasn't ready to tell us which one. That piece of news nearly caused me to drive off the road.

"Whatever are we going to do?" I asked Lucie, who just shrugged and looked resigned. "I suppose I'll have to have a word with her and find out more. But first, we have to get the boxes built, since we really only have a couple of months to do it. That has to be the priority."

Honestly, being the boss was, as I was finding out on a more or less daily basis, a great deal more difficult than I had ever considered (if I ever did).

"Actually, I sort of knew he had arrived before I saw him as a kind of 'ripple' started among the girls."

Be Grateful for Rough Diamonds

IN THE END, I didn't have to say anything to Jana about her out-of-work activities as the day after we returned from Pardubice she arrived in the office in floods of tears announcing that her 'boyfriend' had just dumped her and she was now distraught. I decided not to ask her who her boyfriend had actually been and just made all the right sympathetic noises, along with suggesting that she throw herself into work for now to take her mind off it all. And God, we had so much work it needed more than us just throwing ourselves at it to get it done. We needed a bloody miracle.

That same morning, however, I had woken up at 3.00 am with a brainwave, having spent the whole night wondering whether the Pardubice project was going to be the death of the company. Just a few evenings previously, I had been sitting in The Joyce with Ewan and a few of the others, the boys causing a bit of havoc as usual, when an English guy I hadn't seen before – nice looking but very much a rough diamond – had leant over to our table and said, "Oy you lot! Keep the f'ing noise down will yer?" Ewan had responded with a few expletives of his own before suggesting that he come and join us, but he was too busy chatting up a group the regular Czech girls that were always hanging around the bar.

"I don't get it," said Ewan. "That guy Gary comes in here, rough as shit, and all the girls fall at his feet. He doesn't have to make any effort at all!"

"And what do you do on the effort front?" I responded, raising my eyebrows at him quizzically.

I, as a woman, wasn't that surprised. Gary was one of those guys that had a certain charm about him and, let's face it, most of us girls do like, as they say, 'a bit of rough'. Plus, while not being a head-turner like Jonathan or Simon, he was good looking in a 'cheeky chappy', 'Confessions of a Window Cleaner' sort of way: tall, fittish, brownish, hair, nice eyes. And, possibly more importantly, and despite appearances, Gary was, according to Ewan a bit later, fast becoming one of the richest of the expat boys, having arrived a few months earlier and setting up shop as a builder. And, at that time, English-speaking builders could pretty much name their price.

That evening, I took myself off to The Joyce a bit earlier than usual and waited at the bar until Gary, who I had heard was usually there from about 6.00 until 7.00 pm, arrived. The good thing about The Joyce was that even ladies like me could go there on our own without feeling awkward. Just as I'd ordered my drink, in he walked.

Actually, I sort of knew he had arrived before I saw him as a kind of 'ripple' started among the girls. I was more than a little bit chuffed therefore when he made a beeline for me, introducing himself straightaway.

"I know who you are," I said. "We met the other evening. And, actually, I came down here specifically to meet you as I would like to discuss something with you."

I then gave him an outline of what we had expected in Pardubice and what the reality was and, without even turning a hair, he immediately offered his help.

"Give me a week to finish what I'm on now and then I reckon if I take a couple of the lads and we stay down there we can get it all built in a few days."

"But what will it cost?"

"Don't you worry about that. I'll figure something out."

And so he did. Two weeks later, having camped out in the stands the whole time they were there and causing a fair bit of trouble by all accounts – it sounded as if a lot of the local girls found such charming foreign builders to be quite an attraction and apparently many of them had been visiting the stands on a regular basis – Gary and his crew had worked a miracle and what are now called the 'Weaver Suites' were born. Two floors of supposedly corporate boxes ready and waiting for race-day. No-one that attended that day knew a thing about what had happened beforehand.

It would be wrong to say that the race day itself went by without a hitch, but only we knew that it hadn't. The majority of the people attending in our boxes enjoyed themselves, not least because we had laid on enormous amounts of booze, not only in the boxes themselves but also on the buses we had organised to bring everyone down to the racecourse. In addition, for the first time ever, I had gone along with the idea of bringing in some 'pretty girls' to decorate the place. I know, completely politically incorrect, but with the majority of the people attending being men, the girls definitely cheered the place up and went down well (if you pardon the expression).

Lucie, Jana and I had driven down at the crack of dawn, together with Rhys, a newly-arrived Welshman (don't ask me how I came to surround myself with Welshman at that time, my mother was furious!). Rhys was blonde, brown-eyed and as a fit as a professional rugby player, which, I later learned, he had actually been (of course, as per my earlier comment about the Welsh in regard to Ewan). He was another absolute charmer who could sing like an angel. Just what is it about Welshmen? Rhys had come to Prague to work as a print manager, and we met him when we had been hunting around for someone to get all of our materials printed for the racecourse. Basically, he handled the whole process, using whichever printer he thought would be best for the job. All we had to do was hand the materials over to him and he would do the rest. He and I immediately hit it off, to the point that I did consider briefly that he might be a potential beau, despite the blonde hair (and if he didn't get corrupted in the meantime). Especially since, needless to say, he was a bit of a nutcase. From the day he arrived, everyone loved him, and it was very soon clear that, as far as we JWA girls were concerned, we would be lost without him.

As soon as we arrived at the racecourse, Rhys was off with the grounds-people, hanging banners and blowing up the branded 'inflatables' that were strategically placed all around the entrance and stands, and then it was 'all hands-on deck' to get the huge inflatable and somewhat phallic Staropramen-branded beer bottle positioned in the middle of the parkland. We had chosen the area right next to the Taxis, the biggest and most dangerous fence on the course and one that had been named after the Duke of Thurn and Taxis (who, it is supposed, bred horses nearby some few thousand years ago), on the basis that that would be where the main TV cameras were focused. God knows what the horses made of it. Especially as, in the end, having stayed upright most of the afternoon, it began deflating just as the big race started, ending up at 'half-mast' just as the horses raced past it.

Once all the sponsorship materials were set-up we had to run into the stands to deal with the caterers, and then the gates were opened and the people flooded in. I couldn't believe how many. Most of the locals, of course, were regulars at the racecourse and they had their own places where they stood by the railings, sat on the grass, or milled around the paddock, while the 'big wigs', basically the local mafia, made their way to the top floors of the stands. Our guests arrived on their buses soon after and Jana was outside to meet them and direct the drivers to the parking areas. Lucie and I, meanwhile, were inside, running between the boxes, with a 'yes, the food will be arriving soon' to the hosts of the boxes and a 'get a bloody move on' to the caterers (who didn't know the meaning of moving fast), checking that Gary's brand new toilets had loo rolls, soap, and so on (which they didn't, so it was lucky we had brought some with us) and every so often glancing over at the racecourse to see if there was any sight of animal rights activists, which there weren't, thank God. In the end, we never actually got to see any of the races themselves but were fed with bits of information, in particular one piece of news that everyone was delighted to keep telling us, and that was that 'the fog was getting thicker and soon we wouldn't be able to see the races at all', which we hadn't actually noticed. I jest, as, of course, we had barely noticed anything else. The contract between the racecourse and Bass required that all the sponsorship money would be returned if, for any reason, the big race didn't go ahead and that meant that I was gradually debating suicide, since, at the rate we were going, the unimaginable was about to happen and the plug was going to be pulled. Horses cannot jump fences if they can't actually see them!

By the time everyone got back on the bus to head back to Prague, the race having, thankfully, taken place despite the weather, to say we were exhausted would be an understatement. In fact, as the last people were filing out, the four of us were slumped on the ground by the carpark, more or less unable to move and feeling completely shell-shocked.

"It was good," said Lucie. "Everyone loved it, even those people from Phyllis Morris."

"Who?" I asked.

"Phyllis Morris, the cigarette company."

Which, at the time, seemed so funny we all started laughing. So hard we couldn't stop. And that was how Gary, our rough diamond, found us when he came to look for us.

"Come on, you lot," he said. "My boys will drive the truck home. I'm driving your car."

I could have cried. I probably did.

"Quick!" he said. "Get me inside. There's a bloody great Russian pimp on my tail."

Vicars and Tarts

THE DAYS AFTER the race went by in a blur. We had a lot of people congratulating us for such a successful event. The Bass boys had called us in for a debrief and were generally happy and ready to do it all again next year, and Simon, having promised to keep out of my hair as much as possible until the races were over, was in and out of our offices on an almost hourly basis to discuss the plans for his wedding which were well underway.

I was already realising that there is never any time to relax in a 'PR agency', which is what we now seemed to have grown into. Even when a big project finishes, there is always more work to do and another client breathing down your neck. While I was feeling completely knackered from the stress of the whole Pardubice project and continued to be worried about money – since at that point we hadn't actually been paid a penny, or should I say a crown, by the racecourse – there was no way I could consider taking any sort of break. Also, Simon, whose wife-to-be was off in the country for a few days, had reminded me that Jonathan was organising a pre-wedding party for him on one of the 'botels' that weekend and I just couldn't imagine having the energy for it. Plus, I had thought I ought to go to the UK for the weekend and finally see my mum, after a few too many weeks being stuck in Prague.

Simon, though, is very good at persuasion and, since just about everyone I knew was invited, including Clive and Eva from my old office, I decided that the UK would have to wait another week. Even Lucie was planning to attend, along with a very nice and very quiet English guy that she had finally told me she was dating (I had suspected it but had been keeping her in the office so much that I thought it was probably over).

This meant that my Saturday afternoon was spent trying to figure out what to wear, since I had also forgotten that the party was fancy dress and we all had to go as either a tart or a vicar. Since there was no chance of buying or renting anything suitable in Prague, especially so late in the day, I decided the only things I had that could be vaguely suitable were a very tight black dress I had never had the nerve to wear as it was way too short and tight, together with fishnets and high black shoes. And since, at that time, I lived in suits during the day and jeans in the evening, I felt, relatively speaking, that it was pretty damned tarty.

My plans were thrown a bit when Simon turned up at the cottage in the late afternoon in a mad panic, wanting to borrow something to wear.

"Darling," he said, running up the stairs as soon as I opened the front door and heading for my bedroom. "I've nothing to wear tonight. Surely you have something I can borrow?" He went straight over to my own black dress hanging ready on the wardrobe door. "This would be perfect. Can I wear it?"

"No, you bloody can't," I responded. "That's mine and you've got a bloody cheek thinking that you could get into it anyway."

He wasn't really listening as by that time he was riffling through my clothes, pulling out various different bits and pieces and holding them up against himself while looking in the mirror.

"What about this one?" He had my favourite cream A-line which I kept for posh occasions in his hand.

"Okay, you can try it on," I said, thinking for sure it would be too tight and he would give up. In fact, with his dark skin and black hair he actually looked very nice, even though it was a bit of a tight squeeze.

"I'm going to need to borrow a bra too," he said, heading for my chest of drawers. "I guess I can fit into one of yours. Some socks to stuff it up a bit would be good too." For God's sake, what is it with men and them always wanting to have boobs? "And shoes?" he said, grabbing my black courts and announcing that they should do him perfectly. That left me to wear another pair that were way too high and had been yet another slightly foolish purchase when I was last in the UK, desperate to buy just about anything.

I realised how completely bonkers my life had become when the two of us then sat side by side in my tiny bathroom so I could help Simon to put on makeup while doing mine at the same time. And then, suitably tarted up, we tottered off together for pre-boat drinks at The Joyce and then over to the boat, as if we did this every day of the week.

I don't think I had ever seen a 'botel' before coming to Prague, although I probably had, without realising they had a name. In case you haven't either, it is a docked boat that operates as a hotel. At that time, there was just the one, moored near to my former hotel, The Continental, and the scene, I had heard from my old 'working girl' friends in those days, of some pretty wild and unsavoury goings on. Jonathan, though, does like to put on a show, and for this particular evening he had taken over the whole boat and set up the open top deck as a disco, decked out with fairy lights all around the railings and coloured spotlights along the floor and had even flown in a proper DJ from London or Paris, or something equally Jonathan-esque. Below that floor, at water-level, was a huge buffet area with tables and chairs, and then, under that, in what would normally be the bedrooms, well, I don't think I want to think about those.

Wow. All my previous tiredness was forgotten as we walked down the gang plank into the disco, already packed with many of our regular friends, as well as a lot of new faces. There was Clive with Eva, Clive already being chatted up by a lady banker who we had worked with in the past and who had a bit of a thing for him, despite the fact that he could be heard on several occasions telling her, "It's no good you chasing me, Diana, I am impotent!" While Eva, as usual, was completely over-excited, smoking about three cigarettes at once and flirting outrageously with another of our previous clients, a very good-looking Norwegian that Clive used to refer to as 'that Jessie'. We were never quite sure whether that meant he thought he was gay, too pretty for words or he just didn't like him, but anyway, as he used the term so often, we decided it was a form of endearment.

He clearly deserved some kudos, anyway, since much later on I saw him throwing Eva over his shoulder while doing the jive, which was no mean feat, especially since Eva is what one might call a 'big girl', but then, he *was* Norwegian. Judging from the screams and hysteria coming from Eva, I doubt she had ever been thrown over someone's shoulder before, but she clearly enjoyed it. Then, as

Simon left me to go downstairs to find Jonathan and the other boys, a crowd of others from the pub appeared, led by Ewan, dressed as a very pretty girl, not tarty at all, and another very beautiful, very tall woman – at least from afar – that I had never seen before.

In those days, even though it might sound as if we spent the whole evening and night drinking, all of us, pretty much without exception, loved to dance too. I suppose it was growing up in the 80s, when disco was the big thing, and the music was so great. Ewan, being musical, was a really good dancer, as was Simon when he put his mind to it, assuming he didn't have any other things to do at the time and/ or was sober enough to stay upright. The music on the boat that night was fantastic and, combined with it being a very hot evening and us being outside on the river, the atmosphere on the deck was incredible. And with the stunning Prague Castle lit up on the hill as a backdrop, it would have been difficult not to have wanted to get up and dance, so it wasn't long before the whole deck was heaving with tarts and vicars having a good old boogie.

As usual, I had started dancing with Ewan, and then had a couple of twirls with one of the Bass boys, who had all arrived in a group soon after us, although there was no sign of Maurice or the other senior people. I was a bit relieved by that really as I didn't feel very comfortable letting my hair down in front of a 'big' client (and still don't), unless I know them really well. As I tottered off to find a drink though, I bumped into the tall 'woman' from earlier on, who I realised, once 'she' was close-up, was not in fact a woman, but a very well made-up man with a long black wig, striking blue eyes, huge tits that filled his gold glittery top and pretty strappy sandals.

"Do you want to dance again?" he asked, grabbing my hand and walking back to the dance floor to 'whoops' and cheers from the boys.

"I'm Jeremy," he said, jigging about a bit. "I got here just a few weeks ago. Haven't seen you before."

"No? Well, I can't really say whether I've seen you before or not. But it's nice to meet you anyway," I laughed.

He wasn't a very good dancer, although, to be fair, that could have been something to do with the shoes so, after a few more turns around the dancefloor we called it a day and went off to join the others at the bar. I continued to stay and talk to him for a while though as he was very chatty and appeared interested in everything I was saying, plus, from the way the others were sucking up to him, he was clearly 'someone important', although he dodged the question when I asked him what he did.

The evening continued apace. I briefly saw Lucie in the distance with her boyfriend and spent quite a lot of time dancing with the Welsh boys, Rhys having pitched up later in the evening with a couple of young Czech girls on his arm, but they had been dumped at the bar to wait for him while he did his thing. By the time I had come off the dancefloor, the mysterious Jeremy was nowhere to be seen and, needing a bit of a break from dancing, I headed off to join Eva and Clive at a side table to observe the activities, just like the old days.

I did get a glimpse of Jeremy again later in the evening but, disappointingly, and rather bizarrely, given the circumstances, he was snogging one of Jonathan and Simon's secretaries. Were it ever so. And, as the night wore on, people gradually started to fade away; some sitting down and chatting in the buffet area, while the more notorious headed downstairs to God knows what. So, after saying goodbye to Clive and sitting with Eva for a while in the bar, when she said she was going to head off in a taxi, I said I would go too.

It must have been about 2.00 am when Eva dropped me off outside the cottage, where, of course, I found the front door locked and barred, so it took me a while to get inside and get myself off to bed. I was somewhat unamused, therefore, to be woken up at about 4.30 am to the sound of the outside bell being pressed continuously. I debated ignoring it but then lay there imagining the wrath of the old ladies next door if they could hear it. In the end, I decided I would have to get out of bed and see who was there, as if I didn't know, and, sure enough, Simon was outside, shrieking that I needed to let him in quickly.

Off I went downstairs, dressed only in a T-shirt and pants, and out to the main door I had dutifully locked behind me as I came in, and there was Simon, still wearing my dress, but missing a shoe (one of my shoes, for God's sake), make-up smeared all over his face and out of breath.

"Quick!" he said. "Get me inside. There's a bloody great Russian pimp on my tail."

Needless to say, by this time one of the old ladies from upstairs was awake and had started screaming at us out of her window. I had no choice but to let him in, bolt the door again and then run back into the cottage after him.

Simon being Simon, though, hadn't finished for the night, especially since his wife-to-be was away.

"Darling," he said, plonking himself down in the office and putting his feet and my single shoe on Lucie's desk, "Can you pour me a whisky? I need to recover from the run over here."

Since I always kept a bottle of whisky handy for one of those 'Simon' eventualities, out it came and figuring, 'if you can't beat them, join them,' I poured out two good slugs for the both of us. Simon then smoked about five cigarettes, one after the other, before deciding that the coast was clear and got up to leave, still in my dress, but with the trainers he had been wearing earlier in the day replacing my beloved black court shoe. Leaving meant, of course, I had to let him out and lock up again. Then I was back to bed, out for the count, and asleep for most of Sunday, only waking up briefly in the evening to rattle out a blockbuster *This is Where you Hear it First* bulletin, which I hastily faxed out before falling asleep again.

The following Monday I had a visit from my landlord. I can't say I was surprised.

"I heard about the 'problems' you had on Saturday," he said, making the inverted comma signs with his hands.

"Yes, I am so sorry," I replied.

"No need to be sorry. I haven't laughed so much in years. The old lady from the first-floor flat next door came to see me this morning. She told me that she was woken up by a man dressed as a woman ringing on your doorbell for hours and that you let him in. And that a few minutes later a huge Russian turned up and started looking at the doorbells himself, so she leant out and chucked a bucket of water over him. He wasn't very happy. Mrs Anderova, though, was thrilled. She said she has waited more than 40 years to do just that!"

"Since most of my friends at that time were, as Clive called us, 'puffing billies', we would make our way to the smoking seats at the back."

The Flying Pub

The following week I decided I really had to do a quick visit to the UK before I got completely bogged down by the various projects that were looming. I was fast finding out there is never a good time to do anything other than work, so time off just has to be taken, and to Hell with the consequences. And, also, that being an expat is always difficult when it comes to family.

Despite all the improvements to life in the Czech Republic over those first couple of years, there were still only a few flights a week between Prague and London. The two that everyone took were either the Czech Airlines flight that left at about 6.00 pm on Friday, with a return at 7.00 am on a Monday, or the British Airways flight that left on Friday morning, with a return on the Sunday night. Both of these flights were usually full as there were a lot of people that flew home every single weekend, mainly those guys that led a double life (a wife and family in the UK and a girlfriend in Prague). Actually, I once sat next to a very traumatised-looking guy who told me as we chatted on the plane that he had just said goodbye to his young wife and child at Prague airport and was now going to the UK to see his old wife and children in London. And since he hadn't been home for a few weeks, he was in quite a state. A real-life bigamist! And the thing was, the guys that were doing this kind of thing weren't gorgeous wealthy playboys but regular middle-aged or older married men, who, if they were living in the UK, would probably be at home in the evenings with their slippers on, sipping cocoa. While in Prague, they were dancing the nights away at Lávka and hanging out in the strip clubs, or worse.

Unusually for me, I went back on the BA flight as I didn't want to be out of the office at all the following week. Usually, I preferred to go Czech Airlines (CSA). In those days, the CSA flight on a Friday evening was on an old Russian airplane called a Tupolev. It was a bit like one of those propeller planes that are still in use and was small – I think it sat about 40 people – but the difference was it had curtains in all the windows and narrow slots in the walls of the loo. The planes had been used by the military once upon a time and the slots were for resting your gun through as the plane came into land (or as you sat on the loo, which I have always found to be useful). Since most of my friends at that time were, as Clive called us, 'puffing billies', we would make our way to the smoking seats at the back. Then the pilot would usually say 'we are nearly ready to depart but we are just waiting for one last passenger' and we would all roll our eyes at each other, knowing that after about ten minutes the curtain across the entrance would open and Eva would come bustling in, usually with scarves and red hair flying behind her, heaving her huge 'counsel's briefcase' and hailing everyone that she knew, as well as those she didn't, with a 'hello darling' here and a 'hello darling' there, before joining us at the back. Then, I kid you not, as soon as the engines were fired up and we started bumping our way to the runway, she would have the first of her many fags lit up and, even though various people around her would be shrieking, "Put it out Eva!" the crew didn't particularly care. Eventually, we would be airborne, the curtains along the portholes would be drawn, and off we went on our flying pub until we landed safely at Heathrow quite a few bottles of wine later.

That particular weekend on BA, the whole journey passed without incident. I didn't know anyone onboard, no alcohol was consumed and we landed on time at Heathrow. Unfortunately for me though, the easiest way to get to Royal Tunbridge Wells was to take the underground into central London, then a cab to Charing Cross and then the train, which altogether took longer than flying from Prague to London. I didn't really mind. As much as I loved Mum, the discombobulation of leaving my crazy life in Prague and then having to morph into the 'good daughter' required a bit of time and the train journey down through the lovely Kent countryside allowed me to have that.

In those days my mum was still young and sprightly, so our time together was always fun, a good deal of it being spent pottering around clothes shops and buying things I usually realised when I got back to Prague were completely unsuitable. This weekend was no exception. As usual, we headed to one of the big department stores that bring people into Tunbridge Wells from all around, and, also as usual, I immediately lost her, Mum being only a bit over five feet tall. Within a few minutes, therefore, I was whizzing about between the different franchises trying to find her, rather than looking at clothes.

Then she appeared saying, "Look what I have found, darling," in the posh English voice that she had cultivated carefully since her first arrival in TW, holding up one of the most expensive items in the shop. "This will look gorgeous on you."

"No, it won't," I responded. "I can't wear that colour and it is way too expensive. But okay, I'll try it on."

I headed to the changing room with her following behind and was met with a clap of hands when I appeared and a "Darling, it looks absolutely marvellous on you," which meant that I, not wanting to disappoint her, ended up buying a completely unsuitable dress just to make her happy, and then repeated a similar process again a few times throughout the day.

We also popped into the betting shop as Mum never had the nerve to go there on her own and loved to have a flutter on the horses. She always bet on her favourite jockey, Ruby Walsh, who, needless to say, she regarded as the best looking and deserving of her money. Yes, Mum was a bit of a letch, as you may have gathered, and clearly, I got my liking for pretty boys from her. Then we rushed home to spend the afternoon watching the races on the TV with Mum, as always, bent forward as if she was riding the horses herself, eyes glued on whichever horse she had backed. And if, as happened in several of the races this particular day, her horse started to look as if it might win, she would begin shouting at the telly, "Go on, go on," with a resounding, "Yes!" as her horse stormed over the line first, leaving her a few quid better off, completely overjoyed, and also, I suspected, a little bit pleased that her choice of horse had beaten mine – me being a so-called 'expert'.

Mum was a great cook and would serve up the sort of food that, back in Prague, we could still only dream about, in spite of Zátiši. Plus, she always stocked me up with all sorts of goodies to take back with me. Just as I was cramming my last purchase into an already full suitcase before setting off, she appeared, "Before you go darling," she said with a twinkle, "I have made you a few different cakes to take back. I know how much you like them." And then she handed over a selection, all stuffed full of calories and some, such as the yummy fruit cakes, weighing more than anything else in my bag. I couldn't say no. I imagined it was a bit like how it was for my posh friends when they went back to school after the holidays. But nice.

One thing I always found when I went back to the UK was that my old friends were rarely available to meet up. Since I only ever knew when I could get back to the UK at fairly short notice, I could only give them a few days' warning, and usually they were busy with their own lives and routines that couldn't be changed. As I couldn't really see why any of the reasons they gave me were so important that they couldn't be moved to the next week or whenever, I gradually got the message that we had grown apart and consequently gave up letting them know I was there at all. Yet another thing that makes being an expat quite difficult.

Anyway, there I was on the Sunday evening BA flight back to Prague, suitably rested and cheered up, with newspapers to read on the flight and then to give to my friends on Monday morning and as many books as I could carry. God, how we missed being able to buy books in those days! And, since it was a working day the next day, I allowed myself just one glass of red wine, to go with one cigarette, all the time becoming more and more conscious of someone's eyes on me from the seat across the corridor.

I was sitting on the righthand side by the window in the back row, while by the lefthand side window there was an extremely good-looking bloke, who was half reading his newspaper and half glancing across at me and trying to catch my eye. Since I didn't think I knew him and, you might be surprised to hear, I am generally a little bit shy when sober, I pretended not to notice and got on with reading my book, taking surreptitious glances across when he wasn't looking. Finally we landed and he grabbed his bag and legged it, while I was a bit slower since I had luggage checked-in and there was no hurry.

Luggage duly collected, I found my way outside to where Simon had said he would be waiting, since he had promised to collect me as payback for the previous weekend. There was no sign of him. Annoyingly, that meant heading towards the taxi ranks. Before I got there though, I noticed his car parked (illegally) in the VIP area, of course, and just beyond that, I spotted him. He was hanging onto a young red-haired girl who was wrestling him off while, at the same time, trying to punch the guy from the plane, who was hiding behind Simon. She was screaming at the guy from the plane at the top of her voice, words to the effect of 'you bastard', 'how could you?' and 'I'll kill you' littering the air.

I wasn't sure I wanted to get too near them but also couldn't really ignore them. Plus, I was keen to find out what exactly was going on, as were several other people gathering nearby. Eventually, she stopped screaming, the man from the plane started to walk off and Simon, with his arm around the girl, spotted me and walked over, opening the back door as he got to his car and shoving her inside. I knew her, I thought, and then realised it was one of his secretaries.

"I'm so sorry, darling," said Simon. "I did come to get you but then I spotted Daniela here hiding behind a tree and had to see what she was doing. Transpires she was waiting for Jeremy. Surely you saw him on the plane?"

Of course, I thought. *The beautiful woman from the boat party. The mysterious Jeremy. So that's why he was trying to catch my eye. Interesting.*

"So, who is he?" I asked Simon, after we had dropped Daniela off at her flat. "And why was she so upset with him?"

"He's the new bloke from that big real estate agency just down the road from our office. Turns out though that he isn't staying there long as he has been headhunted to open the offices for a huge new outfit that is about to start up here – bit of a 'blue-eyed boy' by all accounts."

"Hmm, and there was I thinking he was something way more glamorous than just another property boy!"

"Darling, you can't get much more glamorous than a property boy! But why are you asking? Don't tell me you fancy him! Forget it. From what I have heard from Daniela and others, he's a complete bastard. Shags everything that moves. Sounds as if he has some sort of addiction or something. Not like me darling, one of the good ones!"

We headed home with nothing more said on the subject. But I couldn't help feeling that I was going to see a lot more of Jeremy, while also wondering whether that would be a good or a bad thing.

The Sex Capital of Europe

IN BED THAT NIGHT I pondered why I wasn't more shocked by Daniela's behaviour, as she had looked completely deranged when Simon was wrestling with her. I am sure that if he hadn't been there she could have done some serious damage. Not that Jeremy, judging by the look of him, wouldn't have been able to take care of himself, but she seemed like a woman possessed. The reason for my own 'laidbackness' about the whole thing, though, was that in the time I had been in Prague I had seen so much weird and wonderful behaviour by the young Czech girls that nothing really surprised me.

I mentioned before how it seemed that every young Czech girl seemed to be on a mission to bag themselves a rich foreign husband. There were various problems with this, one being that many of the foreign boys, while they might have appeared to be rich when living in Prague, often driving much nicer cars than the locals and/ or living in better accommodation, their lifestyle was mostly being paid for by their companies and they themselves weren't rich at all. The second and most important thing was that the girls didn't always understand that just because they had gone home with someone for one night, that didn't necessarily mean that they were now an 'item'. We heard loads of stories of girls turning up on the boys' doorsteps the following day with their suitcases, or those that refused to leave after their 'night of passion'. There was even one story of a girl turning up the next night with her best friend who had come to join in. Not that that particular boy complained...

The boys I was hanging around with behaved outrageously. They would compete with one another to see how many girls they could shag in a week, or even in a day, in some cases (mentioning no names). Or how quickly they could get someone to go home with them, based on the time between introducing themselves and them leaving the pub, club or wherever we were, which seemed to be, on average, about two minutes. As much as I loved them all, and while I had occasionally dabbled with one or two of them a little (kept that one quiet!), none were 'husband material'. Or, if they were, it was usually because they already one, back home. In my case, therefore, it was much better to stay 'one of the lads'.

The Czech girls, though, while often being very pretty, were *so* predatory. I used to get cross when Ewan – it was usually him – held fort about how beautiful they all were, as I felt it was because we were in the centre of a capital city and the girls that were coming to work for us or to socialise in the 'Western' pubs and clubs weren't necessarily the norm. I reckoned that if you looked at the girls in any city centre – London, Paris and so on – you would see just as many good-looking ones, the difference was that those in Prague made it quite clear they were available and on the hunt. Why they should be so upset when they saw the same boy that they had bagged one night going off with someone else the next, was, on that basis, a bit surprising.

There was something else too. One of the first things we used to discuss in the old days of The Dog & Duck was the clothes everyone was wearing. I know it sounds cruel, but the local fashion was very different from ours. The reason for this was that during communism there were just a handful of department stores and other small shops and the clothes they sold were very different to what we were wearing in the West. Plus, since it was difficult to import anything, and regular people had very low spending power, the choice was extremely limited. This began to change as Western-owned stores started to open, but even then, they were way too expensive for the average Czech. We used to say you could always spot a Czech man in a crowd as he was the one wearing a poor quality, shiny, maroon suit, usually combined with white socks and strange shoes. But a Czech woman, well, she would be dressed in as little as possible, even in winter, priority always being given to making sure that as much cleavage and leg was on show as possible, irrespective of whether either part might eventually be frozen off. You can imagine, therefore, how much the boys looked forward to the summer, when some of the outfits that were on show were simply unbelievable.

I remember one of my previous employees turning up for work in a very short and very low-cut dress that was made entirely out of mirrored coins. I took one look at her and then asked her to pop into my office.

"You look very nice today," I had said. "But it seems a pity to wear such a nice dress to the office. Do you want to run home and maybe change it for something more casual?"

"Oh, don't worry," she responded. "I don't wear this dress for going out anymore as it is getting old. I thought I would start wearing it to the office as it is still smart and everything else in my wardrobe is too revealing."

God forbid!

And another thing. We couldn't buy decent deodorant at that time in Prague and, if we could find it at all, it was very expensive. I used to bring tons of it back from the UK. Most Czechs, though, couldn't afford it and, with their limited amount of clothes and difficulty in washing them – either because they didn't have a washing machine, couldn't afford decent washing powder or just didn't want to – they often smelled dreadful. Funnily enough, the only washing powder on the market at the time was called Colon, which seemed rather apt. Of course, those that wanted to get hold of a foreign man soon realised they needed to clean-up their act (pardon the pun). But, on the whole, standing on a tram or in the metro, especially in the summer, was not a pleasant experience.

Personal hygiene was one of our favourite subjects and, because most of our gang were 'bosses', it usually fell to us to have to do something about this kind of problem in our offices. I remember one of my friends telling me he had put a box full of deodorant bottles in his reception area with a big sign on it saying 'please take one'. However, in spite of the fact that Czechs usually love 'free gifts', no-one actually did! My girlfriend Katy, though, had an even better story one evening:

"I just took on a new secretary," she told us "but something I hadn't noticed at her interview was that she has a bit of a pong. I took a spray deodorant into the office this morning, walked right up to her desk and sprayed it all over her. Then I banged it on the desk and said, 'You might like to use this from now on!' I hope she does, I'm not sure what I will do if she doesn't!"

While Czech girls may or may not be as beautiful as those from elsewhere, what the boys liked the most, though, was their attitude towards sex. We foreign ladies were sure they had all been taught since they were children that the way to a man's heart was through his penis, not through his stomach, as we English girls were taught. And if it wasn't the way to his heart, then it was definitely the way to his money. Prague in those days – sadly, nothing much has really changed – was very much the 'sex capital of Europe', with brothels and strip clubs on every street corner, prostitutes working in the hotels and bars, and some of the first 'modern shops' to open being the Erotic City sex stores. No wonder, then, that Czech attitudes were slightly different to ours! Compare this to the time that a sex shop was opened in my hometown in England and the 'Disgusted of Tunbridge Wells' brigade got it closed down within days, never to be seen again.

One of the best 'sex capital of Europe' stories I heard in the early days was from my still treasured gynaecologist. She spoke perfect English, as well as about ten other languages, and, on my first visit to her, she said how pleased she was to have a British client, as for the last year or so she had mostly only had Russians.

"I suppose you get your patients through word of mouth?" I asked her. "So, when you have a Russian client, she passes your name on to her friends, and so on?" Or do you say that you specialise in specific nationalities or something?" My marketing hat was never far off.

"Not really," she said. "But I seem to go through phases. It used to be Czechs, for obvious reasons, then, since the revolution, it has been Russians. Now, I am seeing more and more Western Europeans: Brits, Austrians and Germans. It makes sense really."

A year or so later, I visited her again and asked if she was still specialising in Western Europeans, or if things had moved on a bit.

"Ah," she said. "I've got a new one: sex workers. They're great clients as they visit regularly and have some good stories to tell."

"I can imagine," I responded.

"Yesterday, though, I heard just about the best story of all," she said. "A very nice-looking lady turned up for a check-up. I hadn't seen her before. but I could tell straightaway she was a sex worker and that she had come from the club just up the road because I've got them on a retainer and the club pays the fees for all the girls. We made small talk as I went about my usual business, and she said she was quite tired as she had two jobs and hadn't had much sleep the last couple of days. After a bit more discussion, it transpired that she works nights as a hooker and days as a policewoman."

Hilarious as it sounded, I was a bit shocked that she would share such a story. But then, as we often used to say at that time, things worked very differently in the Czech Republic, and while my Britishness ensured that I was still taken aback by some of the things I heard, I knew that if I told my girls in the office, they wouldn't bat an eyelid!

"I just feel that they think we are a bunch of girlies messing about with doing business and that if they don't pay us there is nothing we can or will do about it."

Czechs and Slovaks and an Ever-Growing Team

As WE GOT BACK to 'normal' following the big race-day, we headed into my second full winter in Prague with so much work that I thought we would need yet another person to join our team. The constant flood of foreign companies entering the market were still wary of the Czechs and, although a couple of other marketing and PR agencies had opened up, they weren't really going after the same type of businesses as me. One was run by a cuddly, middle-aged Czech guy, who shortly after he opened the business, was 'outed' by the main daily newspaper as a former STB agent during the communist regime. The STB was the Czech version of the KGB, so he clearly wasn't 'that' cuddly, although he became very popular with the big local companies for his 'connections'. The other company was started by a young American girl I had met a few times, but the Americans at that time tended to keep to themselves and she immediately became flavour of the month with the newly arrived FMCG companies, who I didn't think we could approach anyway. Frankly, I didn't even know what FMCG stood for in those days, let alone how to work for them!

In theory, therefore, I should have been feeling comfortable enough that I could afford to take on someone else, but unfortunately, I still hadn't received any money from the racecourse in payment for our various invoices, which made our cashflow very difficult. That was a constant worry, particularly as I had had to pay Gary for all his work. He charged us a very discounted price, but still, it had pretty much cleaned out the bank account for the foreseeable future. We kept trying to chase Little Tomaš, but either he didn't answer the phone or, if he did, he would say that we needed to speak to Big Tomaš, and he was never available. In the end, I decided that we would have to come up with a reason for going down to Pardubice again soon, make sure that both Tomašes would be there, and then deal with the situation face to face.

Among the many newly arrived English expats at that time was Matthew, who had been sent to Prague to head up an Austrian Bank.

I had met him on one of my quick flights back to the UK on the flying pub. As usual, I was sitting at the back puffing away and also, pretty much as usual, we were very delayed. I was worrying how to get down to Tunbridge Wells so late in the evening, when one of the guys sitting with us said that there was someone else from TW on the plane, but at the front, away from the smoking area. I got up to investigate and found a youngish, handsome and very British guy who lived a few streets from my mum. He had a taxi coming to collect him from the airport. I offered to pay half and that was the beginning of a very nice relationship.

I had started to meet Matthew regularly for quick lunches or coffees as he was so grown up and normal and it made a nice break from the usual madness. It was through him I met my third girl, Petra. Petra was a very pretty, young Slovak, small and petite with long black curly hair and big brown eyes. Unfortunately for her, some of the Czechs that she had come across thought she was a gypsy, and Czechs are not good about those. But others, and non-Czechs, looked at her and thought she was gorgeous. Either way, it wasn't always easy to be Petra. Matthew had heard about her when she had gone to the UK to work as a nanny a while back and had told me about her during one of our taxi trips back to Tunbridge Wells.

"It was unbelievable, really," he said. "The whole trip was organised by an unscrupulous Czech agency that I have since heard all sorts of horror stories about. Having arrived in London after a long and uncomfortable journey by bus, she had found the family she was to work for was a single mother with a young child and, once she arrived, the mother pretty much disappeared. Poor Petra then ended up begging on the streets in order to get money to feed herself, as well as the child."

I looked at him in amazement. It was hard to imagine such a story in the UK, which, now that I was living away, I tended to regard with rose-coloured glasses on.

"Well yes, I know it's difficult to believe that something like that could happen at home," Matthew went on, "but thankfully, somewhere along the line, an old colleague of mine found her, took her in as his own nanny and sorted out the situation with the child. He remembered that I am now in the Czech Republic and told me about her when she was working for him. I actually went to see her at that time and told her that if she ever wanted to come back to the Czech Republic, she should come and see me and I would help her. And she has done just that."

Inevitably, therefore, when I mentioned to Matthew that I needed to get another person to join my small team, he reminded me of Petra.

"She's very pretty," he said. I was surprised he noticed, being Matthew, who never seemed to notice any of the girls around him, him being happily married and all. "She speaks very good English and is obviously a hard worker. Why don't you meet her?"

And so, a few weeks later, Petra joined our team. On her first day in the office, she brought in a big box of cakes for everyone, which endeared her immediately to me and Lucie (although neither of us really ate cake, if we could help it) but failed to have any effect on Jana, despite her eating most of them. I had realised very quickly after Jana had started work with us that there was a reason why she was, shall I say, rather large, and that was that she never stopped eating. Also that, when faced with a pretty woman, she was riddled with jealousy and no amount of cake or anything else would change that. And since they didn't get much prettier than Petra, and she was Slovak rather than Czech, Jana went out of her way to be as nasty to her as possible. Which meant that despite her being an extraordinary linguist, she pretended that she couldn't understand a word that Petra said, even though the Czech and Slovak languages are very, very similar. Petra, though, who was met with a very rude *'Co?'* ('What?') pretty much every time she said anything to Jana let it all wash over her and just buckled down and got on with her work. Thankfully, Lucie was fine with her and they quickly become friends, but then she was more 'international' than Jana, who was a bit of an 'old school' Czech. Since Petra was so dark, Jana often referred to her as the 'gypsy' – always out of Petra's earshot, but not out of mine, unfortunately. Which meant that I used to get into all sorts of arguments with her on the subject, even though there was no point, since she wasn't for budging.

Petra, while being petite and frail looking had an iron backbone and coped with whatever was thrown at her. Her English was excellent after her experience in the UK, she was super-organised, and she wasn't afraid of anyone. Despite that, though, I wasn't sure I wanted to disappear down to Pardubice for a whole day with Lucie and leave Petra and Jana in the office together on their own. God knows what Jana might do to her. But then, a solution popped its head up.

One morning, not long after my last trip to London, the phone had rung and on the other end was a very well-spoken English woman who introduced herself as Penelope, the new head of the latest and most famous advertising agency to open in Prague. I had already heard a bit about her as she had just moved into Jonathan's building and Simon, being Penelope's landlord, was a regular visitor as there were lots of things that needed to be fixed and she was quite demanding.

Penelope's agency had just been appointed to prepare and carry out the advertising campaign for the opening of an old building in the nicest residential area of the city, known as Prague 2, the same area her flat was located. The red-brick building was a former market hall that was now dilapidated and a bit of an eyesore among all the lovely art deco buildings that surrounded it. It had been bought by an American architect who planned to turn it into the first shopping mall to open in the city. Since Penelope's agency was doing the advertising, she wanted someone to assist with the PR activities and launch campaigns alongside them and she was calling, she said, to organise a meeting to discuss the whole project, as Simon had given her my name. Bless.

She and I hit it off straightaway. I suppose because we were both British, although she was awfully posh. I, though, am my mother's child and can be posh too, if I need to be and I easily held my own in our first discussion, even though I was, and continued to be, mildly in awe of her. Penelope was a bit older than me and married, although her husband was commuting between Prague and

London. She always wore beautiful clothes and was immaculately groomed, a complete rarity in Prague, apart from when Jonathan's wife, Annabel, was around. I doubted she would ever set foot in somewhere as grubby as The Joyce, let alone any of the other places the rest of us spent our evenings. I quite liked that, though, and regarded her as a 'grown up' sort of friend, as well as, after some negotiating, a client. Within a short space of time, our relationship had got to the point where we would often go and grab a coffee after one of our regular 'shopping mall' meetings, in order to chat about various topics, most of which related to being a businesswoman in Prague and how bloody difficult that was.

It was during one of these coffees I mentioned the problems we were having in getting paid by the Pardubice Tomašes. "I just feel that they think we are a bunch of girlies messing about with doing business and that if they don't pay us there is nothing we can or will do about it."

"Do you really think it's that?" Penelope rolled her eyes. "Maybe the answer is to go there with a man and pretend he is your boss or something. I bet they will behave differently then!"

"What a great idea!" I thought about it a bit, "But who? I can't imagine any of the guys really fitting the mould or, even if they did, having the time to come down there with us."

"Take Alex, my husband," Penelope said. "He's going to be here next week and won't have a lot to do. He'll love it!"

And that's exactly what I did. After meeting Alex on his arrival, the two of us drove down to meet the Tomašes on the pretext of wanting to talk about next year and, as we walked into the meeting room together, I could hardly stop myself from giggling, since all their jaws literally dropped open. Obviously, as usual, they had been expecting me and Lucie, since they were all lounging around looking very smug and un-businesslike, but they soon sat up and paid attention when they saw Alex.

"Hello, everyone," I said, smiling sweetly. "I have brought Alex with me today as he is over from London. He is our global Managing Director."

Alex, a huge and quite tough-looking, but very nice Englishman, smiled broadly and held out his hand as I introduced him to each of the Tomašes and Mirek, who had joined us that day.

"As you know," I said, "we have come to discuss next year's racing and, in particular, the Bass sponsorship, but first, Alex would like to say a few words. Alex?"

"Yes, thank you, Jo," he responded. "This won't take long. Before we start discussing next year, I really do need to stress the importance of us having our invoices paid for the work done to date, as the London office is very proud of our ladies here in the Czech Republic and we value their work very highly. Could one of you give us an update on where you are up to with these payments?"

He looked straight at Big Tomaš, since I had advised him that he was the main man. Big Tomaš, though, took the fairly standard Czech stand of saying that it was nothing to do with him. In fact, he said, "I was under the impression, Tomaš," he looked straight at Little Tomaš, "that you had paid everything up to date?" Little Tomaš wriggled about a bit.

"Not completely," he responded. "We were just waiting for some last payments to come in from other sponsors, if you recall?"

"Okay," said Big Tomaš. "Can I have your assurance that you will pay everything before the end of the week?" directing this at Little Tomaš. Hilarious.

"Yes, of course," responded Little Tomaš, giving him a look that said he might kill him later.

"So, that is all very good," said Alex. "In that case, I will leave it to Jo to briefly summarise how she sees the plan for next year and then we will head back to Prague. And then, as soon as the invoices are paid in full, she, or both of us, will return to discuss it all in more detail."

It couldn't have gone any better. Their whole attitude had changed and, after a bit of arse-kissing (Alex's) and a bit of a blag from me about the plan for next year, which we hadn't even thought about yet, we left. And, sure enough, all the invoices were paid by the end of that week.

A couple of days later, I was invited to Penelope's flat for drinks with her and Alex to celebrate our success. Unbeknown to me, she had invited her 'banker' over too and, needless to say, said banker was, in fact, Matthew, Prague being so small and incestuous. As we sipped our drinks in Penelope's beautiful sitting room, I recounted the meeting in as much detail as I could remember, and we all fell about laughing. Just then, the bell rang.

"I can't imagine who that is," said Penelope, getting up to go and see and leaving the door open so we could hear what was going on. "Oh, Simon, it's you."

"Hello, darling," he said, "I'm not stopping, just wondered, and sorry to ask, I don't suppose you could give me an advance on your rent? Maybe just a week's worth? If you have any cash?"

"Well, I'm not sure. Hold on, I'll see if we have any money here." She came back into the room.

"It's Simon, Alex. Do we have any cash here?" She looked a bit perplexed.

"Don't give it to him," I said, getting up and going out to the hall where Simon, very much the worse for wear, was standing.

"Oh, hello, darling, what are you doing here?" he asked, looking sheepish.

"I'm having drinks with Penelope and Alex. Oh, and Matthew. You?"

"Nothing at all, just popped in to see if all is okay. I'll be off then, love you." And he opened the door and ran off down the stairs. I went back into the sitting room.

"Whatever was all that about?" said Penelope, looking worried. "I hope he isn't in some sort of trouble."

"Don't worry about it," I said. "It's just Simon having a bit of fun."

I should just say here that I had heard from Simon a few weeks previously that he and Jonathan had been having regular meetings with Matthew to discuss his bank's potential financing of a big new project they were working on. Matthew had also mentioned that he had met the two of them and that they had seemed to be such nice and normal boys and doing 'very well' by all accounts. It wasn't for me to put him right at that time, and I didn't think I should say too much now. But he was definitely looking a little bit perplexed.

"Well," said Matthew, "that was an interesting interlude. Does he do that often?"

"Not really," I responded. "Just when the pressure is on, as it is now."

"Yes, I suppose it is. I would love to have seen his face though when you appeared," said Matthew.

"Better would have been for him to see yours!" I retorted. "I am sure he would have died if he had known you were listening into every word!"

"Darling," said Alex, looking at Penelope. "Are you sure you want to live over here? I'm not sure it's completely normal."

"You just wait," I said. "It gets a lot worse!"

Getting set for Christmas

CHRISTMAS IN PRAGUE, how lovely! But not when you are an expat and are torn between wanting to stay put and have a bit of a rest or going back to the UK, or wherever, to see your family. Of course, family always wins. However, knowing that everyone is going to disappear for at least a week means that we all wanted to make sure we lived it up in the build-up to Christmas.

First up, we had what was soon to become an annual event: the Christmas party that the British Ambassador used to host at the embassy for all the British companies and individuals based in the Czech Republic. The British Embassy is in a beautiful old building in the Malá Strana ('Lesser Town') area of Prague, just a few minutes' walk from the famous Charles Bridge. In those days, everything was very relaxed: you received an invitation, turned up on the night, walked through the gates and up two flights of stairs and then you arrived in one of the main reception rooms.

One of the reasons we all looked forward to this event was that everyone who was anyone in the British community was sure to attend. That, and the fact that we all knew we would drink a huge amount of pretty awful wine in the two hours or so that we were there and that, once we had all gathered and left to go into town, the evening was bound to go on into the early hours, and who knew what would happen then. Being at the embassy meant that we had a reason for dressing up, since events there were always very formal. I once turned up to a summer party in the embassy gardens in very smart culottes and the Ambassador looked at me down his nose and said, "Shorts, Joanna? At the embassy?" It was like that, very British.

That particular evening, I had decided to wear a new blue dress, giving my legs an airing after weeks of wearing jeans, and black suede boots, which I had recently brought over from the UK. When I left the cottage, I felt I looked pretty good, especially as my often wild blonde curls had behaved themselves for a change and I felt I had a bit of a Marilyn Monroe vibe going on. However, for some reason, I have always had, and still have, an aversion to arriving at an event on my own, and so had arranged to meet Ewan outside the gates of the embassy so we could walk in together. Simon and Jonathan were on duty that night at their employees' Christmas party, but we had all agreed to meet up later, by which time we expected to have quite the gang with us. When I got to the embassy though, Ewan, being Ewan, had a surprise in store as he had a Welsh film crew following him around for a series they were doing about 'Welsh expats', so we all traipsed in together and made quite the entrance.

Thankfully, once we got inside, I knew just about everyone in there, although many of the people I had expected to see were missing, presumably at some other competing party. I was relieved to see – among all the suits – both Penelope and Katy, although, on second thoughts, Katy is from New Zealand, but never mind. Clive was there too, in a huddle with the ambassador, together with Eva, who I hadn't seen for ages, and who was whirling about kissing everyone and thrusting business cards at everyone she could get her hands on.

The thing about these business events though was that nearly all the people attending were men and they always dressed the same, in dark grey or navy suits. While I may have met them before, I could never remember their names, unless I knew them well, or there was something remarkable about them, such as being incredibly handsome and/ or fit. Unfortunately, that was a bit of a rarity, since they all looked pretty much the same. On the other hand, the men usually clapped their eyes on me and thought, *Oh, there's a bird,* or, *There's a blonde bird,* or something similar, as us few 'business' ladies obviously stood out. Which meant that in the early part of such an evening we were usually ignored and then, as the booze kicked in, we became the most popular people there. Over the years, and with the various changes of ambassadors, there were some pretty riotous evenings at the embassy. In particular, the summer parties in the garden were especially debauched and there was an ongoing competition among the boys as to who could be the first to get a blowjob in the garden loo. I probably shouldn't say that though. No prizes for guessing who won!

That particular evening, I got caught up early on with one of the older expats, a total madman called Roger, who had his chairman in town and had brought him to the embassy to meet some of the others. This was the chairman's first visit and Roger, desperate to get away and drink everything in sight, was clearly wanting to dump him on someone. As soon as we had been introduced, he was off, leaving me to look after the chairman myself; at least us ladies were useful for something at these events.

Anyway, once the ambassador had wished us a 'Happy Christmas' and we were all filing out together, finding the chairman still by my side, I invited him to come with us to the restaurant we had planned to go to next. He was clearly delighted. Roger less so, but, by that time, he had clearly drunk a huge amount and didn't really care. He was the only person that had driven to the embassy but didn't need much persuasion to give us all a lift to the Italian restaurant we were heading to, another new opening in a different part of town. Roger's car was a regular old Škoda, which now probably holds the world record for the most people to get into one car and then actually move. I think there were about 16 of us; the chairman never forgot it.

Off we went, six people piled on top of each other in the front, including Clive and Eva, Clive muttering under his breath about 'todgers', and Eva, having had a bit too much Christmas cheer, with her arm slung around his neck and nose pressed up against the windscreen.

Clive, ever the hawk-eye, suddenly turned to Roger, "Dear boy, best pull over, there's a police-check ahead of us." He then threw open the door and pushed Eva arse-first out onto the pavement, while the rest of us followed suit as fast as we could. The whole group of us then ran around the corner to the next street, while Roger drove on, was duly stopped, paid the police off without a breathalyser – sadly that was the norm in those days and, since it was Christmas, the police were more interested in getting some cash into their coffers than making any sort of arrest – and then hurtled off to pick us up again, at which point, we all piled back into the car and continued on our way.

The restaurant had only opened recently and was authentic Italian. In fact, it was owned by an elderly Italian *mafiosi,* who wasn't overly amused to see such a huge group arriving so late in the evening, particularly when we announced that we were joining Jonathan, Simon and a few others at a table in the middle of the room. Since Simon knew the owner well (don't ask), chairs were pulled up, menus were handed around and we were all shuffled about in order to fit everyone in. The Chairman, thankfully, was shoved at the end of the table with a couple of girls from Jonathan's offices, while I sat myself down next to Katy, who had come with us in the car. I then realised who had ended up sitting opposite her: Jeremy.

I hadn't actually seen him since the airport hiding-behind-a-tree incident and, despite the fact that we had chatted a lot at the boat party, this was the first time I had really spoken to him in a 'normal way'. I have to say we got on very well. Katy, I found out, already knew him as she was acting for his new company and was flirting with him quite outrageously, but then, she seemed to be flirting with everyone, including me! I suspected, though, that she had buttonholed Jeremy to be her 'Christmas present' later that evening. Which was fine, of course…

Dinner went on getting rowdier and rowdier and then we were all off to Lávka to dance off some of the food and drink. By the time we got there, we had dropped Roger and the chairman – who still, to this day, dines out on this particular evening when he recounts his experiences in Prague, especially the car ride – as well as a few others. Needless to say, Simon, Ewan, Jeremy, Katy and I were still going strong at about 3.00 am, which was still early for the boys. Us girls, however, were beginning to fade.

"We have to go," I said to anyone who was listening, while Katy went out to get our coats.

"Already?" said Jeremy, taking me to one side. "I was wondering whether Katy was out to get me or out to get you; seems it's you."

"Don't be ridiculous!" I responded a bit horrified. "We're just sharing a taxi home, but she's dropping me off!"

108

"Why don't you come with me instead then?" he asked.

At which point, Katy swept in, took my arm, and said, "Come on love, time to go."

So that was that, and a good thing too. I did, though, ponder what Jeremy had said for some time after that. I hadn't known Katy for long but liked her a lot. She was such a kind person; she had lent me her car when Simon didn't have one available for driving to Pardubice, had bought me a lovely mirror from one of Prague's antique shops when I was out with her but couldn't afford it and had generally turned into a very good friend. But she was very difficult to read, and we didn't really talk about relationships – not that I had one to talk about – so it hadn't occurred to me that she might, as the boys would put it, 'bat for the other side'. Not that it made any difference to me, it was just a bit of a surprise.

Two nights later, I was off out again. This time to the Christmas party of my old firm, to which only a select few of us had been invited. This, I told myself, will be very grown up, and I therefore vowed not to drink too much or do anything silly, since it would be one of those occasions when one should look 'professional', with so many potential clients likely to be in attendance.

A few weeks previously, I had been invited by the owners of a new restaurant called Peklo (which translates as 'Hell'!) to come take a look. It was in the Castle area of town and was about to open. They wanted PR people like me to know about them as they had a basement wine cellar that was the perfect place for private functions. Since Clive had asked if I could sort out a venue for the firm's Christmas party, I figured this place could be perfect. We agreed on a very nice menu, booked a DJ and then, on the day, had gone to dress the whole place up with Christmas decorations, lots of candles and glittery things to add atmosphere. It looked amazing. Then we rushed back to the office to get changed and, since we knew Clive would be stressing about everything, Lucie, my date for the evening, and I headed back there early to be ready to meet him when he arrived. I wore my favourite black trouser 'work' suit, but with a green sparkly vest underneath, boots, and lots of fake jewellery. I had also slung my old mock fur coat on top since it was completely freezing outside. Lucie, who would look gorgeous in a dustbin liner, was also in black, but had chosen a longish dress and her mother's fur stole. I felt we would do Clive proud. He had always liked Lucie, who, as mentioned before, he regarded as a 'good strong girl' (his highest accolade), and she had most certainly scrubbed up for this particular evening.

What a party! As expected, the food was great, especially for Prague at the time. While there were a lot of people we didn't know, in true Prague-expat fashion, they were mostly men and once they had started drinking both Lucie and I were in demand to get up and dance with whoever was asking. My old assistant Monika was there, happily jigging away with spotty old Michael, who I had once threatened to murder. And who, I now knew, was having an affair with him. I say 'affair' as, in my day, she had been living with her very nice Czech boyfriend who, I believed, was still on the scene, but who knew with these girls. Clive was twirling various of his new chickens about, Ewan and Rhys had turned up with two unknown girls and were telling jokes at the bar, and Simon and Jonathan were dressed in their very best suits and were standing about together, drinking whisky and looking very dashing and serious.

It must have been past midnight, and the party was still going strong when the last few guests arrived; the banker Diana, together with some of her directors, along with Katy and then Jeremy. Of course, I knew they had been invited as had seen the guest list but was beginning to think they wouldn't show up. They had come straight from Diana's firm's Christmas dinner and were dressed to the nines. Jeremy was wearing a dinner jacket (who doesn't look good in one of those?) and Katy had on a very nice red dress and looked great. I hadn't seen her since she had dropped me off after the embassy party night and Jeremy had made his rather strange comment. I didn't plan to mention it. She, however, had obviously been told something by him as the minute she came over to me she said, "Don't worry about what you heard the other night, love, I'm bisexual. Surely you knew that? I'm very happy with it too!"

And then – okay, I have been kind of avoiding this bit – there I was on the dancefloor with Ewan, dancing to his absolute favourite song from that time, 'I'm Too Sexy' by Right Said Fred, when out to join us came Jeremy, jacket off, bow tie around his ear, and looking 'way too sexy for his shirt'. In fact, he looked rather irresistible, especially after about a gallon of nice red wine. It was Christmas, after all, and I had long since given up on my earlier vow 'not to do anything silly'.

Obviously, I'm not going to go into all the details, and besides, we had drunk so much by the time we left the party that I don't remember many of them. I do know, though, that we went an awful long way out into the country to get to his house, with the result that I couldn't get back into town the following morning and had to wait until Jeremy could give me a lift back in, which took forever. I remember thinking that his house was so much nicer than anywhere else I'd seen in Prague at that time – it even had its own swimming pool and games room – and that when we first got there we danced wildly to Billy Idol's 'White Wedding', and I surprised Jeremy by admitting to being a former 'rock chick' and not at all into all the 'smoochy girly stuff' he had assumed I would prefer. And then, of all things, we played table tennis for a while, since he had made the mistake of saying that women cannot play ball games – maybe that was a joke? – and I wanted to prove that some women, especially me, a once-upon-a-time very good junior tennis player, were very good at them. And then the next day I realised that, despite trying not to, I might quite like him. *Oh dear.*

"What a cracker!"

 **It's Christmas Time**

BY THE TIME I got to the office the following day – in other words, having appeared at the front door, instead of arriving down the stairs from my flat – the ladies were all getting a bit concerned as to where I was since it really wasn't 'me' to stay out all night. Lucie, in particular, seemed to be in a bit of a state. That touched me, until I found out why! And since we had more or less finished everything we needed to do for the time being and there was only one more working day before we closed the office for the period between Christmas Eve and New Year, I suggested we all have the rest of the day off and see each other the next day, when we would have our 'office Christmas lunch'.

One good thing about our lack of any sort of efficient form of communication at that time – we still only had our one phone line, which connected with the telephone for calls and fax for all of our written communication – was that if we simply took the phone off the hook, to anyone calling in it would just sound as if it was engaged. Which could mean anything, from us being super-busy and on the phone a lot, to the Prague telephones just having a bad day. This meant that no-one thought badly of us if they couldn't get hold of us. It was quite a handy way of avoiding talking to anyone, especially on days like this. And so, once the girls had disappeared, I spent the afternoon trying to sort out everything work-related in readiness for my leaving for the UK over Christmas, while trying not to sort out anything 'personal', particularly relating to the previous evening's activities. Of course, as mentioned, Jeremy had given me a lift back into town that morning, but our conversation had been fairly non-committal. I had been determined I wasn't going to be the one that said, "So, what's next?" Obviously, we would cross paths again in the not-so-distant future, so the best thing, I kept telling myself, was just to see what happened and to focus, as always, on work.

By early evening though, I was starting to fade and decided I would just stay put in the office until it was late enough to take myself up to bed and give up on the rest of the day. Easier said than done. I was just locking the office door when the doorbell rang. *Bloody Simon*, I thought to myself, imagining that, at best, he was turning up to get the dirt on whatever had happened with Jeremy or, at worst, he was still 'out' from the previous evening and in need of money, whisky or somewhere to sleep. But instead of Simon, there was Jonathan.

"Oh," I said, probably looking pretty unfriendly. "I didn't expect to see you. I thought it would be Simon!"

"Sorry, it's me. I won't stop though. I'm just on my way home and wanted to quickly talk to you."

"Okay, so come on in." *Whatever could he want*, I wondered. I liked Jonathan, even though he is not the easiest person in the world and most people were terrified of him. But we got on well and he was a fantastic friend to Simon. I just never saw him very much on his own. "I've got something to tell you,", he said. "I thought I should do it now, before you hear it from someone else. You'll never guess who I took home last night."

You're right, I thought. *I have no idea. And why should I need to know anyway, especially as I'm his wife's friend*?

"No, you're right, I can't guess. Tell me."

"Your lovely Lucie. What a cracker!"

"Oh, bloody hell, Jonathan!" I couldn't believe it. What a potential mess that could be! "How could you?" I said. "She's so fragile!"

"She's not fragile at all!" he responded with a bit of a nasty look in his eye. "Far from it! Anyway, I thought I ought to tell you as I'm sure she will want to tell you herself sooner or later and I wanted you to be prepared."

And with that, off he went, pleased as could be, leaving me to deal with the potential fallout.

After a reasonable night's sleep, albeit a bit tormented – I never sleep that well at the best of times and there was a *lot* running about in my head – I was up early for our last day in the office. Before I even got downstairs and put the coffee on, in walked Lucie, looking dreadfully pale and near to tears. Out it all came at a hundred miles an hour. How she hadn't meant to go off with him, how she knew he was married and so on – but not happily, of course – how he wasn't a bastard as everyone said and how, when she was a child, she had dreamed of meeting a prince and living in a castle. Jonathan was that prince.

"Lucie!" I said. "Slow down. What you do outside the office is nothing to do with me. As long as you are happy and you work hard as usual, the rest is up to you. But be careful, it could get very complicated."

Thankfully, the other girls turned up as I was finishing my grown-up bit and Lucie got herself together enough for the morning to continue without any further drama. We had a nice lunch together to 'celebrate' Christmas, but I must say, I was glad when the day finished, and we said our goodbyes and 'Happy Christmases' and so on. And then, feeling a little bit sad, I sketched out the final *This is Where you Hear it First*, which I had somehow managed to keep going up until then, announcing that, since it was the end of the year, this would be the last ever edition. And Happy Christmas to all, et cetera. In the circumstances, I couldn't really see how it could continue.

"Everyone that comes to live somewhere like this is running away from something."

 **New Year**

Coming from a bit of a broken home, Dad having died when I was little, and then various other dramas as I grew up, I had never really liked Christmas as it was always a bit quiet and a bit sad. I always assumed that everyone else was having a high old time, with loads of people, children, dogs, presents and happiness around them, but of course, as I got older, I realised that that was not really the case but, you know, Christmas can be a time for feeling sorry for oneself too.

Added to that, I had the feeling that I suppose all expats have of complete and utter discombobulation whenever we go 'home' for any length of time. Because, of course, we are not really sure where 'home' actually is, and trying to fit back into the clothes of our previous existence is nearly impossible.

But I did eat a lot of nice food, saw various friends and family and gave a lot of Czech presents. There may not have been a lot to buy in Prague at that time, but the glass was, and is, amazing. Plus, Russian caviar and Russian sparkling wine is yummy and very cheap, and there were a few other 'ethnic' bits that made for very good gifts. But a week was enough, so, on the afternoon of New Year's Eve, I was on my way to Heathrow to wait for the flying pub to arrive and take me back to Prague again.

As was the norm in the winter at that time, the inbound flight was late arriving, due to bad weather in Prague. Eventually, we took off just two hours late and I figured that if all went according to plan, I would still be back in time to maybe go off to The Joyce or meet up with one or other of the gang that had stayed put over Christmas. What I mean by 'if all went according to plan', though, is that it often didn't. I have a theory that the previous communist regime had purposely built Prague airport in the highest area of the city, where the weather is always at its worst and fog was a constant problem. I figure that they thought it would make it even more difficult for people to leave than it was already and, if that was their plan, it worked. Eventually, the special equipment that was the norm in other European airports was installed and things became a bit easier, but, at that time, the last half an hour or so of coming into land in winter was always a bit nerve-wracking, as we were never completely sure we would actually get down. More likely, somewhere midway through our descent we would hear the announcement that, "Due to the weather conditions at Prague airport we are now diverting to Vienna," or somewhere else nearby, and that, as we all knew from regular experience, was a total nightmare.

If anyone could land a plane in bad weather though, Czech pilots could. Another of our theories in those days was that having originally been military pilots, the worse the weather, the more they enjoyed themselves, and we would often come into land without any sort of visibility at all, only to touch down and take off again, or be held circling before suddenly bombing down and landing with a huge crash. However bad the landing, it was definitely preferable to diverting, since, when that happened, it usually meant being taken off the plane in whichever airport we had arrived in and then being put onto buses to bring us back to Prague. In bad weather, that could take anything up to 10-15 hours, and it happened a lot. I kid you not.

Luckily, this particular flight did land in Prague, and we all piled off. There was no-one around I recognised, and I therefore made my way quickly by taxi through tons of snow, back to the cottage and back to my 'normal life' again.

Except that it wasn't really. Once I had unpacked, put on the heating, and got myself sorted, I tried to call a few different people but either couldn't get through or there was no answer. I contemplated going to The Joyce but, with no guarantee of anyone that I knew being there, I wasn't that keen. For the first time since being a grown up, therefore, I went to bed at about 9.00 pm on New Year's Eve! Not much of a welcome into the New Year!

The following morning, though, I woke up feeling quite cheerful, despite the fact that the temperatures in winter in Prague can be quite scary. In those days, we could go two or three months with the temperature never getting above zero, and January onwards was always the worst. But, if the snow had fallen, and it usually had by then, the sky was blue and the sun was shining, walking around the Old Town, as long as you were well wrapped up, was almost ethereal. This was especially the case in the early days as there were not as many tourists at that time and I would often walk up to the edge of the Old Town Square, look across at the clock tower and see that I was the only person there.

When I say 'well-wrapped up', in my case this meant piling on layers and layers of clothes, without caring too much about how I looked. I had a big sheepskin jacket that I wore all winter, fur-lined boots, a furry hat and gloves and, underneath all of that, I would usually be wearing jeans, leggings and sweaters, in various different colours. My Czech girls wore more or less the same, but then – as far as I knew – they weren't total maneaters, like the rest of them, many of whom would still be wearing skirts up around their bums and very high-heeled boots, irrespective of the snow or ice on the ground. More recently, I remember asking one of my ladies how she managed to walk in the snow in five-inch-high stiletto boots, while looking at my own furry flatties, to which she responded, "I just have a very strong core." I felt mildly insulted by this, since she obviously thought I didn't, and since, by that time, I was at just about my fittest, that didn't lie at all well.

So, that first full day back, having slept in, I called Katy, since she was one of my only friends I knew had stayed in Prague, and asked her if she fancied a New Year's lunch somewhere. As she hadn't been outside for more than a week and had spent most of the previous few days reading, all her family being back home in New Zealand, she was more than happy to venture out to Zátiši, despite the weather.

I liked Katy, as I have said before, but in the days before any form of mobile communication – and it therefore being impossible to get messages to one another – she was always a bit risky to meet on her own as there was never any guarantee she would turn up on time, or even at all. This was partly due to her high-pressure job, which she didn't really talk that much about but, when she did, it sounded bloody tough, but also due to her general scattiness. This time, amazingly, she was already sitting in Zatisi waiting for me when I got there, all dressed up, which set a good tone for the rest of our lunch, as did the bottle of champagne that was immediately offered to us as I joined her.

One of the things about Zatisi is that not only is it cozy and pretty, with its low ceilings, colourful walls and big velvet-draped windows, but the food is always great and, as we were such regulars (well Katy more than me), we knew all the waiters and always received 'VIP treatment'. In fact, Kumar, being a proper marketing expert, was the first to start a real loyalty scheme type set-up, when such things were completely unheard of. If you went to the restaurant often enough you were automatically added to the 'list of regulars' and would receive little cards with points on them when you got your bill. I think it was something like one point for every 100 crowns you spent, and then the points could be redeemed against your next meal, something that happened generously often.

On this particular day, Kumar, who had been sitting in the corner having lunch with what appeared to be his family, joined us while we were tucking into our main course (beef wellington, delicious!) and, after a bit of general chat, asked me if I wouldn't mind talking 'shop' for a few minutes. He was planning on opening a new restaurant later that year and wondered if I would like to help with the launch; a prospective new client and it was only the first of the year! That deserved another glass.

Just as we were finishing off our last bottle of wine and wondering whether to order more or take ourselves off home – and also at the point where I thought I had gotten away without an interrogation – Katy looked at me slightly shiftily and said, "Well, love," she called everyone love, "are you going to tell me about your evening with Jeremy, or shall we just pretend it didn't happen?"

"Um, pretend it didn't happen?" I replied. "I could probably like him, but he is clearly a bastard from what I have heard and seen, and I really don't want to be stressing about a bloke when I have enough to cope with on a daily basis with work."

"You're right in a way," she responded. "But I don't really think he's a bastard. I think the poor love has probably got that sex addiction problem that Michael Douglas had. Either that or he is so

120

insecure that he just has to try and pull anyone he meets in order to fluff up his ego."

"Well, yes, exactly. But who needs that? I think, for now, I'll try and steer well clear. What about you? How has your love life been recently?"

"Me? Oh, I'm a bit of a mess. But who isn't? That's the nature of the beast. Show me an expat and I'll show you a fuck-up."

I was taken aback, but she clearly meant it.

"Look, love," she said, gazing at her chewed down nails as if wondering whether to have another gnaw. "Everyone that comes to live somewhere like this is running away from something. Why would we come otherwise? I am, aren't you?"

"Are you?" I was surprised. "I'm not sure I am. I really did come just for the money! Not now, but in the beginning. But I suppose you are right, I'm probably running away from various things too, I just never thought about it in that way."

"I see that. But let's face it, if it was just for the money, we could all have gone anywhere. But this is a place where we can reinvent ourselves completely and no-one will know. Isn't that what you're doing? Did you really plan to be a marketing queen? I bet you didn't. But now you are, and everyone believes that you are. And that's fine."

"I suppose so," I said. "I need to think about it a bit more; we definitely need to have that next drink now!" It was a habit learned from Mum. Never let one's guard down and talk about real feelings!

Soon after, we went our separate ways, having agreed that we would have at least one of these dinners every month. I headed back to the cottage pondering everything she had said. It reminded me of something a guide had told me when I was first in Prague and he was showing me around.

"You see that building," he said, pointing at one of the beautiful painted houses on the Old Town Square. "It's beautiful, isn't it? But it's just a facade, and behind the facade lies something very different. That's how life is here."

I wondered if that was what Katy was alluding to. We might all have beautiful facades, but behind them is something very different, sometimes quite ugly. I wasn't sure I liked that thought.

Getting Back to Normal

WE OPENED OUR DOORS properly again on the second of January. Despite my mixed feelings about the past week or so, I was happy to get back to work and to see the ladies when they arrived on what was a hideously cold and grey day.

From a business point of view, I was feeling quite positive about the coming months. That said, despite always thinking of myself as being 'good with money' – I had, after all, trained for that side of things, even if not for marketing, as per Katy's previous comments – I had been a bit depressed to see how little profit I had come out with after my first full year of business. When I said as much to some of my friends though, they all replied, "Oh, don't be depressed, 95% of businesses fail in the first year so you have done well." I'm sure they were right. I probably had. But I had definitely miscalculated how lots of what seemed like relatively small payments for all the different monthly running costs could add up to one very big amount each month. And then, how much work we needed to be doing in order to even just cover that. On the other hand, I told myself, the monthly running costs did actually include my own 'life' since the company paid all of my rent, travel and so on. I was hardly on the breadline.

I think, though, that part of my financial stress was down to the fact that it was impossible to have any sort of debt in the Czech Republic at that time, although in some ways that may have been a good thing. Banks wouldn't lend money to small businesses like mine, overdrafts didn't exist, and I had no access to other funding. If the cashflow got difficult – and working for a few big companies that paid, but paid slowly, meant that it often did – I was guaranteed a few sleepless nights. One time I even had to draw cash out on my English credit card in order to pay my ladies' salaries. Even that wasn't that straightforward since credit cards were still relatively new to the country and this was well before the days of the holes in the wall. Luckily, I had Matthew in the bank who managed to sort it somehow.

I decided that this being the New Year, it was time to do something radical about cashflow. I would set up a budget, something I hadn't bothered with before, since it was my company, so why would I? And I would try to charge more for the work we were doing. I realised too that I needed to clean up my own life as well and thought about getting a TV and investigate getting some foreign channels added as there was a rumour that this was now possible. I even thought that I might try to smoke less or to give up entirely, although that wouldn't save me much money, since cigarettes cost next to nothing in the Czech Republic. But even if it didn't save me money, cutting down or giving up could only be a good thing.

And then, I thought, what about sub-letting a bit of our space? My friend Rhys the printer was working from home and before Christmas he had mentioned he could really do with having a desk somewhere, if not a whole office. I wondered how he would feel about paying something into the pot each month and using our meeting room as his base. It was definitely worth asking him.

There were also various administrative things that needed to be dealt with and that, of course, required money. First up was the need to organise my accounts and that was going to require a local bookkeeper as I would need to file proper Czech accounts for my first full year of trading. And how to do that? I would also have to renew my residency permit, since the Czech Republic was not yet in the EU and we foreigners needed to get an annual visa in order to be able to work. That was also something that was not easy to organise.

All in all, therefore, I agreed with myself that we needed a lot more organisation and a more active approach to generating income, which led me to decide that, as of now, we would have a team meeting every Monday morning and brainstorm where we could cut back and where we could look for new and more lucrative work on an ongoing basis.

Having said that, our income looked to be pretty good for the first quarter. We had Simon's wedding at the end of February, for which I would be charging a flat, albeit discounted fee, then we had a press visit from the UK for Bass in the coming couple of weeks, two brochures to prepare for two different companies, and the ongoing work for Pardubice, if we could be sure we would get paid. Plus, looking ahead, we had the work with Penelope on the shopping mall which was planned to open in early summer, and I had the potential new work from Kumar to look forward to too.

"So," I said to the three ladies at the end of our first Monday morning meeting, "We have a lot of work to do in the coming weeks and need to be on top of our game. If anyone is at all stressed or worried about anything, then please let me know now so that we can see where we can support each other." *Good speech*, I thought, but no reaction. Lucie looked worried, but then she always did. The others, well, not a flicker. Obviously, all was well in everyone's world. I couldn't help but think how nice it would be if one or other of them piped up with a suggestion or two, or even just a bit of understanding as to just how stressful it all was to have every decision and every plan weighing on my shoulders. That would be the day.

During the first few weeks of the New Year, while I did venture down to The Joyce most evenings, I managed to get quite a lot of things sorted that, I hoped, would make life in Prague a lot easier, and even cheaper. I sent Petra off to hunt down a TV and research how to get the new channels on it and soon had it set up in the small room upstairs, opposite the kitchen, where I could now feast on both CNN and Eurosport when I felt like staying home in the evening. Not only that, but it was finally possible to buy a washing machine in Prague with the opening of one of the big white goods companies and soon, a mini version of a washing machine/ dryer was also installed. That was possibly one of the most exciting things that had happened to me since starting the business. What does that tell you?!

All of this cost money I didn't really have, but I figured I would soon make it up through all the cash I was going to save from not going out. Except that I still *was* going out, pretty much every evening; initially to The Joyce, and then, as if someone somewhere was playing a nasty joke on me, to the newly opened Molly Malone's Irish pub that had opened immediately across the road from us. It

125

seemed almost churlish not to pop over there for a couple of glasses or so after work.

Things were generally a little bit easier though since as soon as I had asked Rhys if he would like to rent a desk with us, he had jumped at the idea and moved straight in, and what a difference that made. He wasn't actually in the office that often since he had to be out and about dealing with clients, and then the print-houses, but when he was, he cheered me up enormously. He also helped us with our regular work, not only in Pardubice, but in the preparation of what was often a huge amount of different promotional materials. When we had finished the preparation of a brochure, for example, he would take it off to various different printers to see who could do it the quickest and for the best price, and then we would leave him to get it done with whichever one he chose. With so many new companies opening up in town and lots of them needing the printing of business cards, brochures and so on, it seemed to be a very good business for him. But, of course, as with all small companies, cashflow was very difficult, hence why he had not yet taken on his own office.

Rhys, like Ewan, was Welsh, was a bit of a womaniser, but not as bad as some, and he had a fantastic singing voice. That meant that if we needed a bit of cheering up in the late afternoon when he tended to be in the office, he would be quick to turn on the 'beat box' that he kept in the meeting room that doubled as his office and sing along to one of the Elvis CDs he loved to play. Then, once the other ladies had left for the evening, out he would come, saying, "Right then, J'ver," (his pet name for me, pronounced 'Jay-ver'), "time for a sharpener?" and the two of us would head off across the road. I would prop up the bar with Gary, who was a more or less permanent fixture at that time, while Rhys would go and chat up whichever Czech ladies were around, or to join any of the other boys that had turned up for the start of their evening.

Having a man about changed the whole dynamic in the office. The ladies were always happier when Rhys was around and he was someone that I could talk to about whatever was worrying me, since he was in a similar position to me, having just started his own business. It wasn't long before we were practically inseparable.

It wasn't that we stopped going to The Joyce – that was more of a 'later in the evening' or a weekend place – but Molly's, being right across the road, was a good starting place for whatever we were going to do for dinner, or after. And, at that time, the most likely place for me to spend the rest of my evening was in a new and tiny restaurant just a couple of minutes' walk away from us called U Zlatá Ulička ('at the Golden Lane'). It had been opened by a very handsome Bosnian guy called Nenad who had recently arrived from Sarajevo, where he had run a successful restaurant chain. When the war between Croatia and Serbia started to rumble, he had fled to Prague, leaving his business and some of his family behind. Some did turn up later, hugely traumatised.

There were just six tables in the restaurant, mostly occupied by other Yugoslavs who were mostly friends and family of Nenad, and each table was decked out with a red checked tablecloth and bunches of flowers in old food cans. No matter how busy the restaurant was, I, and whoever I arrived with, but usually Rhys, were always made welcome, and most evenings we would end up staying until late, drinking lots of Yugoslavian wine and eating delicious local food. By which time, two of the Yugoslav guys would get out their guitars, start singing old Bosnian songs and cry, while Rhys sang along, making up the words as he went.

It was a hidden away place and I kept it a bit quiet as I didn't want it to become an expat hangout. Sometimes Ewan would come over to find us and Katy was also a regular visitor, but that was about it. Katy loved Nenad, almost as much as I did, plus she was convinced that one day Rhys and I would waltz off across the horizon together. But, while I thought that it wasn't beyond the realms of possibility, I was pretty sure the feeling wasn't mutual, however much she tried to push us together.

At about that time, a very Jewish-looking and slightly older Englishman started turning up regularly at Molly's. Jacob was always impeccably dressed, to the point that I had decided he was probably gay, since no other man I knew smelt quite so good or took quite as much care of his appearance. He should have been my type (if he wasn't gay that is!), with his black, wavy hair and grey eyes, but he had slightly buck front teeth with a large gap between them and I found that rather off-putting. Most evenings he would be sitting at the bar telling dirty jokes to Gary when we arrived and, after meeting him a few times, but only briefly, I sat and chatted to him one evening and it turned out he was an accountant.

"An accountant?" I said when he announced it. I felt sure he was joking as he didn't look or sound anything like any of the accountants I had met before. He was far too naughty for a start!

"Yup, I run a small English firm here. Actually we have had an office here since before the revolution as we used to act for a couple of the big state companies that were able to operate outside of Czechoslovakia."

"Do you have Czech bookkeepers and so on?" I asked.

"Of course," he responded. "Why, do you need one?"

And within days, I had been set up with a nice young Czech accountant called Ondrej, who not only sorted out my books, but advised me on how to get my visa organised. He prepared the paperwork for me and said, "You just need to go to the Foreigners' Police with the paperwork and your photo, hand it all over and then they will ask you to return after a few days and collect your visa. You need to get there early – they open at 7.00 am – as there is always a long queue. The Ukrainians and Vietnamese take forever."

"And how long do you think I would need to queue for?" I asked.

"Well," he scratched his chin, "it can take a whole day. But what you could do is send one of your ladies there first thing, let them queue for a few hours and then go and join them at, say, lunchtime."

"And there is no other alternative?" I asked.

"No. Well, the other alternative is to bribe them." He looked rather shifty as he said this. I figured that he had probably never actually said these words out loud before.

"And how does that work?"

128

"I prepare the paperwork, you give me the photo and 5,000 crowns, and I talk to the right people and get it for you." Okay, so maybe he had, and maybe sweet young Ondrej, who looked like Harry Potter's brother, wasn't quite as sweet as he appeared.

"Okay, so let's do that," I said. And a few days later, after everything had been handed over, Ondrej appeared, visa in hand.

Incidentally, this story reminds me of another similar situation much later on, when I asked my then team of employees whether any of them could drive and one of them answered that she could.

"When did you pass your test?" I asked.

"Oh, I never passed a test," she said, smiling. "But I have been driving for a few years."

"What do you mean, you 'never passed a test'?"

"Well, I gave my instructor some money and he gave me my driving licence." She seemed baffled as to why I would ask such a question.

"And how many lessons had you had with the instructor at that point?" I asked.

"Oh, none. I couldn't afford them. But I soon learned. And, besides, there weren't so many cars on the road in those days."

Only in the Czech Republic!

"Beautiful ex-model forces herself on young unsuspecting journalist outside hotel room and refuses to leave if he won't let her in and shag her…"

A Piss up in a Brewery

ONE OF THE FIRST projects we worked on in the New Year was for Bass. The past year they had spent millions on the brewery they'd bought, completing the reconstruction of the old brew house and the other main areas, while still maintaining the old and historic look, training the existing and new salesforces, re-branding the famous beer and even bringing some of their own beers over to sell on the Czech market. We were already discussing with Maurice the potential launch of one of the traditional English ales on the Czech market, which, in both of our books, seemed complete nonsense – talk about 'bringing coal to Newcastle', since the Czechs are one of the world-leaders in the production of beer – but that wasn't for us to say. But, anyway, and more immediately, the first bit of publicity about the work they were doing in Prague was getting started.

The Bass PR agency in the UK had organised a trip for various top-level journalists to visit Prague for a long weekend and learn all about the investment Bass had made, and it was our job to plan what the journalists would do while they were here, and, most importantly, to ensure that everything ran smoothly (which wasn't always easy, as you have probably gathered by now).

The plan was for the journalists to arrive on the Friday lunchtime plane, be met at the airport by Jana, who would accompany them into town on the coach we had hired for the weekend, and then they would be involved in various activities, including tours of the brewery, tours of Prague, and lots of eating, drinking and sightseeing, both of the city and its inhabitants! And, most of the time, Jana, Petra or Lucie would be accompanying them to make sure that everything went smoothly.

This wasn't really the sort of work I aspired to be doing, since it involved an awful lot of standing about in the cold, sitting around at the back of restaurants, or worse, and, often, arguing behind the scenes; with hotels or restaurants due to bad service, or coach drivers because they had turned up late or parked in the wrong place, or just about anyone that might want to put a spanner in the works. On the

131

other hand, it was what Mum would have called 'bread and butter money'. In other words, relatively easy and relatively well paid. We charged a fee for the general organisation of the trip, plus we often got commissions from the bus company, the hotel and even the restaurants. In the beginning, I didn't actually expect or even realise that I could ask for such commissions, but just about everyone paid them without us even asking, bribes and kickbacks being standard in the Czech Republic at that time.

For this particular trip, and as these were high level journalists, I planned on being around most of the time, plus as Lucie had done most of the organisation beforehand, I expected she would be helping Petra and me. I wasn't overly happy, therefore, when, on the Thursday before they all arrived, Lucie asked to speak to me and explained that Jonathan had invited her to go skiing with him for the weekend and that would mean her leaving the next day at lunchtime. Since we had returned after the New Year, I had tried to make it a rule that we didn't discuss our personal lives too much in the office. Especially not the relationship between Lucie and Jonathan, which, I felt, could only end in disaster, and was sure to impact on her work. And now, here we were, exactly as I had feared.

Anyway, Lucie being gone meant that Petra would have to deal with the bus drivers and, I suspected, that could be problematic since they could be quite difficult and would, for sure, behave worse to a young Slovak girl than someone like Lucie. Plus, we would need one of us to be in the background when the group arrived in the hotel, the restaurants and so on and, since Lucie had made all the arrangements and knew the people involved the best, it would have been way easier for her to be that person. In the end, I decided that Jana would need to take over those bits, since while she could be very difficult, mainly due to her inability to do anything without arguing about it first, there was one good thing about her and that was that she never seemed to have much planned in the evenings or weekends, so never minded turning out to work. And, for this particular weekend, she said she had kept her diary clear just in case, which was nice, although I rather doubted that it was quite like that.

Despite all of my early misgivings, however, in the end I felt that the whole event went off very well. The journalists were happy to be in Prague and seemed to take the whole trip very seriously. The buses turned up on time at the airport and the drivers did as they were told in regard to waiting, parking, picking up and so on. The hotel, a newly renovated and quite smart boutique one in Wenceslas Square didn't tell us that we didn't have rooms booked, which is what often happened, and which only tended to get resolved when we produced endless fax confirmations, called the manager, or threatened them with murder. And the journalists loved the brewery and the various drinking and ogling activities on the Saturday night as they were all horribly hungover and sheepish when I turned out to take them to the airport on Sunday. All in all, therefore, it was a success.

I was a bit surprised and concerned then, when, first thing Monday morning I had a call from Maurice asking me to come to the brewery and meet him that afternoon.

"We have a very serious problem," he said, speaking very quietly, which I found a bit unnerving.

"Whatever can it be?" I whispered to Jana, my hand over the receiver, as she was clearly listening in and had been on edge, I realised, since early that morning.

"I have no idea," she said. "I thought that everything was fine. It must be something unrelated."

I set off to the brewery a bit nervously in the afternoon. It's a bit of a drag to get to at the best of times, being in what was, at that time, an industrial and undeveloped area of Prague. On that particular day, I had to walk to the nearest metro station in the snow, travel a few stops and then walk quite a long way again in slush, so there was plenty of time to convince myself, in my usual catastrophist way, that we were going to lose the contract with Bass. And that was a 'best case' scenario.

Being a good PR girl, I managed to arrive at Maurice's desk looking happy and fluffy.

"Good afternoon, Maurice," I said with my biggest smile. "How are you feeling after the weekend? It looked as if everyone was enjoying themselves?"

"Yes," he responded. "They certainly did. I just hope it was all worth the effort."

"For sure it will have been." Another big smile from me. "I spoke to several of the journalists, and they were all raving about Prague, the brewery, and the trip generally. And they all assured me that there would be loads of nice articles written."

He didn't look convinced.

"So, come on Maurice, you're making me nervous. What's the problem? It doesn't sound like there was anything wrong from what you have said."

"Well," he said, looking a bit embarrassed. "I am sorry to tell you this, as you did such a good job. But I am afraid that there was something very wrong. It was Jana. She made herself a bit of a nuisance…" He stopped and the words hung in the air.

"What do you mean a 'nuisance'?" I asked eventually. "I was there most of the time and didn't see her doing anything wrong."

"Well, it seemed she misread the situation a bit. On Friday night, after she took everyone back to the hotel and made sure they got in okay, one of the journalists – actually, from our perspective, the most important one – asked her if she would like to stay on and have a drink with him at the bar, so she did."

"Okaaaaay," I said, raising my eyebrows. "Was that so wrong?"

"Well, no. The problem was that after one drink he asked for the bill and said to her that he had to get to bed as there was an early start in the morning. She refused to go. In fact, she followed him up and tried to barge her way into his room with him. It seems that he had to fight her off."

"Oh God."

"And then, on Saturday evening, he tried to pretend nothing had happened and was very polite to her but, once she took everyone back to the hotel, after going to the strip club, she made a bit of a scene again as she had had way too much to drink. Apparently, she started crying, begged him to let her stay and generally made herself an embarrassment. In fact, he called me on Sunday to say he wanted to make a formal complaint."

"Oh, bloody hell, Maurice. I am so sorry. I will deal with it," I said. "This is the last time she will come on one of these trips, don't worry."

"Well yes, you had better do *something*," he responded. "For now, though, we'll keep it to ourselves."

On my way back, I pondered what I actually could do about all of this. But, at the back of my mind there was something that niggled me about the whole situation and made me want to wait a bit before I did anything radical. By the time I got back to the office, anyway, the ladies had all left for the evening, so there was no need to get into it straightaway, since only Rhys was still there, manning the fort. "Come on," I said to him, "I definitely need a drink. Plus, I need to ask for your advice on something."

He downed his tools and off we went across the road to Molly's.

As usual, I cheered up a bit as soon as we entered the pub. Not because it is a pub, but because it was so cozy with its dim lighting, clouds of cigarette smoke, Irish music playing and beaten-up old sofas and chairs. One table even had an old sewing machine set inside its frame. It looks pretty but is difficult to sit at. Once we found a seat in one of the corner alcoves, I told Rhys what had gone on and he burst out laughing.

"Fuck me, J'ver. The bugger made an official complaint? Do you think he would have done if it had been Lucie? Imagine the headline, 'Beautiful ex-model forces herself on young unsuspecting journalist outside hotel room and refuses to leave if he won't let her in and shag her…' That's the stuff dreams are made of! I'm sorry, I know you don't always like Jana, but this one, I dunno. I think it's completely unreasonable."

"You're right." I said. "I knew there was something off about it. Hmm, I think I'm going to leave it for now. If we have to do an event like this again, well, I'll worry about Jana's involvement then. Poor old Jana, eh?"

135

"I have personal training in the morning. But okay, just a small one."

 **Fat Cows**

THE FOLLOWING MORNING all was quiet in the office. Jana looked up anxiously when I walked in from upstairs and barely gave me time to sit down before saying, "So, how did it go with Maurice yesterday? Was he happy with everything? I waited around for you last night, but I had to leave at 5.30."

"Yes," I responded. "I was there quite a long time, but mostly just chatting generally. I think that there was some misunderstanding with one of the journalists, but he seemed happy enough."

She looked relieved and rushed off to make both of us a cup of coffee to go with the cakes that she had brought in, clearly to butter me up, so to speak, if there was any issue. No sooner had she sat back down, Lucie arrived, a bit late and looking dreadful. Despite not wanting to get too involved in her situation, I couldn't help but ask if she was okay, at which point she started to well up and rushed through the meeting room to disappear to the loo. After a while, I figured she needed to come out and tell me what was happening. I bashed on the door and asked her if she was alright.

"Yes, I'm fine," she said, opening the door.

"So, what's happening?" I asked.

It turned out Jonathan had taken her to some very posh hotel in the Alps for the weekend, where a whole load of his friends from London were staying. After meeting them all at a party in the resort on Friday night, where, she said, all the women were dressed in amazing clothes and all knew each other and looked down their noses at her, she refused to come out of the hotel room again until after they had left on Monday morning. Apparently, Jonathan had gone mad. And then, to cap it all off, on the way back to Prague, he had told her that if she was going to come with him to other functions in the future, she needed to get some good clothes. But, in order to look good in them he said, she needed to lose some weight; Lucie, who was a size 10, if that! God knows what he made of the rest of us elephants.

137

"That is complete and utter bollocks," I said. "Sorry, Lucie, but that is not at all good, you look absolutely great, and you absolutely don't need to lose weight."

"But he's right," she said, pulling at some non-existent flesh above her jeans. "It's okay. I can lose it easily. I've done it before."

None of this boded well, I felt. But what could I do? I kind of understood how she must have felt, having been a 'poor girl' myself, growing up in a very well-to-do town and hanging out with horses and horsey people. I knew how intimidated I had felt sometimes, when everyone around me came from money and I didn't. For Lucie, it was multiplied ten times over, since she was from a completely different country, spoke a different language and had so little experience of the things that even regular people in the UK took for granted, let alone Jonathan's circle. The whole situation reminded me of something Mum once said to me, that, "It is difficult enough to be married, let alone married to someone from a different culture, who speaks a different language and who has had a completely different upbringing."

Something else that bothered me too was that if anyone needed to go on a diet it was, first of all, Jana – but that was a 'no-go' area since I had such a weird relationship with her I couldn't imagine ever broaching the subject – and secondly, me! I had been a fat baby, a fat child and a sometimes fat and sometimes very thin, verging on anorexic, teenager. Had it not been for my doing hours and hours of sport pretty much every day of my life – until I got to Prague – and being about five foot eight inches, so I could just about carry off my 12-14ish size, I would have been able to give Jana a run for her money in the fatso stakes. And just as Prague was a terrible place for someone with Simon's drink, drug and gambling problems to pitch up, so it was for someone like me too. It wasn't just the food; after a lifetime of being careful with my eating, I could tell the calorie value of a piece of food at about a hundred metres and worried about just about everything that I ate when I was out and about. But boozing every night and the difficulty of getting hold of healthy food regularly, combined with very little exercise, was a disaster for me. In the first two years alone, I had put on about 10 kilos, or possibly more (I didn't really want to know). Sitting in the office that afternoon and contemplating how ridiculous it was for Lucie to be talking about going on a diet, I wondered whether it might just be time for me to take myself in hand.

At a recent lunch with Simon, who was going through a 'good as gold' period and liked to lecture everyone, especially me, on the perils of an unhealthy lifestyle, he mentioned that he had recently met an American girl called Cheryl who had just arrived in Prague and was setting up as a 'personal trainer' in the newly opened gym in the hotel around the corner from our office. Simon planned to become one of her first clients.

"That sounds like a great idea," I had said. "But what's a personal trainer?"

Growing up in the countryside, riding horses, playing tennis and generally being a tomboy, I had never been in a gym, apart from the weird old-fashioned torture chamber that we had at my girls' school. I refused to go in there very often. It had wooden ladders up the walls and a variety of boxes to vault over and, since I'm unable to jump in the air, unless I'm sitting on a horse, and am scared of heights, it wasn't for me.

"Well, to tell you the truth, darling, I'm not that sure myself," said Simon. "But I plan to go and see her next week and find out. Thing is, she is pretty bloody sexy and if she wants to manhandle me and get me fit in the process, who am I to say no?"

Before I could think about it again, I decided to walk around to the hotel later to see what a real gym looked like and then find out how much it might cost to go there, assuming I could work out what to do. While I was standing looking around in the reception area – the door had been open, but no-one was there – a very fit looking, all muscle and no fat girl bounced in and hailed me with a huge bright white smile.

"Hi! Can I help you?" she asked in a strong American accent.

"Hi, well yes, maybe. I wanted to have a look at the gym and find out a bit more about membership and so on."

"Sure," she said. "Come with me, I'm Cheryl."

139

The gym itself was nothing like I imagined. It was very clean and bright, with big windows looking out onto a grassy lawn that ran alongside the main road, parallel to the river, and lots of different bits of equipment that looked nothing like the stuff from school, but appeared fairly easy to work out. Plus there was no-one else there.

"So, how does it work?" I asked. "Can I just pay a fee to come here, or do I have to become a member or something?"

"It depends on what you want to do," she said. "If you haven't been to a gym before you might like to sign up for a few training sessions with me first, just to get used to it all and take it from there."

Before I could have second thoughts and, more importantly, before I could figure out whether I could afford it, I had signed up and was ready to start with her the following morning. Except, I realised I really didn't have anything suitable to wear to such a place. That meant a trip to the one store I could think of that might sell something vaguely appropriate, the hideous old eyesore in the centre of town known as Kotva.

Kotva was the first shop I ever went into in Prague on my own. Mainly as, at that time, it was the only place that boasted something that vaguely resembled a supermarket on the lower ground floor. When it was built in the 70s, the old regime was very proud of Kotva, as not only had they brought in a Swedish architect to design it, which was unheard of at the time as the communists kept themselves to themselves, but they had also gone to pains to make sure that it looked properly 'communist'. Five or six floors of large square blocks with lots of darkened glass and concrete, and a complete contrast to the historical buildings at either side. Despite that, Kotva has always been one of Prague's real landmarks as it is situated just a little way down from the 13th century Prašná Brána (the 'Powder Tower'), the blackened archway that is the entrance to the main street, Celetná, that eventually leads to the Old Town Square.

The old regime may have been proud of it, but Kotva is a horrible beast. However, if you really dig about, you can find quite a lot of useful stuff among the huge amount of rubbish. On the ground floor there's a dodgy looking café with a lot of very unsavoury gangsters hanging about doing deals, plus a sort of 'perfumery' that is supposed to be a bit like the ground floor of Selfridges but couldn't be further from that if it tried. And then there are a few floors of clothes, including one huge and fascinating fur coat department and, I vaguely remember, a shabby sort of sports goods area. The whole depressing shopping experience is topped off by the fact that Kotva has just about the surliest shop attendants, if you could ever find one, in Prague, which is saying something.

I did, though, find some black, stretchy leggings and a white T-shirt that I figured, while not actually labelled 'sports', would do. I got some plimsolls too. Who remembers those, eh? White, flat soles, very light and very far away from the trainers that we are all used to now, but as good as it got at that time.

This, I told myself, was the start of a whole new and healthy regime. And, in Molly's that night, followed by a 'light' dinner in U Zlatá Ulička, I held forth about how I had been an athlete before and could be an athlete again; just wait and see. Which Rhys, being a still fit rugby player, looked vaguely surprised to hear but, to give him his due, he did make all the right encouraging noises.

Unfortunately, though this was one of those evenings when a small crowd had gathered in the restaurant, and once the 'closed' sign had been hung on the door, Nenad had brought out a whisky bottle and was off telling his war stories.

"I really have to go soon," I said to the world in general. "I have personal training in the morning. But okay, just a small one."

Safe to say, the small one turned into a big one and 2.00 am saw me staggering back home, knowing that in five hours' time I was going to be up and over to the hotel for my first personal training session with Cheryl. Not a good thought at all!

However, since I never sleep very well, especially if I know I have to wake up early, I was up in plenty of time to put on my new gear underneath various other sweaters and overcoats in order to walk around to the hotel. I wasn't feeling great but also not so bad and the first training itself was quite fun, if you can call running on the treadmill, doing sit-ups and lifting weights fun. But it was good to start moving again and I was determined that I would keep it going, especially as there was the added benefit of Cheryl loving to gossip., although it was clear she didn't know too much about the boys just yet.

One morning, soon after I had started, I arrived for one of my training sessions and Cheryl was standing in reception looking very worried.

"Simon's here," she said in a bit of a whisper. She had a slight speech impediment which meant she whispered a lot and did a kind of breathy 'ah' at the beginning of some words which, I imagine, the boys found very sexy. "I don't know what to do about him, he's clearly pissed. He just staggered in here, told me he was going for a lie down and now he's on one of the sunbeds out for the count. Should we wake him or call someone?"

"No," I said. "I would just leave him to sleep it off, unless anyone complains."

And that's what we did, that morning and many mornings after.

My own training, though, started going very well. It's funny how the body remembers things and, after the first couple of weeks, when everything hurt, my muscles started to take shape again and slowly – very slowly, sadly – a bit of weight started to come off. Back in the office, however, while Jana seemed to grow bigger and bigger every day and Petra stayed small and petite, Lucie was shrinking in front of our eyes. And that started to become a major concern.

The Buck Stops Here

ONE MORNING I WAS training with Cheryl and, while I jumped about and did my stuff, she was asking me about my work and why I always seemed to be stressed. Personal training is about more than just fitness, as she was always telling me. It also has a lot to do with nutrition, mental health and so on. I pondered this, as I hadn't actually realised that I was *that* stressed, definitely not enough to actually look it.

"I suppose," I said after a while, "it is partly due to being on my own, not just living on my own and not having any sort of partner, but also knowing that the buck stops with me for *everything*. I'm responsible for paying all the bills, the salaries and so on, ensuring that there are no mistakes, finding clients and just being 'the boss'. That, and having a team of such young girls with absolutely no experience and no real idea of what they are doing. Plus, I'm not that much older than them and I don't have much experience either! Especially not of being a boss, which is really bloody difficult."

"It's funny," said Cheryl. "I hear the same thing from everyone. It's the people, they keep saying, so why can't you find better ones?

"I suppose for us foreigners, in particular, it's the need to have people that speak English. Which means, for the most part, young girls. They are the only ones that have really learned to speak it, which they do most of the time by going somewhere to be a nanny. Blokes haven't really had the chance to go anywhere to learn English, or anything else for that matter, and macho Czech guys definitely wouldn't want to be nannies!" This was a constant discussion among us, and not really one that had a solution.

"But why can't you at least find people with experience? Or couldn't you hire a translator or something? Or even learn to speak Czech yourselves?" Cheryl looked puzzled. I, though, had had this conversation many times before.

"The thing is," I said, "people with experience of working under the communist regime mostly have 'bad' experience. Besides, the things I'm doing, like 'marketing' and 'public relations', didn't really exist in those days, so there are very few people that even know what those words mean! Really, what we all need are Czechs that escaped from Czechoslovakia and are now coming back, but they can name their price and the big companies always grab them. They would be way too expensive for the likes of me."

"Yes, I see what you mean," she said. "Still, I suppose if everyone here knew what they were doing, could speak English, and had had the experience you are talking about, there would be many fewer opportunities for all of us." And wasn't she exactly right?

I was reminded of this conversation later that day when I went for my first meeting with Kumar. He had just taken on the lease of a building close to Lávka which he was in the process of renovating and staffing in readiness for the grand opening later that year. It was that opening I was there to discuss.

The venue was incredible. Right by the river, looking directly out at the Charles Bridge and the river, it was entered by a door into a long corridor that opened into a huge space for the restaurant, which had amazing floor to ceiling windows with the best view imaginable. I had never really noticed the building before, possibly due to usually being in that area in the dark and/ or the worse for wear from drinking, but you couldn't really imagine a better location for a restaurant.

I opened the door, walked down the steps and stopped. I could see the end of the corridor, where it widened into the main room and could hear Kumar shouting at the top of his voice. I walked a few more steps to see what was happening and saw about a hundred young people, all standing in lines, while he was at the front shouting and pointing at something I couldn't see. *Hmm.* I was not at all sure I wanted to disturb whatever was going on so I turned around, crept back out the door and stood outside having a cigarette. Cigarette finished, I opened the door again, walked down the steps and there was Kumar, all smiles.

"Hello, Jo," he said, kissing me on both cheeks. "Great you're here, let's go into the meeting room and talk about my plans."

There must have been something in my face as he sat down, looked at me and then said, "Did you come in earlier? Maybe you heard me shouting?"

"Well, yes," I said. "But I didn't want to interrupt, so I went back outside."

"Yes, well, sorry about that," he responded. "The thing is, working with these people, especially in the restaurant business when you are dealing with waiters, chefs and so on, you have to be tough. They really only understand it if you behave like a dictator and tell them 'do this and do that', you can't give them any sort of flexibility or ask them to use their initiative, they just don't have it yet."

I was sure he was right. The problem was that, however hard I tried, I couldn't be like that as I always wanted to be nice and have people like me. Which is probably why Kumar became so successful, and a millionaire several times over, and I did not.

The meeting seemed to go well, although I could see that working with Kumar could be very demanding as he is just so much smarter than everyone else! Whatever I suggested he could cap with something better and more inventive. But I must have said a few reasonable things as we got the job and I left feeling very excited about the possibilities that lay ahead.

From there, instead of going back to the office, I headed to The Joyce, where I had arranged to meet Katy for our monthly dinner in Zátiší. I was early. Katy was, as expected, late, but, keeping in mind my 'new regime', I nursed a Diet Coke while waiting and chatted to a few of the regulars at the bar.

Soon after that, Katy arrived, and we walked up the road towards the restaurant. "I hope you don't mind," she said. "I wanted to prepare you beforehand but didn't get a chance with the other guys there. I invited Jeremy to join us."

"Mind?" I asked. "Bloody hell, of course I bloody mind! I haven't seen him or heard a dickie bird since that Christmas party!"

"I know, love," she shrugged. "I couldn't really help it. I had a meeting with him this afternoon and told him I was meeting you tonight and he asked if he could come along. I didn't think you would mind that much."

I had, of course, realised that Jeremy and my paths would cross sooner or later, as was inevitable in Prague. I suppose I had vaguely thought I would look amazing by that time, and he would be regretting he hadn't made contact earlier. Unfortunately, that wasn't the case, and I was in thick trousers and a sweater, with all my woolly bits and pieces on top, and hadn't done any sort of tarting up since the morning, which wasn't quite how I would have planned it. But it was too late to do anything about it now.

And, actually, it didn't really matter. I had forgotten that even though Jeremy was a bit too handsome for his own good, he was actually very good company, and having Katy there as well meant that we had plenty to talk and laugh about. It only got tricky towards the end, when Katy announced that she was heading off early, paid the bill and legged it before anyone could stop her, and we were left there alone.

"So, what do we do now?" said Jeremy. "We can go our separate ways, or we can go home together. What do you think?"

Go our separate ways, I thought. But what came out was, "Go home together."

Home, I found out this time, since we went to his rather than mine, had a new lodger whose name was Colin and Colin was staying with Jeremy until he found somewhere of his own as they were now working together. I already knew a bit about him as Simon and a couple of the others had been talking about him in the pub one evening, particularly the fact that he had once been a male model and that he was in Prague to be Jeremy's righthand man. I hadn't realised, though, that he was living with Jeremy, and was a bit taken aback to see him sitting on the sofa in the living room when we arrived, and also, I have to say, just how good looking he was! Tall, well put together, with jet black hair, brown eyes and very white teeth, and this was before people had their teeth 'done'. But I also thought that he wasn't very sexy as he had too much of that 'clean-cut American boy' look for me, even though he was English. Mind you, the minute we walked in, he got up and left the room without saying a word, so I didn't really get a good picture of him. just the feeling that all was not that harmonious between the two of them.

Back to my resolve, or lack of it. Hopeless, at least on my part. I suppose I did like Jeremy a little bit more than I let on, otherwise I would prefer to think I would have had more will power. And, even though I found him attractive, the fact that we got on very well when we just sat and chatted was as important. I could even imagine, on a good day, with the wind in the right direction, having a normal relationship with him. But I wasn't sure that he was in any way ready for that himself, plus the temptation that he had around him every single day made it quite difficult to imagine him ever being faithful to just one person. Definitely any sort of meaningful conversation, such as, 'Shall we go out for a proper drink one day?' or, 'When will I see you again?' would be pointless. Better, I felt, not to think too hard about the whole situation, if there even *was* a situation, and just see what happened next.

"I didn't really expect to see me
here either! I got persuaded."

Relationships, who Needs Them?

PRAGUE IS VERY SMALL, which means that everyone knows everyone, and if they don't know someone, they know someone else that does. That goes not just for the foreign expat community but for the Czech business world too. In those early days we all knew way too much about what each other was up to, whether that was in work or in our personal lives (hence the success of the late and much lamented *This is Where you Hear it First!*).

In some ways, especially in the work environment, being such a close community could be a good thing. For example, everyone in my world knew I worked for Bass, so no other agency (and there were a few gradually starting up) was going to try to pitch to them as they knew we were in there already, at least that was the theory. On the other hand, it also meant that companies didn't believe they needed to 'market' their products or services very much. Word-of-mouth was everything and there was a general belief that a company could build its customer base on its owners' or directors' friends alone. On that basis, they questioned the need to spend money on any sort of promotional activity, which made selling our services, which I now clearly defined as 'marketing and PR', to many local companies was near impossible.

On a personal level, life could be even more complicated, since we all moved in the same circles, went to the same bars and restaurants and even, by then, the same gym, which meant that nothing ever stayed a secret. I was happy there had been very little gossip about me until recently – hardly surprising, as I had barely done anything worthy of a gossip, sadly – and actually, my first hook up with Jeremy went fairly unnoticed, probably because it was just before Christmas and most of us had disappeared for a while. Then, by the time we all came back, life had moved on. In his case, I was sure there had been many new 'conquests' in the meantime. In mine, I had just been keeping a low profile. But this time, well, everyone in my social circle seemed to know where I had been the night before and with whom, which wasn't great. Simon, in particular, was full of it, and for a couple of weeks after could barely finish a sentence without asking in a teasing sort of voice, "How's Jerry?" or similar. I'm sure the same was happening to 'Jerry' himself.

A couple of days after the dinner with Katy, I was working late and had popped over to Molly's for a couple of drinks with Rhys and Ewan when they suggested we head to a new nightclub called Radost. I wasn't keen. I was tired. It was cold, plus, I had an early start the next morning. Much better, I felt, to just go back across the road and call it a day. Plus, Radost was a total dive and not really my thing. It was outside the centre for a start, which meant taking a cab there and back, and the ride home could often be very late since it stayed open until about 7.00 am.

The entrance to Radost was at street level, and then you went downstairs into to a dark and dingy bar area, which then led to the dancefloor, where you couldn't see much apart from the vague outlines of hundreds of bodies gyrating about in the thick smoke that filled the air. I also wasn't so keen on the music there since it was much more focused on 'techno' than the usual 80s and early 90s that was played in the other clubs. Actually, as far as I could see, the only vaguely interesting thing about Radost was the loo cleaner, since he had been one of the three main people that had led the Velvet Revolution of 1989, alongside the soon-to-be and now was President, President Havel. So, now he was a toilet cleaner. What does that say?

However, being the middle of winter, Lávka had lost its appeal, since the best thing about it was the wonderful terrace overlooking the river. It was not somewhere to hang out in the freezing cold and snow, and Radost had quickly become the new 'in' place to go. I knew the boys spent a good deal of time there and Simon, despite the wedding not being far off, had become a more or less permanent fixture, since, rumour had it, it was a good place to buy banned substances. But anyway, that evening, since I'm not very good at saying no, my arm was twisted and the three of us hopped into a taxi and made our way there. And even though it was a Tuesday, the place was absolutely heaving.

Ewan was soon off hunting, but Rhys and I headed to chat to a few of our regular group who were propping up the bar, and we were soon joined by Simon, bobbing and weaving about, with various different girls hanging off each of his arms. I was nursing my drink and wondering why I had agreed to come with them, when down the stairs came Colin, Jeremy's new housemate, looking a bit lost, as he hadn't yet met many people other than Simon, who he immediately made a beeline for. Then he saw me.

"Hello," he said. "I didn't expect to see you here."

"No," I answered. "I didn't really expect to see me here either! I got persuaded. But why *wouldn't* you expect to see me? I'm always out and about with these reprobates!"

"Sorry, I didn't mean to sound strange," he replied. "It's just that I heard Jeremy coming in with a girl just before I left home and thought she sounded like you. Must have been one of his others."

I still don't really understand why his saying that upset me as much as it did. I suppose I liked to think I was a bit different to the regular Czech girls and that he should have assumed that I may not like the idea of someone that I had just spent the night with being with another person a few days later (and who knows how many on other nights). But then I wasn't really sure why I *did* care. Whatever it was, I must have looked as if I was going to cry or something as Simon immediately dumped his entourage, grabbed me, and rushed me out the door and up the stairs saying, "Don't break down here, it won't look good." Before I knew it, I had been shoved in a taxi and whizzed back to his place to spend the night! But before you get any wrong ideas, that meant me being given the sofa and some blankets to sleep on while Simon hovered about to check that I was okay, before leaving for the rest of the night, only to be seen again briefly in the early morning creeping past the living room with two girls in tow. At which point I got dressed, let myself out and walked all the way back to the cottage, arriving in time to get showered, dressed and start work before anyone else even arrived.

The fall-out from that story though was quite spectacular. Simon being Simon had told Jeremy what Colin had said to me that evening and Jeremy, being Jeremy, had gone into the office the following day and punched Colin in the face. Which was, I believe, the beginning of the end of a relationship that was fast going down the drain. As, I had decided, were any future shenanigans of my own, especially with Jeremy. Which also had its own implications, since I was living in a country that I still found quite difficult to live in and running my own small company, which had put an end to my ever going back to my previous life. And, as far as I could see, little to no chance of meeting anyone I could ever have a normal relationship with. Which meant, potentially, that with so few even vaguely attractive Czech men in the vicinity, the only real solution for me was to become a nun.

February Blues

FEBRUARY IS PROBABLY the worst month in the Czech Republic as it's just so cold. Some days it feels as if it never really gets light plus, by that point, we have usually had a huge amount of snow, which means that the pavements are covered with ice and slush. Not a good month to have a birthday, but there wasn't a lot I could do about that. And since Petra's birthday was just one day after mine, I wondered whether we should have a dinner or some sort of party or do something a bit special to celebrate. I discussed the party idea with the ladies one morning and they seemed to like it, so we decided that we would ask Nenad if we could take over the restaurant for an evening, have a buffet and lots of Yugoslavian wine and maybe the guitar boys that played there on an irregular basis could come along and sing a bit. And then, of course, we would probably all move on to one of the clubs. After a bit of discussion about dates and, whizzing over to see Nenad, we settled on the last Friday of the month and agreed that Petra would be in charge of preparing the guest list.

Since the beginning of the year, we had been working flat out. Jana was getting very annoying with her constant bitching about Petra and jealousy of Lucie, while Petra herself got better and better each day. But all of us, in our own way, worried about Lucie. She was literally disappearing in front of our eyes and even her newly bought designer clothes were hanging off her as if she were a clothes-rack. While I had tried to ignore it, I realised she very rarely appeared to eat anything, and if she did, then soon after she would wander off to the loo and come out much later, having cleaned the whole cloakroom. If it hadn't been so worrying, I would have suggested that when we were less busy, she could also clean my flat, but that wasn't really appropriate! Petra, who was tiny but ate like a horse, used to bring all sorts of goodies into the office and offer them around, but they only really got eaten by Jana, since Lucie would turn her nose up as if she had never, ever, eaten such things in her life before. And me, well, despite the ongoing boozing, I was still hoping to get some more of my weight off by working harder in the gym.

I obviously realised that Lucie's state of mind was caused by Jonathan, who, despite Annabel being in and out of town quite regularly, often turned up at the office to sit and chat with Lucie and then suggest they go for a quick drink 'or something', at which point Lucie would disappear for the rest of the day, arriving the following morning looking even more stressed than usual. To be fair, she worked very hard when she *was* there, but had started to grumble about various things, especially the office; it was too dark, her eyes were being affected by having to work under electric light all the time or that it was too small for us, and so on, to the point I wondered if she would actually leave if I didn't agree to move.

"You should have seen the offices I worked in in London," I said to her one day. "We had an open plan space that was probably smaller than our ground floor and we had about twenty desks in it with about a square metre of space for each of us."

"Yes, but that was London," she responded. "Most people I know here have their own office. Maybe we Czechs just like to be more comfortable at work?"

"Of course, I would like us all to be more comfortable," I said, inwardly snarling, "and once we are earning more money and we can afford it, I am not against moving somewhere more modern and bigger, just not yet." That, I hoped, would be the end of it for now.

That night, I sat in Molly's with Rhys, and we pondered what we could do about Lucie and how it seemed her whole personality was changing.

"She was such a lovely girl when she started," I said. "But I barely recognise her now. She's so thin, so pissed off all the time. I just don't know what to do. Plus, she hardly does a full day's work anymore, which doesn't exactly lie well with the others."

"She'll come out of it," he responded. "We all know Jonathan is never going to leave Annabel, and sooner or later she will realise it for herself. I think you just have to hang in there and hope that it doesn't affect her work for too much longer."

But, of course, it did. On a more and more regular basis. You can imagine, therefore, how annoyed I was when on the Friday night before the week of our party she asked me if she could speak to me in private and then said, "I'm really sorry, Jo. I won't be able to attend the party as Jonathan has asked me to go away for the weekend again. Actually, we have to leave Thursday lunchtime. I hope you won't mind?"

"Well," I said. "I do a bit. First, we have quite a lot of work on at the moment, so being off at all is not great. But second, and in terms of the party, I had wanted it to be a nice thing for all of us, not just for me, and that meant you being there too." At which point she burst into tears, and not just tears, but howls of hysteria, which ended with her kneeling on the floor and sobbing.

"Lucie," I said. "This is no good, you can't continue like this. Jonathan is my friend and I like him, but he is not for you. You're not eating, you're not happy. You need to stop it."

"I can't stop it," she wailed. "I love him and he loves me. He will leave his wife, you'll see. It's just that he doesn't understand that I can't just take time off when he wants me to. Please don't sack me for asking."

"Don't be silly, I'm not going to sack you. But you need to think if this is really what you want."

Being a boss was not at all easy. And being a boss who is only a few years older than the people working for her is even more difficult. Which meant, really, that I had no idea what to do about the whole Lucie situation. So even though it was a Friday, and in spite of all of my usual gang trying to persuade me to go out, I decided to stay in and have an early night, hoping that in the morning, I would wake up with a solution.

At about 1.00 am, however, I was woken by the phone. I had just had an extension phone put in in my bedroom, since such sophistication had recently arrived in the Czech Republic, and that meant that if anyone called us, both the office and the bedroom phone rang. Since I don't sleep well anyway, I answered it within a couple of rings.

155

"I'm so sorry to call you in the middle of the night," said the voice at the end of the line, "but you need to come to Radost and collect your husband. He is in a bad way." Hmm.

"My husband?"

"Yes, he says his name is Simon and we should call you to come and get him."

"Okay, I'm on my way," I answered, pulling on my dressing gown. As soon as I put the phone down, I picked it up again and called for a taxi (another new phenomenon in Prague was a taxi company that prided itself on being both honest and reliable) who said that a car would be with me in just two minutes. *Sod it*, I thought, *I'll just go as I am*. Shoving my feet into my boots, a scarf around my neck and then throwing my sheepskin on top of my dressing gown, out I went, into the cab and off to Radost, where a small crowd had gathered by the bar around Simon, who was clearly drunk and possibly on something nasty too and in a heap on the floor.

"Simon, come on, get up,' I said, taking his arm and trying to pull him to his feet.

"Okay, let me help, come on mate," said another voice, and there was Jeremy, newly arrived and elbowing his way through the crowd. Between us we got him up and outside and then wondered what we should do.

"I think we have to take him to my place," I said. "I don't have keys for his and we can't leave him here."

The taxi driver got out to help us shovel Simon into the back of the car and then the two of us piled in as well, back to the cottage and into the office where, I suggested, we could put him on the sofa in the meeting room and hopefully he could sleep off whatever he had drunk/ taken there.

"I'll get him some water and a bucket," I said. "In case he wakes up feeling sick." I went upstairs to get both. By the time I came back down, Jeremy was sitting in the office, with a glass of 'my' whisky in his hand.

"Give him his water then and come and have a drink with me," he said.

I put the water and the bucket on the floor by the sofa – Simon was already out for the count – and returned to the office.

"Why've you still got your coat on?" he asked.

"Well, I went out in a bit of a hurry and don't actually have anything underneath other than my old dressing gown," I replied.

"What? You went to Radost in your dressing gown? That's a bloody first. But great. Less to take off." *Hmm,* I thought, *no chance of that after the Colin 'putting his foot in his mouth' incident and my new resolution.* But then, for God's sake, I can be quite ridiculous sometimes, and Jeremy, when he is being nice, can be very difficult to resist. And, you know, sometimes you just have to grab these opportunities…

Simon woke up the next morning, realised where he was and then got up, feeling the worse for wear, and marched upstairs to find me. How he laughed when he found me and Jeremy sitting in my 'lounge', watching Eurosport on the TV and chatting about sport, something that I can do indefinitely and that Jeremy was, I think, surprised to find that a 'mere girl' could actually hold forth on.

"I'm not entirely sure how I came to be here," he said, "Nor what's going on with you two. But whatever it is, I like it."

Shortly after, the two of them got up and left and I went downstairs to clear up and then figure out what to do for the rest of the weekend. With very few options, other than the usual coffee/ lunch/ pub scenario, I decided to do what I always do when there isn't a lot else to occupy me, and that is to sit down at my desk and plough on with work.

"Oh, look down there!
There's a beautiful swan
wearing a man's overcoat."

Birthday Bash

THE WEEK BEFORE our party flew by, partly as we had so much work to get done by the weekend, and partly as the weather was freezing cold, with dark grey skies and snow, which meant that going anywhere further than across the road to Molly's in the evening or over to the gym in the morning was out of the question. Everyone we had invited was attending the party – everyone, that is, except for Jonathan and Lucie – even Clive was staying in town for it, as was Eva, who had barely been in Prague for months. She had arrived on the Wednesday and planned to stay until Sunday and insisted on us having lunch the day before in Zátiší, her birthday treat.

Off I went in the freezing cold to meet her the day before the party and we chatted all through our lunch, before she looked at me with a funny expression and said, "Darling, haven't you noticed anything new about me?"

I looked at her: long reddish hair, lots of very nice makeup and jewellery, lovely clothes that disguised her slightly larger-than-she-was-happy-with figure. Nothing different that I could see.

"I'm very sorry, Eva," I said. "But I can't see anything new. What am I missing?"

"I'm not smoking! How can you not have noticed?"

I was just so used to seeing her with a cigarette attached to her hand that it had become an appendage you took for granted and no longer noticed. But once she had pointed it out it became very apparent. "Bloody hell, Eva! However did you do it?" I exclaimed.

"I was hypnotised," she said. "I went to this amazing place in London. It cost just a few quid, and now, *bam*. Here I am. Haven't had a ciggie for a week and no cravings for one either."

"Give me their details now!" I said. "I'm going there too, as soon as possible." The minute I got back to the office I called them and made an appointment for the following week. *To hell with it.* I would take a few days off, if necessary, if it was going to work.

Friday night then, Petra, Jana, Rhys and I headed to U Zlatá Ulička early. The place looked gorgeous; lots of candles and lanterns, soulful traditional music playing on CDs. Various friends started to arrive, including the Bass boys, Ewan with one of his regular girls in tow, Clive and Eva along with Tom, a new arrival in the old office and who Jana immediately clapped her eyes on *God help him.* Also Petra's nice Slovak boyfriend, Milan, and Matthew together with Katy. Simon turned up a bit later than the others, complaining that he couldn't find the place since he had never been invited before, and with a message from Jeremy that he was on his way from some God forsaken place in the south of the country. Just about everyone I loved and cared about was there.

The food, as usual, was fantastic, and, as we worked our way through endless bottles of red wine, the two guitarists arrived to play, and Rhys got up to join them and sing as usual. And then Ewan, not wanting to be overshadowed, asked them if they knew any Tom Jones – *What, two young Bosnians*? I thought to myself. It transpired, however, that they did, so, before we knew it, Ewan's amazing voice was belting out 'Delilah', 'Green, Green Grass of Home' and others, which we all sung along to, applauding ourselves wildly at the end of each song.

Unfortunately, since U Zlatá Ulička is in a residential area, and Nenad is very law-abiding, we had to quieten down by midnight. But then, just as we were debating heading for Lávka, Jeremy appeared, carrying a magnum of champagne, which he insisted on opening and sharing around, giving himself and me the largest glasses and clinking them with a twinkle in his eye and a big "Happy Birthday to my favourite lady" in front of everyone, in what felt like him asserting his 'ownership' over me. With all of that going on, it was about 1.00 am before we eventually left and headed to Lávka for yet more boozing and a bit of dancing. I had walked with Jeremy and Katy, so when we arrived the receptionist grabbed our coats, including Jeremy's new and rather smart Prada overcoat, and hung them all on the one hanger. I wondered what Jeremy would make of that, since there was a bit of a hidden implication in it.

At about 3.00 am, I started to flag and was thinking it was probably time to leave, possibly alone, but I was never quite sure with Jeremy, especially after the previous weekend. But while I was dithering about wondering whether to just head off or speak to him first, Katy came over, grabbed my arm and said that she was leaving and that I should probably go too. I said my goodbyes to those of my friends that were still around and looked to see what Jeremy was up to and there he was, in the far corner of the main room, smooching and snogging a young girl I had never seen before.

"Okay, let's go," I said to Katy, and the two of us walked out to the reception desk together, where the receptionist handed us back all three coats. And then, well, I don't really remember what happened next, but it is possible I may have walked to the barrier at the side of the pathway and accidentally dropped Jeremy's coat over the edge and into the river, I'm not sure…

The following day, I was woken quite early by the telephone ringing and it was him.

"I don't suppose you've seen my coat?" he asked. "It was on the same hanger as yours when we went into Lávka last night."

"Hmm, no," I said. "I have no idea what you are talking about."

He slammed the phone down.

Later on, I met up with Katy and Eva in a small restaurant near the river and we sat by the window nursing our hangovers and carrying out a postmortem on the evening before. I had just got to the bit where we were leaving Lávka, having watched Jeremy snogging someone, when Katy said, "Oh, look down there! There's a beautiful swan wearing a man's overcoat." We all burst out laughing.

"Katy did tell me what happened," said Eva. "But it must never, ever, be mentioned out loud again."

"I don't know what you mean," I responded. But, despite the smile, I was also resolving, *again*, that that was the end of any sort of 'relationship with men' for the time being.

Over the years, we have all reflected a lot on how the 'boys' in Prague behaved towards women. And not just the boys, even older, married men, many of whom were as bad, if not worse, than those of my age. I knew of one, the managing director of one of the multinationals, who was, according to those that knew, completely addicted to going to one of the 'knocking shops' (brothels) called K5. Apparently, barely a day went by without this MD paying a trip there, sometimes during the day, sometimes in the evening. Then, there was another executive, fairly newly arrived in Prague from Hong Kong, who, despite having a very beautiful and glamorous wife living in Prague with him, would turn up at one or other of the bars or clubs most nights with a different young Czech girl on his arm. We used to think that he and his wife must have an 'open relationship' and that the wife must know about his string of girls but, when he was eventually found out, which was inevitable since he was so open about his womanising, the shit hit the fan like there was no tomorrow.

What we concluded, generally, was that the majority of foreign men were perfectly normal and decent before they got on the plane to Prague. But then, once they settled in and realised so many of the Czech women that crossed their path were, as they would say, 'up for a jump', irrespective of whether the women were married, were their age, had two heads, or were just about anything really, the majority reverted to 'male sex maniac mode' and off they went, pretty much shagging anything that moved. And, of course, they gave very little thought as to whether anyone might get hurt or if there were any other consequences. And that meant that us foreign ladies were rather lumped together with all the Czech girls as far as behaviour towards us was concerned. We didn't like it, and nor did the more 'normal' local girls.

Those rampant Czech girls though could be ruthless in the way they went about their hunt for a foreign partner. I saw the perfect example of this when I was having tea with Rhys at a coffee shop just around the corner from the office one afternoon after 'the coat incident'. We were sitting on high stools by the bar and, for once, I was listening to his problems, rather than boring him with mine. Within a few minutes of our tea arriving, a Czech girl in her mid-twenties, I suppose, and reasonably pretty but tarty, came and sat on the bar stool the other side of Rhys. There were only three stools in total, but plenty of other seating around the café, so it seemed a bit strange.

"Do you have a light?" she asked, tapping him on the arm at the same time.

Rhys, ever the gentleman, and always an outrageous flirt, lit her cigarette and then turned back to me to continue talking.

She tapped him on the arm again, "Are you new in the area? I haven't seen you before," she asked.

"No," he said. "I work just around the corner from here."

"Oh really? What do you do?"

And off he went, describing what he does, where his office is, why she hadn't seen him before, because we usually go to Molly Malone's (very subtle, Rhys). Meantime, I was sitting with his back to me, sipping my tea and getting angry. Eventually, I got up, looked firmly at Rhys and said, "I'm going back to the office, you can pay," then marched out.

"What was all that about, J'ver?" he said when he arrived back an hour or so later. "I hope you weren't jealous? That would be weird."

"No Rhys," I said. "I'm not angry because I was jealous. I was angry with her! Bloody hell, she didn't know who I was and what my relationship was to you. We could have been married for all she knew. She didn't care. She was clearly after you and wouldn't care if she snatched you from under my nose. God, they make me sick sometimes."

"Oh, yes. I suppose you're right. I dunno though. I don't think she was after me? Was she?" He looked hopeful.

"Sometimes, Rhys, you are just as hopeless as the rest of them. Men; can't live with them, can't live without them."

"My name is Vladimir.
'Vlad' for short."
Or 'Vlad the Impaler',
as we later called him.

The Only Way to go is Sport

The following weeks were fraught on various levels. First, I had a bit of a fall-out with the Tomašes in Pardubice again. I had called them to suggest us going down there to discuss in more detail the following season and Bass' sponsorship. The agreement between Bass and the racecourse had been for Bass to sponsor the big race for one year and then have 'first refusal' on whether they would continue the following year. I reminded them of this when Little Tomaš said, "Actually, Jo, we don't need to discuss the sponsorship for this year as we already have a sponsor of our own. We won't be needing Bass."

"But did you discuss this with Bass before you agreed the new sponsorship?" I asked him.

"No, why would we?"

"Because they have the right of first refusal, it is quite clearly stated in the contract, which means you were supposed to ask them if they wanted to continue to be a sponsor before you agreed anything new." *Oh God*, I thought, imagining going to Maurice, him saying that they wanted to continue the sponsorship, and me having to say, "Sorry, no, they have someone else."

"Oh well," said Little Tomaš. "They won't mind, I'm sure. And anyway, the contract doesn't mean anything. What are they going to do? Sue us? We don't have any money!" He laughed.

This wasn't the first time I had been told by a company that a contract that they themselves had been so difficult about now doesn't mean anything. Such was business in the Czech Republic. I just wasn't sure that Maurice and the others would understand it.

"Well, let's hope they're as relaxed as you think they will be," I said. "I'll talk to them. In the meantime, though, I hope you're not going to change your mind about my having five of the boxes to sell to our clients for the season?"

We had agreed during our discussions about money previously that even though they had eventually paid me most of what was owed, thanks to Alex, they still hadn't refunded me in full the money

I had given to Gary. Their suggested solution had been that I could sell five of 'my boxes' for whatever I wanted this coming racing season and keep the money.

"No, we haven't changed our minds. But, unfortunately, we have sold some of them already, so we can only give you three this year. I hope that's okay?"

"No, it's not okay," I said. "But what can we do about it?" I didn't want to make it easy for him and tell him that we actually didn't want five boxes as that would be a lot of people to try to sell tickets to. I let him squirm a bit, as much as Little Tomaš ever squirmed.

Later, I spoke to Maurice about the sponsorship.

"It was okay last year," he said. "We got some good publicity for it. But this year, well, we are thinking to investigate some other sponsorship, maybe ice hockey. Could you start looking into it?"

And as is the way of these things, ice hockey soon became one of the most important things on my mind, following on from a call I received the next day from Bjørn, my old friend and client, who was coming to Prague the following week.

"I'll be in town for a few days as I am coming with the Swedish ice hockey team who are going to play the Czechs. The manager is an old friend of mine." I remembered how Bjørn always knew everyone. "I thought you might like to come with me, and bring a friend? We will be there as their VIP guests. You'll enjoy it!"

I would generally say that I love all sport, both doing and/ or watching it. But if there was one that I really couldn't cope with, it was ice hockey. We had never really played it in the UK since we don't have the ice rinks for it, nor do we have any teams or players to follow or look up to – or, at least, we didn't then – and the only time we would watch it on the TV was during the Olympics. But even then, it was on for so much of the time in the early stages, and the rules were so impossible to understand, that it only really got our attention when the players started to bash each other up. The Czechs, though, are brilliant at ice hockey and have regularly been world and/ or Olympic champions, plus they have loads of players that are good enough to be wanted by teams all over the world.

Being an ice hockey player in the Czech Republic was and is a bit like being a top footballer in the UK or Spain; however ugly and/ or thick you might be – or not, of course, in the case of many, no offence meant – you are still a god in most people's eyes, and the ultimate prize for any self-respecting Czech girl.

However, while I might have been a bit horrified at the idea of spending an evening watching such a sport, it did mean I would also get a crash course in what it was all about, which would help in my research for Maurice. That said, I never meant to research it quite as much as what happened next.

At this time, while we continued to be super-busy, I had been throwing myself into my fitness training, determined to get more weight off and tone up before the spring came. I had tended to go to the gym on my own more often than doing any personal training, partly due to my schedule and partly due to my lack of spare cash. But then, at one of my infrequent training sessions with Cheryl, she mentioned that she had made the mistake of getting together with one of the most notorious of all the expat real estate boys. I asked 'which one' with a sinking feeling in my stomach that I wasn't going to like the answer. It was unlikely to be Ewan as I didn't think he even knew her, and I doubted it could have been Simon as he was trying hard to behave with the wedding just around the corner, so that left the most obvious one.

"Jeremy," she said. "I know, I know. It was a mistake. I know he's a bastard and he screws everyone. I had just had way too much to drink and somehow ended up in his bed. And now, you know, I don't want to like him, but there is something about him."

Well, I might not have wanted to be with him myself and might have also treated Cheryl like a 'personal trainer' and told her about my woes sometimes, but never about him. But one thing was sure, I really, really, didn't want to hear about the ins and outs of her thing with him, if you pardon the expression, on a regular basis. In fact, I kind of thought that this might be the opportunity to move on from Cheryl. She had been the perfect person for me at the beginning, but now, I wanted to step it up a bit. If I could find a way to wriggle out of training with her carefully, who knows, maybe this would work out okay.

Over the past few weeks, a new trainer had appeared in the gym. He was a huge beast of a Czech bloke with muscles in his toenails, a shaved head and a training method that looked absolutely terrifying but was clearly very effective. And with a view to the new regime that I had in mind, I figured this kind of training might just be what I was looking for. I wasn't sure if he could speak English since I had only heard him speaking Czech, but that was easy enough to find out. So, the next day, when I was running on the treadmill and had seen that Cheryl had left the gym, I went over to him and asked him, in my not very good Czech, first, whether he could speak English. To which he replied 'of course', without an accent, even. And second, whether he could train me.

"But aren't you training with Cheryl?" he asked.

"Yes. Well, I have been. But I was once a fairly serious sportswoman, even if I don't look like it at the moment. And I think I need a bit of a tougher regime."

"Okay, so when would you like to start?"

"Well, I need to clear it with Cheryl first. Then I'm going to London to give up smoking in two days' time."

He raised his eyebrows.

"How about next week? Thursday?"

"Okay, I'll see you here at 8.00 am on Thursday and we can take it from there. By the way, my name is Vladimir. 'Vlad' for short." Or 'Vlad the Impaler', as we later called him.

Cheryl seemed to be okay with it. Obviously, I didn't say anything about Jeremy, but I explained that I wanted to do things a bit differently and I think she kind of understood. In any event, at that particular time, I didn't really care.

Lucie, then, was back from her latest jaunt with Jonathan and was just as stressed-looking as usual, still not eating, and still doing a lot of cleaning. To be fair though, she seemed to be working as hard as ever, even though she would often disappear for an afternoon or two, so, with everything that was going on, I decided to keep the status quo and just watch and learn. She and the other two girls had, anyway, settled into quite a nice routine, with a lot less bitching from Jana than usual. I felt I could go off to the UK for a couple of days and not have to worry too much.

One thing about being an expat – I'm sure I'm repeating myself here – is how much we miss our families or, in my case, my mum. For me, being the youngest of three by a long way, my mum was relatively old. Despite being as strong, mentally and physically, as an ox, I still worried about her, especially as she was living on her own and I was a million miles away. I knew that, really, she would prefer me to be living around the corner from her in the UK, but she would never say that, and, of course, she was proud of what I had achieved. But, with the phones still playing up, and no other means of communication, my trips to the UK always felt a bit too short and often left me feeling a bit sad and guilty.

This trip was no different, of course, but it did achieve something good. Well, two things: first, even though I headed straight to Tunbridge Wells upon my arrival in the UK, the following morning I was straight up and off to London for my hypnotherapy treatment. I won't go into too much detail here, since the session lasted four hours, except to say I was in a room with about six other people, and we spent ages discussing with the therapist why we smoked. About every two minutes he would say, rather irritatingly, "Go on, have another cigarette, you know you want to." That was until we got near to the big moment when he said, "Okay, you can throw your cigarettes, lighters, matches – whatever – into the corner, as you won't be needing them again."

Then we were all told to recline in our seats and think about our favourite smell. I chose the sea air, a rarity in the Czech Republic! And then, one second later, or so it felt, he said, "Okay, you're done." And swept out of the room.

What a bloody waste of money, I thought. "As soon as I get out of here, I'm going to have a cigarette and curse myself for spending all day doing all that rubbish." Then I left and got into a cab which had a sticker saying 'No Smoking' on the window. Got out of the cab, got onto a train, still thinking, *I'll have a cigarette soon*. But then remembered that the trains were also now 'No Smoking' in the UK.

I then arrived at Mum's house, where she opened the door with a cigarette in her hand and said, "Well, did it work?"

"I don't know," I responded. "I don't think so."

"Do you want a cigarette now?" she asked.

"No, not yet."

I never smoked again. Not only that, but after a few weeks of battling with her, I eventually persuaded Mum to go to the clinic herself. It worked for her too, and that, we later found out, probably extended her life by about twenty years. In fact, I sent about ten different people there over the course of the next few years and it worked for all, bar one of them. Guess who? Poor old Simon. Just too addicted to everything for it to be possible to cure him.

Arriving back in Prague as a non-smoker and feeling that I had kicked one vice so could now concentrate on getting rid of another, I thought, *To hell with men. The only way to go now, is full-on sport.*

Changing my Life

THURSDAY MORNING, I woke up as a non-smoker, ready for my first training with Vlad. Since I was scheduled to start at 8.00 am, I got up extra early and put on my new blue leggings and white T-shirt, brought especially from the UK the day before, along with some new, hi-tech trainers which, apparently, 'changed your life'. I was looking forward to that. Then, after bundling myself up in my usual extra sweaters and sheepskin coat, I walked around to the gym with a few minutes to spare and warmed up. Vlad was already inside, training someone else who looked vaguely familiar and who I later found out was one of the many top Czech tennis players he worked with, which was very exciting. I watched them while doing a bit of cycling until, on the dot of 8.00 am, he came over.

"Carry on cycling for a bit while I ask you a few things, okay?" He leaned against the handlebars of the bike, causing it to quake in its shoes as his huge muscles rippled.

"Okay," I said, pedalling along and trying not to look as if I was breathing hard.

"I have seen you training with Cheryl, so I know that you are reasonably fit. Tell me what you want from your training now?"

"Well," I said. "I spent the first 20 years of my life doing serious sport, probably four or five hours a day, either riding horses or playing tennis, but the last two years, since arriving in Prague, I have turned into a drunken lush. I want to get back to being more of an athlete and less of a lush."

"Okay," he said, looking me up and down. "You look as if you need to lose a few kilos; we'll do a weigh-in next, as your nutrition is going to be as important as your training. You understand that don't you?"

Bloody hell, a bloke telling me I need to lose a few kilos. I didn't like that at all. But that paled in comparison to me having to strip down to my undies in order to be 'weighed', for God's sake. I was already hugely regretting starting this.

"Do I have to?" I asked.

"Yes, and then, from today onwards, I want you to write down everything you eat and drink each day and show it to me every Thursday, starting next week."

By this time, I had decided I hated him. But there was no going back. All I could do was show him that, while I might be a fat cow, I was still a very fit fat cow. Weighing and humiliation over, I said, "I know you may not think it, especially after that, but I am not some housewife wanting to do a bit of gym stuff. I am really serious about getting back to super-fit, so please treat me like that."

"Don't worry," he said, and then half-killed me. Well, no, not quite. But each time I thought, *I can't do one more sit-up, one more bench press, or one more anything really*, he would insist that I really could. And then I did.

"Not bad for a first training," he said. "We'll step it up gradually and I'll see you next week," and off he went to his next victim, while I showered and crawled my way back to the office to start my working day.

I had only just sat down at my desk with a cup of coffee, which was duly noted in a new exercise book, as per Vlad's instructions, when the doorbell rang. Not expecting anyone other than my ladies, none of which had arrived yet, I wandered out to the courtyard, opened the door and in flew a large and very beautiful blonde woman, dripping in jewels and perfume, looking as if she may well kill me.

"You utter bitch," said Annabel, throwing the door to the office open ahead of me and plonking herself down on my chair. "I know what you have been up to; you must think I'm stupid. You're supposed to be my friend."

"Hold on, hold on," I said, thinking fast. "I know, I should have told you," I said, stalling for a bit of time while praying that the door wasn't going to open and Lucie walk in (or worse, Lucie walk in with Jonathan). "But I have barely seen you for months and wanted to talk to you in person about the whole situation."

"What? Did you think that just because I was in London you could carry on with my husband and then you would just 'talk to me about the situation' when I got back to Prague?" she said in a sarky

172

sort of voice. "Well, you're too late. I have had a private detective watching your office for months, so I know all about the two of you." Clearly the private detective wasn't very good.

"Look," I said. "Let me make us a cup of coffee and then let's talk about everything calmly." I tried to smile.

"Forget it," she replied. "I'm not talking about anything with you. I'm going home and will tell Jonathan I want a divorce; you're welcome to him." And out she stormed again, narrowly missing Lucie and the others as they arrived, literally one second later.

Well, this was turning into quite a morning. But it wasn't finished yet. No sooner had we all sat down and started work, none of the girls knowing a thing at this point, than the doorbell rang again. Petra went out to open up, and there was Simon.

"Hello darling," he said, rushing past her. "I need to speak to Jo in private. Can you bring me a whisky please," and he shot into the meeting room, me following after him.

"Want a cigarette?" he asked, waving one in front of my face.

"No, thank you. I don't smoke." I laughed.

"Well, you're going to start again once you hear what I have to tell you. Annabel has found out about Jonathan and Lucie. She's had a private detective watching your office. She's gone mad, and now Jonathan is panicking that she is going to try to take him for everything, and his dad will disinherit him or something."

"I know. Well, I don't know all of it, but she has already been here. It seems that somewhere along the line she has gotten the wrong end of the stick and thinks it's me!"

"You? Bloody hell, she really has gone mad!"

Thank you, Simon, I thought. Obviously, Jonathan wouldn't be interested in a fat cow like me.

"So, what did you say?" he asked, taking a swig of whisky.

"I didn't say much. She shouted at me a bit and then stormed off, thank God. Presumably Jonathan will put her straight and I will then deal with the complete and utter disaster that will be Lucie when it all comes out."

173

"Yes, bloody hell, Lucie is a mess at the best of times. Petra!" shouted Simon, getting up and opening the door. "Bring us two more whiskies, would you? Your boss has just had a nasty shock!"

That's great, I thought, wondering what Vlad would make of my food diary today, if I told him the truth: coffee and boiled egg at 7.30 am; another coffee at 9.30 am; a double whisky at 10.00 am. Even he might think there is no hope!

By lunchtime, the girls all knew what had happened. Lucie had gone as white as a sheet and headed out to 'buy a sandwich and have a walk' which meant, in fact, 'go and meet Jonathan and try to find out what will happen next and whether she will still be a part of his life'. Jana, who was always taking pot shots at Lucie about Jonathan was sniggering away to herself, while Petra worked on, not saying a lot. She was always difficult to read.

I regaled all of this to Rhys later that evening, once he had turned up in the office to do a few things and we then walked over to Molly's for a 'sharpener', for him, and a Diet Coke for me.

"Honestly, J'ver," he said, downing half of his beer in one go. "I did wonder how all of this Jonathan stuff was going to end up. I never expected that there could have been a private detective hanging around outside our office though."

"Nor me," I answered. "It's hilarious though, isn't it?" The private detective was clever enough to work out that there was something going on with someone in our office, but not who it was. I wonder what he made of all the other to-ings and fro-ings. I mean, if he thought Jonathan was visiting me, then what did he make of Simon, Jeremy – even you – turning up at all times of the day and night?'

"Good point. It makes you wonder, doesn't it... was there really a private detective? Or maybe someone else spilt the beans?" Rhys raised his eyebrows.

"Ah, I see where you are going with that. I'm not sure I want to know. What I do know is that, as of now, I am changing my life. No more boozing and partying. I'm keeping out of other people's problems. I'm going to be fully focused on work and fitness for the next few months. And, by the way, haven't you noticed something?"

"No?"

"I'm not smoking, in spite of everything."

And with that, I was off, back to the office and back to work, full of yet more good resolutions. But, of course, the thing about resolutions is that they only really exist in order to be broken.

"Well, you know, it does get a bit boring for us ladies to watch girls taking their clothes off all the time."

Big Fish in Small Ponds?

I KNOW I CAN be quite rude about the Czech Republic, and there are lots of things, as you have heard already, that could and do drive the most patient person in the world completely mad. But there are also some good things, and one of them, if you can call it that, is the way it is very easy to feel like and/ or become a very big fish, because it's such a small pond.

One of the reasons for that is that everything and everyone is so accessible. Even when we were driving to and from Pardubice, I used to muse about the fact that this was a 'world famous' racecourse that we were visiting and trying to help, and could we really imagine being in such a position in the UK? A couple of young(ish) ladies, holding themselves out to be marketing queens and advising on such things as the size of the fences at, say, Aintree or Cheltenham, or organising an event in one of the function rooms in Buckingham Palace or the Houses of Parliament, as we had done in equivalent places in Prague? Hardly. But that was how it was for us, especially early on.

I'm not a 'name-dropper' sort of person, but I couldn't help talking about these things sometimes, especially when I continually bumped into 'famous people' at the gym or got to meet the boss of a large multinational company. With the Czech Republic being such a great place to invest in and, as it was becoming more and more popular with tourists, and, of course, as it is relatively small for a capital city, we could just walk down the road or pop into a restaurant or pub and see a familiar face at any time. I was always amazed that the much-loved President Havel, the leader of the Revolution, and the President of the country at that time, was a fairly regular customer at The James Joyce; he would sit behind a newspaper, his flat cap on his head, watching the goings on, safe in the knowledge that, he thought, no-one would recognise him, us being mostly foreigners, even though we all did. In any case, we would never bother him. I am not sure whether he was there when

Ewan set his arse on fire, but he probably wouldn't have batted an eyelid even if he was.

I met both of his wives; his first when we organised an auction to raise funds for her charity, and his second in the loo of a restaurant one evening when she nicked a cigarette off me. That was before I gave up, obviously. So, being as sports-mad as I was, and having the secret hope that I could one day turn our general marketing agency into one that focused more on sports, training with Vladimir, as if it wasn't already exciting enough, became even more interesting once I started to meet some of his other clients and realised that many of them were exactly the sports people that, I hoped, we could one day work with.

As I got to know him, I realised that behind the huge, brutish exterior was a soft teddy bear, so we often got into quite heavy 'life' discussions, which, I guess, is what a really good personal trainer should be doing; I even found myself telling him things that I had probably never told anyone else. Even better than that, though, was that after only about three trainings with him, I was starting to see muscles I had never seen before, and my excess weight was definitely coming off. One of Vladimir's favourite motivational things to say to me was, "If you want to work with sports people, you need to look like one," and that was enough to keep me on the straight and narrow for a few more days!

He didn't only work with sports people, mind you. He had two regulars that were both top models. The Czech Republic was as well-known for its models as it was for its sports people; there was an infamous billboard that was splattered all over town in those days of Eva Herzigová advertising the Wonderbra, another reason there were so many car crashes on Czech roads at that time. Anyway, if you think that working out in front of top sports people is stressful, try doing it when there is some gorgeous, skinny model in next to nothing prancing about all over the place! Vladimir, however, was in his element, especially as, I soon realised, a lot of ladies had crushes on their personal trainers. He was never really my type, thankfully, since he had the standard Czech-man look (and I am not going to explain what that is for fear of offence...), and I definitely wasn't his, since he preferred girls with boys' bodies. But it was quite obvious to me that a lot of the girls training in the gym at that time were largely there to try and get off with him.

Actually, he often asked me what so and so looked like naked, since Czech girls, unlike some other nationalities, have absolutely no concerns about walking about naked in the gym changing rooms and you could always tell the Brit or American, as they would be the ones huddled in the corner wrapped in a towel and trying to get undressed without anyone else seeing a bit of naked flesh. It was not the same for the Czechs. As soon as they arrived, off came their kit, and then they would go about getting ready – walk to the loo, brush their hair, put on lipstick, even shave their pubes at the wash basins, for God's sake – completely naked. Hence Vlad's curiosity. I, however, would usually answer that they looked like 'Belsen victims' without their padded bras on, as it made me feel better! Czech men are also pretty uninhibited and, going into a sauna – assuming it is mixed, and most are in Prague – is not for the faint-hearted, as I found out on several occasions much later on.

On the morning of the ice hockey game that I was due to attend with Bjørn and Katy, who I had invited along to be my 'guest', I was in the gym early, doing a bit of jogging on the running machine before training with Vlad. I was keen to get some info from him about what we could expect that evening, especially, of course, what one should wear to such an event.

"We will be in the VIP box," I said in a rather pleased-with-myself sort of voice, "but we're not really sure if we have to dress up or how it works?"

"I wouldn't think you should dress any different to usual," he answered. "I doubt it will be that posh, these things never are. Plus, it will be cold, not just outside, but inside too, so you want to keep warm."

"And what do we do?" I asked.

"Well, you watch the hockey and cheer when the Czechs score! What do you think you do?" Vlad rebuffed.

179

"I don't know, I've never been to an ice hockey match. I suppose we'll figure it out." I have to say, though, figuring out an ice hockey match is still way beyond me. I've never really let on about that before though, for what will become obvious reasons.

Katy, amazingly, arrived on time at my office and we then headed over to the hotel where Bjørn was staying, which was the same one as my gym. We both had made a bit of an effort; me in a dress and boots under my posh coat and Katy in a very nice navy and red dress that she had put on, she said, to be a proper 'Czech' supporter.

The hotel, we soon realised, was hosting the whole Swedish ice hockey team, as a great big bus, that said as much down its side, was waiting by the entrance. We waited while what appeared to be a bunch of blonde schoolboys streamed out and piled on board, together with various older and slightly sinister looking guys, and then went to find Bjørn at the bar. As usual, he was dressed immaculately and was waiting for us with two very grand looking gentlemen who were, apparently, the senior directors of a new Swedish telecoms company that was about to hit the global market and, as part of their launch, were sponsoring the national hockey team; this is what I mean about 'big fish in a small pond'. In my former life, someone like me would never, ever, meet someone like them. At least, not until I was so old I didn't care.

Despite the fact the Czechs and the Swedes were – and still are – two of the biggest teams in ice hockey, as we drove through the gates into the stadium, I was rather taken aback by the shabbiness of it all. I had imagined it would be something like turning up at the Arsenal football ground (something I had done a lot of as a kid). Far from it. The entrance was right by the carpark and populated by two bored-looking stewards (X-ray machines were clearly not for them, as they are in the UK) and then you had to go through two big double-doors that appeared to lead to something like an aircraft hanger, and, as we made our way up the steps to the 'VIP salon', all you could hear was what sounded like a large number of people bashing something that sounded like dustbin lids. Once we got inside, the noise was incredible. The Czech supporters were mostly standing on various levels around three sides of the arena, all banging drums and chanting some completely ridiculous and impossible to understand sort of war cry that sounded something like 'Cheshy, doh toh hoh', while the Swedes took up much of the fourth side and were also making as much noise as they could. And then, in the middle was the ice rink where both teams were, I presumed, warming up by bombing around the ice and banging the puck about between each other. We had made our way to the 'VIP room', which was really a box along the lines of ours in Pardubice, with a buffet table running down one side, a few tables and chairs, and scantily dressed waitresses walking about, serving huge jugs of beer to the other so-called 'VIPs' in attendance. I say VIPs but really, they looked more like the money changers and mafia types we usually saw out and about in the city and probably, on reflection, that's what they were. The Swedish VIPs looked bemused, but Bjørn, who had spent half his life in Nigeria which, he used to say, made working in Czechoslovakia seem like a walk in the park, took it all, as usual, in his stride.

The two main things that stood out to me during the course of the match were how a load of angelic-looking Swedish boys could turn into ferocious and, dare I say it, rather manly, great brutes once they got kitted out in their gear and started to really get moving around the rink. I couldn't quite believe how fast they skated, nor how difficult it was to actually see the bloody puck, let alone whether it had gone into the net or not! And the other thing was the 'entertainment' that was going on at one end of the rink on a sort of raised stage. Here, the 'in-house' female cheerleaders were strutting their stuff to loud disco slash rock music with a view to exciting the crowd along the lines of a US baseball game. In fact, though, they looked more like a junior school aerobics team, only with fewer clothes on and absolutely no sex appeal. Katy and I both agreed that we could both do a lot better than them, after all of our disco dancing practice at Lávka, and pondered offering our services at a later date. I'm not sure they whipped anyone into any sort of frenzy, but they certainly worked hard. I later found out they worked even harder than I had realised, as apparently there was more than one cheerleader team at each game, and they rotated between 'dancing' on the stage and 'entertaining the players' in the dressing room during the breaks. Need I say more?

Don't ask me what the final score was. I have absolutely no idea, but from what the other VIPs were saying, it seemed the Swedes had won. And, on that basis, after the match had finished and everyone had disbursed, we were all invited back to the players' hotel for a celebration. This took place in the main bar area, the scene of many a shoot-out not so long ago, where the team had gathered with all their supporters and a few fans from outside, and where Katy, Bjørn and me and the telecom boys soon joined them. First there were a few speeches by some of the Swedish sponsors at the end of the room. Then one of the main guys announced there was a free champagne bar where we could all drink as much as we wanted. Then the lights were dimmed, and a pole descended from the ceiling, bang in the middle of the bar area, followed by a group of girls running in from the side for the obligatory strip show. This time we were treated to the added benefit of a bit of pole dancing, something that, at that time, was very new to Prague, and that certainly showed, since the girls were rubbish at it.

After a few minutes of watching the show, and also observing that Bjørn and Katy were now cooing at each other, I edged over to the bar to grab a glass of champagne. After about a gallon of really vile wine at the match, I wasn't quite sure that was a good idea and wondered whether I could make my way out without being noticed, when a Swedish-accented voice behind me said, "Didn't you like watching the show?" I turned to see one of the players – at least, I assumed he was a player, since he was younger than the VIPs, but a bit older than many of the other boys and, it must be said, FIT – standing on his own, drinking a beer and looking almost as unimpressed as me.

"Well, you know, it does get a bit boring for us ladies to watch girls taking their clothes off all the time," I responded.

"Not just you ladies. I stopped finding it interesting after about my second year of playing! I am Lennart, by the way. Do you want to come and get something to eat upstairs?"

"Why not?" I responded, and in fairness, I should just say that, at that point, I had not quite realised what a good-looking beast he was, since the bar was generally very badly lit. Once we got outside though, blimey; tall, with unusually jet-black hair and piercing blue eyes which, I couldn't help but notice, were boring into mine with 'that sort of look', and, well, what I suppose Vladimir would call a 'very well-put-together frame'. I felt it could be rather intimidating in certain circumstances, but decided it was best not to think too much about that, otherwise my cool exterior might start to crumble.

By 'upstairs', he meant the restaurant area that was just closing but, on seeing us – well him, I guess – they immediately sent a waiter over to show us to a table, where we sat and chatted for hours over a burger and chips (sorry, Vladimir) until he said at about midnight, "It has been really great meeting you Joanna (yes, I had given him my full name and he said it in a rather delicious way, more of a Yo Hanna), and if you want to come and watch a match in Stockholm one day, give me a call!" Then he got up, kissed my hand – my hand, is there anything more romantic? – and walked off to the lifts. And I, like a very good girl, took myself home and went to bed cursing myself and my new resolutions, but smiling nonetheless.

"Extrovert, good looking,
clever and completely wild."

A Whole new Perspective on the Dating Game!

THE NEXT MORNING, I woke up still feeling happy about the night before and, while I was getting up for work, I pondered why that should be. Yes, it had been fun at the ice hockey, and it had been great to feel like a VIP, albeit in a rather shabby setting. And yes, he, Lennart, seemed like a very nice man – not to mention pretty damn hot – and, as I had found out over dinner, divorced and generally available. But an ice hockey player living in Sweden? That clearly wasn't going to be the start of some sort of relationship, even if I had wanted it to be.

I realised, though, that last night was probably the first time since I had arrived in Prague I had met a man I didn't know already, started chatting, and then sat down and really talked to him like a grown-up person. And not only chatted, but flirted, and it had been reciprocated without the evening ending in a quick shag that was completely meaningless and could have been with anyone. I think that, up until that point, while I wasn't very happy with how things had panned out with Jeremy, and while I joked a lot about the bad behaviour of the boys in general, I tended to put all of that down to the Czech girls being so predatory and easy, without ever really placing any blame on the boys themselves.

Staring into the mirror as I cleaned my teeth, I was reminded of what Katy had said some time ago about expats, especially in 'crazy' countries, like the Czech Republic at that time, being 'on the run' from issues back home. I remember thinking it was a bit of a generalisation but, on reflection, I realised that maybe the guys we were hanging out with and that were arriving in those days, more generally, were a certain type and that maybe she was right. First, they and we were very young, even though we didn't think it at the time. And second, to actually cope with living and working in such a difficult country required a certain type of person, and most of the boys were just that. Extrovert, good looking, clever and completely wild. And most were unlikely to stay for long if they didn't make it.

All of that added together meant they mostly preferred a different girl every night, rather than any form of commitment.

If I looked at it that way, I could feel better about myself, and needed to, as my own self-confidence was generally pretty low. I doubt that any of the guys I was hanging out with at that time ever stopped to think that I, and the few other women in our group, might find it demoralising, to say the least, to be told over and over again how beautiful the Czech girls were. I also imagine they never thought about whether we really wanted to hear all the gory details of their latest trip to the K5 'knocking shop', or one of the other similar places. Or, as was the case with Jeremy, what a horrible thing it was to see the person you slept with one day going off with someone else in front of you the next, even though next week, or whenever it was, you might then be the chosen one again. I would say that, prior to coming to Prague, I was generally pretty confident, but the past couple of years had whittled away at that, due, mainly, to my having to continually question whether someone else was being chosen over me because they were prettier, funnier, more intelligent, or just better in bed; none of those were good thoughts.

Once I realised it was not so much about the girls' failures but more about the boys' own inadequacies, I could see that I could rise above it all and, who knows, maybe I would meet someone local after all. And with that, I slapped on a bit more makeup than usual, sprayed myself with my favourite perfume and went downstairs to start the day as a new woman.

Since Annabel's visit, Lucie had been very subdued. Despite her insistence that "Jonathan was going to leave his wife" earlier on in the relationship, I think that when it looked as if that just might happen, there was a part of her that was completely terrified. That was mainly due to Jonathan, now that he could be out in the open about their relationship, popping into our office more frequently and being ever-more demanding about Lucie's time. The last two weeks, at the very last minute, she had announced that she had to take Friday off, as they were going someplace, or Monday, as they would be arriving back late from another, and the other ladies were getting fed up with it. I was trying to be okay with her comings and goings since, generally, as long as all the work got done, I wasn't too concerned about hours and days off. But one thing I wasn't okay with was Lucie's health. Every time she came back from lunch, or even if she was just staying in the office and eating a sandwich, she was still disappearing off to the cloakroom soon after, where, quite obviously, she promptly threw everything up. When I finally worked up the confidence to ask her if she was making herself sick, she was so outraged that I didn't dare to bring it up again.

The consequence of that was that she was as skinny as she could probably ever be, even though Jonathan had apparently suggested she start going to the gym to train with Vladimir, and he would pay. And her whole personality seemed to be changing. She was bad tempered, tearful, complained about her eyesight all the time, and was generally a shadow of the bubbly girl that had first started to work for me and who, at that time, had regarded herself as a nutcase; that girl was completely normal compared to the latest edition.

After such a memorable evening with Lennart, I was determined to keep my good mood going for as long as possible. Unfortunately, that was just a few hours. We had been working away all morning, Lucie had been out for lunch with Jonathan, and when she had returned had asked if she could talk to me. *Here we go again*, I thought. *Another weekend away?*

"I have been talking to Jonathan about the offices," she said. "As you know, I find it really difficult to work here without any natural daylight and my eyes are getting really bad because of having to work under the electric light all the time."

"That's not good," I responded. "But are you sure it's the light that's causing your eyes to get so bad? I haven't really heard of such a thing before and know a lot of people who have to work in worse conditions than these."

"No, it definitely is the light. Plus, I don't like that we all have to share one room. I really don't get on with Jana, as you know, and when we are all here it is so noisy. I was telling this to Jonathan just now though and the good news is that he has offered us an office in one of his buildings!"

How lovely that would be, I thought, *an office in Jonathan's gorgeous historic palace at a cost of about ten times what we are paying. Just the thing!* "When you say, 'he has offered us an office,' Lucie, do you mean for free? Or at a discount? I mean, I know the office building he has just bought and know it's amazing, but it would be way too expensive for us."

"No, he doesn't mean that building. He has another building he bought in an auction that has some good space which is much cheaper. It's in Žitná."

"Žitná?" I pronounced it 'Shitna' on purpose, since it's a horrible, busy main road leading from Prague 2 towards the centre of town and is very polluted with lots of dodgy bars and strip clubs; just the place for us.

"Yes, but it's okay. I've seen it. I said I would ask you and we could all go and see it together. What do you think?"

What I thought was that I didn't much like being pushed into a corner when I, personally, was happy in the cottage. Plus, if we moved to a new office, I would have to find somewhere to live as well, something that neither Jonathan nor Lucie had thought about. On the other hand, if I said no, would I run the risk of losing Lucie? And perhaps a proper 'office' wouldn't be so bad, as the cottage, when we were all there, did feel a bit small. And maybe a proper flat, if I could afford it, would be good too. What I said, though, was that I, 'Would think about it,' and that I would, 'Let her know.'

As usual, I ran it all past Rhys later that evening. "The thing is, Rhys, I have been vaguely thinking about moving anyway," I said, watching his expression to see if I could gauge how he might feel about it. "We have so much work that we should probably take on another person soon, but where would they sit? And of course, if we did move, you would come too."

"That's good to know," he responded. "But I can't advise as it has to be about whether you can afford to move, and, besides, where would you live?"

"Oh, bloody hell. I really don't like the idea of Lucie being in control of everything. But I guess I need to talk to Jonathan about it."

188

And that's exactly what I did. Jonathan, of course, while not necessarily knowing how guilt felt, was, at heart, a good guy. When I explained the whole situation, he came up with what seemed like a pretty generous solution, which was that I would take the offices, subject to seeing and liking them and he would then give me a very reduced rate on a flat that had become available in his residential building, actually the one where my friend Penelope lived. In total, it would be an additional cost of about Kč 20,000 a month – which, at the time, was about £500 – so a stretch, but doable. In the end, it seemed almost too good to be true. Which, as I later found out, it probably was.

"This is going to be the biggest thing ever to happen in Prague and my agency is going to be moving offices right in the middle of the most crucial period?"

Welcome to Shitna

OUR LANDLORD AT THE COTTAGE was surprisingly good about us terminating the lease as it seemed his son was keen to have more of the space anyway. And the offices in Žitná, when I went to see them, were actually very nice; two big airy rooms that would easily fit at least two or three desks in each, large windows looking out on the main street, a high-ceilinged and chandeliered meeting area at the back overlooking an attractive courtyard, and then the usual loo and kitchen. Plus – unbelievably luxurious – two telephone lines, which meant that we could have one for the phone and one for the fax; that sold it for me.

In lots of ways, the offices were ideal for us as they gave us the ability to take on more people in the future, if we needed them, and we were able to invite clients to us, rather than us always going to them. As much as I loved the cottage, I never quite felt it gave the right impression to clients from outside the Czech Republic, although locally-based people thought we were operating in the height of luxury. On the other hand, the costs involved in moving far surpassed my original budget as, of course, it wasn't just the cost of the move itself, but also the need to buy more furniture, the re-printing of all our letterheads and business cards, and all sorts of other bits and pieces I hadn't thought about and hadn't planned for. But then, I knew that we were already on track to bring in a lot more income than originally budgeted as well, so I wasn't too worried.

The flat, though, was what clinched the deal. It was lovely, had a big parquet floor sitting room and a bedroom with high ceilings and huge arched windows, a modern grey and white kitchen with a proper big washing machine and a smart bathroom and separate loo. The only problem I could see when I first moved in was that it was going to be very bare, since I literally only owned a bed, a wardrobe, a tiny sofa and a TV. But that would have to do. The furniture was the same as I had had in the cottage, there was just a lot more space to go around it all!

191

The time between handing in our notice and moving into the new place flew past, as it really was the worst time to be packing up and moving, since we had so many projects on the go. We had been putting everything together for Simon's wedding, which had been delayed until the end of May, as somewhere along the line he had forgotten to 'post his banns' (a legal requirement for a foreigner, whereby he needed to have a notice of his intention to get married posted at the Embassy in case anyone had any reason why that shouldn't happen. No wonder he had forgotten!), and even him offering the appropriate person a bribe couldn't get the paperwork ready in time! Then, just when we thought we had everything in place, some of Simon's very grand North London Jewish family descended on us unexpectedly, with a view to checking everything that was planned, and that didn't quite go as we'd hoped.

First, his mother and grandmother insisted on coming to meet us on their own the day after they arrived in Prague; the doorbell rang and a very bossy woman demanded down the intercom, "We are here to see Joanna. Can you please open up straightaway as it is cold out here?"

We buzzed them in. Mother was slightly less intimidating than Granny, who looked me up and down snootily.

"You do know that we are planning a Jewish wedding, don't you?" she asked. Clearly, she didn't like the fact that I am tall and blonde. Possibly Aryan race?

"Yes, of course," I responded. 'I am Jewish myself and have attended many Jewish weddings." Okay, that was a bit of a fib, but better than my having to tell her that this wasn't actually going to be one, at least not as far as Simon was concerned.

That took the wind out of her sails.

"Oh," said Granny, looking a lot more cheerful, "you don't look Jewish at all."

"No, I know," I answered. "But I can assure you, I am; my father's family perished in Auschwitz." I smiled back at her.

"Well, that is marvellous," she responded. "Clearly, then, you are the perfect girl for the job." She was almost ecstatic.

Unfortunately, the ecstasy only lasted until we took them both on a tour of the city and they commented on how dirty everything was. It was true that, at that time, a lot of the biggest buildings, such as the National Museum and the stunning Týn Cathedral, were still in their blackened state from the old days. But the grubbiness wasn't usually the first thing people said about beautiful Prague. Their mood didn't improve once they saw the venue for the wedding, which was non-Jewish, and the hotels that they would be using for their guests, which were the best in town, but still not that good. By the time they left, I was sure that the whole thing was going to be pulled and moved elsewhere, so that rather stopped everything in its tracks while we waited to see who would win between Simon and his family.

We were also busy with the opening of the shopping mall in Prague 2, just across the road from my new flat. We had started off by working with Penelope, who was handling the advertising campaign for the build-up and launch of what they had called, in Czech, Vinohradská Tržnice – now you can see why we foreigners struggle with this language – but to the expats would be known as 'Pavilon'. But, as we got nearer to the time of the opening, we began to meet up more with the developer, Stewart Morris. He was American, short and bald, with a little moustache that gave him a professorial look, and very charismatic. He was also one of the most difficult men I had probably ever met, although it did appear as if difficult male clients might eventually become my specialty.

He was clearly brilliant and an amazing architect, and what he had done with the rundown old building that had originally been a marketplace was incredible. Now it looked like a mini-Covent Garden inside, with food and drink areas on the lower ground floor and small boutiques running around the corridors on each subsequent floor, with the whole central area open from the ceiling down to the very bottom. The look of the place made me think that we had to go with a Covent Garden theme for the opening, and that, I could imagine, would be a lot of fun!

Stewart fired people on an almost daily basis, so we could be going to his office to meet one person, only to find they had disappeared, and another had taken over, plus no-one could ever tell when he might suddenly lose his patience and start screaming at one or other of us. It was all a bit terrifying. I had once been in the office when he had hurled a coffee cup at the wall, narrowly missing the head of one of his people. I'd also seen him reduce several of his girls to tears in front of everyone else. I, myself, had had many different arguments with him, usually about his need to reduce costs (especially ours) while also getting a lot more work from us for his money.

When I told Stewart we would be moving offices just a few weeks before the start of the build-up to the opening of Pavilon he nearly blew a gasket, since he was sure that our work for him would suffer –he was probably right – but I wasn't going to say that. His suggestion was that we postpone our move until the opening was over and I said that was impossible.

"Well, if you won't postpone the move, I will have to look for another agency," he said again on the phone, a day or so after the meeting where he had thrown all his toys out of the pram.

"I can't," I said, trying to stay calm. "We have given notice and everything is set up. But don't worry, it will all be fine."

"Don't worry?" he screamed down the phone. "Don't worry? This is going to be the biggest thing ever to happen in Prague and my agency is going to be moving offices right in the middle of the most crucial period? Right now, I have to say, I'm really close to firing you."

"I tell you what, Stewart," I responded, imagining him spluttering into his moustache and rubbing his bald head. "I'll make it easier for you and resign. How is that?" I slammed the phone down.

Lucie, Simon's wedding, and money woes were all getting to me, which meant that I was sleeping even less than usual and my temper was getting shorter. And on top of everything else, we had a trip for 50 people down to Pardubice at the beginning of May and another event for Bass at the end of the month, as well as several

194

other projects that were ongoing, not to mention our own move to organise.

Then, with just one week go and with everything more or less packed and ready to go, Lucie announced she wouldn't be able to help us on the day of the move because, guess what, she was going to be away again that Friday, and over the weekend (we were moving on the Friday to give us time to get sorted over the next couple of days).

"Bloody hell, Lucie, this is getting ridiculous," I said, folding my arms and fixing her with a stare. At which point, she more or less collapsed on the floor and started wailing and crying again that it wasn't her fault, Jonathan put these ridiculous demands on her and that she didn't want to upset me, but she really did have to go. And, as usual, I felt sorry for her and guilty for being mean, so finished off with saying, "Okay, it will be fine, we will manage."

And, of course, we did manage. Rhys, as usual, was a star, as was Gary, who took a couple of days off and moved all the furniture for us, then put it all together in the office, and the flat, while we scurried about putting all the files away, and so on. By Friday evening, everything was in place, and, by the end of the weekend, we had sorted our papers, put up our pictures, bought some flowers and plants to make it homey and were pretty much ready for our new life in Žitná to begin. But even then, I had a feeling in my bones that our time in 'Shitna' may well live up to its name.

From the day we moved in, until about the middle of May, it rained pretty much every day. And since the journey from my flat to the office, while not being that far, meant two different tram rides, my journey was about half an hour longer than it had been in the cottage, where it was about ten seconds. And that meant leaving home a bit earlier and, potentially, getting a good soaking. Plus, the gym was much further away, which meant that, rather than just finishing training and going home to shower, as I used to do, I needed to take all my kit with me, set out earlier, and then shower and get ready for work in the changing rooms. I know, it all sounds a bit spoiled. Just saying!

What I hadn't really bargained for, though, was the effect that the move would have on my non-working life. There was the fact that we couldn't just pop across the road to Molly's after work, or around the corner to U Zlatá Ulička, which soon became quite a big issue for both me and Rhys. Most mornings, if I was up early enough, I went to the gym, either on my own, or for training with Vladimir, before going straight to the office. But that made for a very long day, since we often didn't finish until about eight or nine in the evening, and I really didn't fancy schlepping into town on the metro or walking for what felt like a good 20 minutes across the Old Town, if it was only going to be for a quick drink or a bite to eat. Often, the effort of going out was too great and I just ended up going straight home after work. Of course, Rhys and I still headed to Molly's some evenings to meet up with Ewan and some of the others, and I often had dinner in U Zlatá Ulička on the weekends. Plus, I made an effort to see Katy for dinner in Zátiší at least every couple of weeks and to do a few lunches with Matthew, whose office wasn't far away, but it wasn't quite the same.

Added to this, the atmosphere in the office wasn't great. Jana was moodier than ever, and a moody Jana meant a Jana making even more mistakes than usual. I put her sulking down to the move, as the new office was further for her to travel too but, unfortunately, I found out much later that it was down to more than that. Petra was her usual, sunny self, but, as the only member of the team that was even a little bit sane at that time, I was giving her more and more work to do, which kept her very quiet. And then Lucie, whose whole bloody idea it had been to move in the first place, didn't seem any happier in Shitna than she had been in the cottage. First, I think she had somehow visualised that she would have a room to herself, or, at the very least, share with one other. Instead, she sat with the other two girls, while I was in the second main room, either on my own, or with Rhys, if he was in. Where Lucie actually sat, though, seemed unimportant since she was mainly, of course, spending even more time than ever in the loo and, if she wasn't in the loo or cleaning it, she was out doing something 'Jonathan-related', rather than any actual work.

I don't think of myself as a jealous sort of person, but I have to say there was a little bit of me that was irked sometimes to hear that she was being carted off to this hotel in the Alps, or that hotel in the south of France, returning wearing clothes the rest of us could only dream about, especially then, when I had so little money to spare myself and we were all working so hard. But wherever she was going, and whatever she was being bought, it definitely didn't make her happy. In hindsight, I realised that what happened next was probably a good thing all round, it just didn't feel like it at the time.

Rather surprisingly, after my earlier fall out with Stewart Morris, he started to take a bit of a shine to me. The week after I 'resigned', I heard from Penelope that she had had to do quite a lot of negotiating to get him to calm down, which was helped by the fact that, despite trying, he couldn't find anyone else to take on the job and then, shortly after we opened our doors in Shitna, I had an invitation to join him for tea in his office. I duly met him, and we drank tea, ate cake and chatted about all sorts of non-work things, until, after about an hour, he said, "I am so sorry to have been so difficult about your move. I know I was taking out my frustration about the project on you, wrongly. Please can we start again and get moving on it?'

"Of course, we can," I said, letting out a huge deep breath. And from then on, everything started to run smoothly.

The launch campaign for Pavilon started with a press conference in Stewart's offices late one afternoon, where he explained how he had come up with the concept for the new shopping mall and announced which tenants were already signed up and then showed slides of the interior – which only a few of us had seen at that point – and images of the advertising campaign. We had a huge turnout of journalists – which was another 'phew' from my side – and they all stayed behind for drinks and the opportunity to have one-to-one meetings with Stewart. In the end, Penelope, Lucie and I were all standing about feeling very pleased with ourselves, when Simon came over with a big smile on his face and invited us to join him for a dinner to celebrate the end of 'Phase One', as he called it. This was not, of course, the kind of invitation that you should say no to, so both Penelope and I immediately said that we would love to, while Lucie grabbed me and said, "I'm really sorry, Jo. I can't do dinner tonight, I have to be at Jonathan's for a dinner party."

"Okay," I said, slightly irritated, but sure Stewart wouldn't mind. "I'll see you in the morning then."

"Yes," she responded. "Have a nice dinner," and off she went.

A couple of Stewart's team joined us, and the evening turned out to be great fun as, I was gradually finding out, he could be very good company, with his Groucho Marx impressions and indefinite number of 'New York Jew' jokes to tell. But then, the next morning, still feeling pleased about everything, I walked into the office, sat down, and then saw a bunch of keys on my desk with a note.

"I'm sorry Jo. I have left. Here are your keys. Sorry, Lucie."

I didn't see her again for nearly two years.

Worse than a Divorce

I READ LUCIE'S NOTE and felt sick. It was early in the morning and the other girls weren't in the office yet. Where could I go? I put the keys and note in my pocket, locked the office door and walked around the corner to the bank where Matthew worked, walked into his office and burst into tears.

"Whatever is the matter?" he asked. "Is your mum okay?"

"It's not Mum," I said, trying to pull myself together. "Read this," I said and handed him Lucie's note.

"That's not at all good, is it? Of course, she can't just walk out as she has a contract with you, she needs to give you proper notice and so on. I think you need to try to get hold of her straightaway and talk to her. She's clearly not herself."

"The trouble is, Matthew, she will never be herself while she is with Jonathan. And even if I try to get her to come back, I don't know if I want her now. I feel too hurt by her behaviour. Bloody hell, we even moved into these bloody new offices because of her. I feel as if a long-term boyfriend has just dumped me or something."

"I see that. But, you know, maybe your pride doesn't want to allow you to 'beg her' not to go. But wait a day or so until you feel less upset and then speak to her. She may even change her mind. Perhaps it was all a spur of the moment decision? Whatever. But don't shoot yourself in the foot by refusing to talk to her about it all. For now, though, how will you manage?"

"That's a very good question."

I went back to the office, still shaken and tearful, but decided I wouldn't tell the other ladies yet. Part of me hoped that, at some point during the day, I would hear from Lucie, and she would apologise and say it had all been a mistake. Another part of me thought that I would never speak to her again.

Jana and Petra, apart from realising that Lucie wasn't in the office, didn't seem to notice anything particularly wrong, and quite honestly, over the last few weeks, she had been so weird and had done so little work they probably were relieved to have a day without any drama, even though there was so much work to do. Rhys though, smelt a rat and, at the end of the day, suggested we head down to Molly's, for what he always called a 'sharpener'.

'Sharpener' in hand, we sat down and straight away he said, "What's the story with Lucie?"

"She's gone," I said. "She left me her keys and a note that said she has left and she isn't coming back. Bloody bitch."

"Oh, J'ver. What will you do? Are you going to call her and try to persuade her to come back? What are you thinking?"

"You know what, Rhys. I was in tears this morning about it all and for the first half of the day kept hoping she would appear or call. But now? I don't think I'll hear from her again and don't think I want to, anyway. I'm sure we'll figure something out. Come on, let's have another one and then go to The Joyce and let our hair down for a change!"

The next few days went by in a blur. I explained to the other ladies that Lucie had left and that, for now, we would manage everything ourselves and start to look around for a replacement. They didn't ask much, and I didn't volunteer anything. Petra, as usual, handled everything I threw at her, and Jana, also as usual, argued with me and bitched about Petra until I thought I might just chuck her out too, but resisted.

Then, every evening, stressed to the eyeballs, I dragged Rhys down to Molly's or The Joyce for a few too many drinks, usually getting back to the flat way too late to contemplate an early start in the gym the following morning (although that resulted in a call from Vladimir, demanding I come and train with him that Saturday morning, or else). By Friday night, I was completely exhausted and wasn't at all keen on joining Katy for dinner when she called to suggest it. She wouldn't take no for an answer.

"Come on, love, a nice dinner will cheer you up no end, and, besides, I have a suggestion for you."

We met in The Joyce, as usual, and it being a Friday, all the usual culprits were there, which was a good start in the cheering up process, particularly as no-one had yet heard about the 'Lucie situation'. Knowing how we all loved to gossip, I was worried that everyone would be talking about it. That said, they were all too busy chewing over the news of a new arrival in town, a young Englishwoman called Mary. Mary had just turned up in Prague to work for one of the multinationals and was young and mousy, with round pebbly glasses and the general look of a librarian about her. I put her look down to the fact that she had had a very strict convent education in the UK, and the reason for all of the excitement was that, according to Ewan and Simon, she was something that was very rare in the Czech Republic: a virgin. And that, of course, was cause for a lot of discussion, in particular who was going to be the first to have a go at her. I don't think I need to offer any prizes for guessing who I would have put my money on if there *had* been a prize.

Poor Mary turned up in The Joyce a bit later that evening, fortunately accompanied by a couple of older guys that no-one knew, so everyone was on their best behaviour. I only met her very briefly, as Katy and I were on our way out as they arrived, but having another woman around was a good thing in my book, added to which, I later found out, she was to be a new neighbour, since she was moving into the flat below mine. Clearly our building was soon going to become known as a home for sad and lonely English ladies, although at least we had Penelope on the second floor, who did have a husband, even if he was rarely there.

Dinner in Zátiší was, as usual, lovely, and we had a good old chat, only getting to the point of why, according to Katy, I had been behaving so weirdly that week by dessert.

"I hadn't realised I was acting strangely," I said when she asked. "We are just so busy at the moment, and I am still not feeling completely at home in the new offices. I suppose that is the main reason."

She didn't look convinced.

"Plus, and even now it upsets me to say it, Lucie has left."

"What do you mean she has left? What, has she handed in her notice?"

"No, she just left me her keys and a note saying, 'I've left, sorry.' It's unbelievable. I am so upset, I'm not even ready to talk about it." I looked at Katy a bit teary eyed.

"But what did you expect, love? You have treated her like a little sister the past two years, rather than an employee. I felt you should have chucked her out ages ago, just didn't like to say. It's not surprising the poor girl couldn't bring herself to do the right thing and tell you properly, she was probably too scared as she knew that you would be upset and that she would feel so guilty she wouldn't be able to carry it through."

Now, that was *not* what I had expected from Katy.

"So, are you taking her side then?" I asked, in a bit of a hostile voice.

"Not at all," she answered, smiling. "I just want you to remember this conversation and make sure this situation will never happen again. If you want to build a successful business, you have to keep a distance between yourself and your employees; you can't get emotionally involved with them as they will always end up disappointing you. Remember that."

I mulled over what she had said and realised that, of course, and as usual, Katy was right.

"You're a very wise old girl," I said. "I feel a lot better now. So, what was it you wanted to suggest to me?"

"Well, you know I've been seeing a bit of Bjørn when he's been here in Prague?"

"Yes," I said, thinking, *Of course, you are not* always *a wise old girl.*

"And I was wondering if maybe you quite liked that Lennart too?"

"Well, yes, I suppose so. But I haven't spoken to him since he was here. I just called him to tell him our telephone number was going to change once we moved. That was a few weeks ago now. Since then, I haven't heard a thing," I replied. And just to explain, one evening when I had got home late after having had way too much to drink, I had thought, *What the hell, I'll call him and use the new telephone number as a pretext, so as not to look too keen.* In the end, though, I had just left a slurry message on his answering machine as he didn't pick up.

"So, why don't we take a trip to Stockholm one weekend soon and surprise them both? I could get my secretary to research flights and a hotel. What do you think?"

What I really thought was that Lennart still wouldn't pick up when I called and Bjørn would probably have a heart attack if he heard that Katy was in the same city as his wife and family, but I didn't say as much since, you know, a weekend away to somewhere new is always a good thing in my book.

"Okay," I said. "I'm up for that, let's do it!"

"they say they want to work together too. If you want one, you have to take both!"

Finding People

HAVING HAD A good talking to from Katy on the Friday night, I trained with Vladimir on Saturday morning and he had a very similar view of the Lucie situation as she had. Actually, I wasn't really sure why her leaving had affected me so badly since she had been a bit of a deadweight the past few months and her not eating was very worrying. But her just upping and leaving had hurt a lot. I did, though, vow to myself that I must take note of Katy's, and then Vladimir's, talking to, and toughen up.

After a weekend of lying about and doing very little, by Monday morning I was feeling almost back to my old self and, instead of feeling sad about Lucie, I was more focused on finding someone to replace her than worrying about how to get her back. The week started well too. Simon had calmed things with his mother. and we were now going full steam ahead with the wedding. Plus, I had spoken to Penelope, and she was happy to announce that Stewart had liked our Covent Garden concept and was even talking about another project on which we all could collaborate. Things were looking very positive, I just needed to find a few more pairs of hands to help Petra and Jana to do it all!

As I have mentioned before, finding good people in the Czech Republic has always been a major problem and, in those days, it was almost impossible. It wasn't just that there were no such things as recruitment agencies, very few places to advertise and that, of course, the internet was still a long way away in the future; the people we needed just didn't seem to exist. Ever since the Wall had come down, Czechs who had emigrated to other countries had started to return, but those that spoke English and had some form of international education or work experience were in such huge demand they could name their price. And that price was way out of my league.

Then there were the older Czechs who had grown up and worked under communism, but they had a whole load of baggage to carry around and, besides, they were unlikely to speak English, which was a must for most of us foreigners. That really only left the youngsters who had hit working age at around the same time as the Velvet Revolution in 1989, and then started to look for work. The girls, as mentioned before, often went off to become nannies, learn English and other skills and then return to find work, while some of the boys took off to the US, studied, returned, and were immediately offered high-level jobs that were way beyond their experience or know-how, and which often led to disaster. In any event, boys weren't interested in working in marketing and PR, let alone working for a woman, and a young one at that! Those boys that did speak English usually had their eyes firmly focused on the banks, law firms, accountancy practices and the multinationals, where all the big money could be earned.

There was one other group of potential employees, however, and they were the foreigners that were heading to the Czech Republic in droves. I don't mean those that were sent, like me, to work for a foreign firm, but others who, for whatever reason, fancied a spell in a former communist country and thought Prague sounded nice. And, of course, in the case of most of the men who moved here, they were usually following a Czech girl. The problem with a lot of them, though, was that they had very unrealistic ideas as to the sort of salary they could expect.

Over the past couple of years, I had met several different people, usually in one of the Irish pubs, who told me they were looking for work and that they were ready to do more or less anything, but that, in the UK, or wherever they came from, they had been earning, for example, £2,000 a month, and they wouldn't, therefore, be able to accept less than that here in Prague. I would tell them that the average salary in Prague was, at that time, about £500 a month, and that it would be very difficult for an employer to pay a foreigner much more than that, even if they could afford it, as their Czech staff would find out and it would create too many problems. At which point, whoever I was talking to would look at me in horror and decide that I was obviously some sort of slavedriver, or worse, and move on to talk to someone more sensible.

206

The thing was, though, the cost of living in the Czech Republic at that time was very, very low, and the Czechs generally lived quite a comfortable existence, even on what appeared, to a foreigner, to be such a small salary. Most Czechs lived in virtually rent-free apartments; electricity, gas and other utilities cost very little, transport around Prague was basically free and even food and other necessities, while a bit scarce at times, tended to be a lot cheaper than elsewhere. The problem for foreigners was mostly that the accommodation available to them was quite expensive, so they had a bit of a point when they asked for much more money than the locals. But the Czechs would never see it like that.

Over the weekend, though, I did have a bit of a brainwave (it's amazing how many of those you can have if you manage to sleep a good few hours and don't drink too much). My old friend Rory Jones, of the red jacket fame, having spent his first year in Prague setting up and running one of the handful of international advertising agencies now successfully operating in the city, always said that a year of trying to find good people to work for him had nearly sent him to an early grave. But, instead of giving up and going back to the UK, as he had been tempted to do several times, he had done a very brave thing, and something that most of us at the time felt to be quite crazy. He gave up his 'proper' job and set up his own headhunting company to specialise in finding people to work in the marketing and advertising worlds. I remember saying to him at the time that he needed to be prepared to be bored; I couldn't imagine where on earth he would go hunting to find even one suitable head but, despite all of our doubts, he did seem to be making a good go of it. At least, he definitely had a lot of big clients asking him to work for them, although I'm not quite sure he always found the people, at least in the early days.

Anyway, I thought, *don't ask don't get,* and one of the first things I did on that same more optimistic Monday morning was to call to him.

"I know you only work for the big guys," I said. "And I'm sure that even if you have someone that could be suitable for me, they will be way too expensive. But I thought I'd ask, just in case."

"It's funny you should call me now," he responded. "Because I have literally just interviewed two young girls that could fit the bill. I was thinking that they will be impossible for me to help, but, you know, they just might suit you."

"Well, that's amazing. How soon do you think I could see them? Will you fax me over their CVs? Is there one that you would favour over the other?" I was full of questions.

"So, here's the thing," he responded, sounding a bit shifty. "They are from California and travelled here together, and they say they want to work together too. If you want one, you have to take both!"

"Oh, God. Well, okay. Shall I meet them anyway? Do you think they could come this afternoon?"

"Let me give them a call, I'll let you know."

That afternoon, while we waited for Annie and Christie to turn up, I wondered why on earth I had agreed to meet them. Of course, I couldn't afford to take on both of them, and even if I could, to have me and two foreigners and just two Czechs (and one of those was Slovak!) would be completely unbalanced. But it was too late now, since, just as I was deciding that I should try to call Rory and cancel the whole thing, the doorbell rang.

Petra went to open it, and a loud shout came from outside.

"Hi!" screamed a US-accented voice that nearly smashed the light bulbs. "I'm Christie, this is Annie." And in walked two 'American sweethearts', both pretty, both nicely dressed, both with huge white smiles, but one with a voice that was so 'loud' I flinched every time she spoke.

Annie was from San Diego and Christie from LA. They were both in their mid-20s and both had some form of marketing type degree. Both, of course, were unable to speak Czech, but I didn't want to think about that yet.

The three of us sat in the meeting room and chatted. I say 'chatted', but actually I said only a few words and Annie very little, while Christie shouted that they were in Prague for at least a year, had already found somewhere to live, 'loved it' already and were 'so excited' to think that they might be able to work in marketing since

208

they thought they would only be able to get some form of bar job or something, that it is so 'good of me' to see them at short notice, and so on . At one point, I debated falling on the floor or fainting in order to stop the non-stop stream of near hysterical shouting, or even bursting into tears. But I managed to contain myself. I did ask Annie, when Christie drew breath for what appeared to be the first time in about half an hour, if she could quickly tell me about her own work experience and in a couple of sentences she managed to squeeze out that she had done a marketing degree at the University of California and also spoke Spanish. Which meant, she said, that she hoped she would be able to learn Czech relatively easily. Not because it is in any way like Spanish but because she had an aptitude for languages. But then Christie jumped in and gushed a bit more about how 'marvellous' Annie was. Eventually I managed to get a few more words in and the 'interview' came to a close.

"I will talk to Rory," I said. "I'm sure he will come back to you quickly."

And then they left, leaving me feeling as if I had been beaten around the head with a wet fish. I called Rory.

"They have just left," I said. "I may have to go and lie down in a quiet room for a while, you could have warned me!"

He laughed. "I knew that if I warned you, you wouldn't see them! But Annie is great, isn't she?"

"Yes, she definitely seems perfect. But even if Christie was normal, there's no way I could take on both of them. And she definitely *isn't* normal! Can you imagine having her sitting in your office all day? It would be exhausting!"

"Okay, shall I see if I can persuade Annie?"

"Well, you can try. But I barely spoke to her and have no idea what sort of money they or she wants. If you can get her to come on her own, and if she is ready to take an average Czech salary, well, why not? I'd give it a go. I guess it is over to you."

That evening Rory called back. "I spoke to Annie," he said. "She loved you. If you will have her, she's yours for just 15,000 crowns a month."

I could hardly say no, and that meant that within just a couple of days of Lucie walking out, we had a replacement person. What a team we would be: me, an already world-weary and battered English woman; a hugely overweight, messed up and sex obsessed Czech girl; a young Slovak 'gypsy' look-alike (I shouldn't say that, but the Czechs are awful about their gypsy population, so the fact that Petra was black haired and dark skinned didn't always work in her favour); and a newly-arrived-in-Prague American. World-beating.

I say that sarcastically, obviously, but in fact, within just a couple of days of Annie joining us – and she started right away, turning up promptly at 9.00 am the next day – wow, what a difference she made. We all loved her and there were so many good things about her; not only was she super-smart, with loads of good ideas and very hard-working, but when Annie said, 'Have a nice day,' in her earnest Californian way, you just knew she meant it, in just the same way as, 'You're welcome,' really did mean what it said.

By the time Friday came around, therefore, I felt a lot more relaxed about disappearing for our planned Swedish weekend, although neither Katy nor I had had much success in getting hold of either Bjørn or Lennart in advance of our trip. Admittedly, I had only tried calling once, even though Katy was urging me to keep trying. I just didn't want to look that keen and had only reached his answer-machine again. I left a vague message about being in Stockholm on business this coming weekend, if he was around, blah, blah. I know, a lie. And I suspected that Bjørn was lying low and wondering quite how it was all going to pan out with Katy just around the corner from his marital home. I wasn't too concerned. Sometimes, well, often, it was just really good to get out of Prague for a few days and I decided I was going to enjoy the trip, whatever happened.

The Swedes

IT DIDN'T START WELL. I'd been invited to a dinner that Friday evening by one of our old gang, Andy – 'the Bish', as we used to call him; don't ask me why, I have no idea – who had his big boss from the UK in town for the first time ever and wanted to impress him by hosting a dinner for him and a few 'interesting expats'. The dinner was at Kumar's new restaurant, and I thought it would be quite a tame affair as the Bish himself was an ex-soldier, always very polite, always immaculately dressed, and, relative to the other boys, always well behaved. Actually, in the early days, The Bish had been desperate for me to include him in *This is Where You Hear it First* but I never could, other than as just 'a bystander', as he never seemed to do anything naughty enough to be included. Anyway, I had assumed that the big boss would be the same reserved type and that, after a quiet evening, I would be able to slip away early and be up in plenty of time to get to the airport for my 8.00 am flight to Stockholm the next morning; not a bit of it.

As usual, the flight from London to Prague had had its usual effect on male passengers and Will, the big boss, was no different. Clearly, he had already started the transformation from a normal senior English businessman into a sex-crazed alcoholic, and by the time we sat down at the table for dinner we had already shared quite a few bottles of champagne at the bar. Will led the way to our table and in his welcoming speech to the 12 of us that had turned out he included the fact that he was very much looking forward to seeing the famous Radost nightclub later, as well as some of the other attractions he had heard so much about. My heart sank.

This was obviously going to be a very difficult evening to get away from early, since my willpower was generally proportional to the amount of booze I had consumed, and I became even more concerned when we were led to our table and I saw that I had Jeremy sitting opposite me, Ewan next to him, and my accountant friend Jacob next to me. Jacob had just flown in from LA, as he had been doing his regular two weeks there with his wife, who was based there. He had just got back and, he said, was feeling extremely weird from the jet lag. I hoped he would leave early so I could then follow suit and not be ribbed for being the first to leave. Incidentally, we had always assumed Jacob was secretly gay because he never showed the slightest bit of interest in any of the ladies hanging around our group; which just goes to show that at least a few of the guys were able to resist the charms of the Czech girls. Jacob, despite being an accountant, can be very funny and was soon regaling all of us with some very far-fetched 'meeting famous people' stories that I doubted were true but were hilarious all the same. I mentioned, of course, that I'd interviewed a girl from LA just that week and that she shouted the whole time and barely drew breath, to which Jacob responded, "Everyone in LA shouts. It's because of all the space around them and they like to be heard. Parents teach their children to shout rather than speak the minute they are born. They're all like it."

I'm still not sure if that is true or not, but anyway, it was the cue for Jeremy and Ewan, being naturally boisterous, to talk very loudly in US accents the whole way through dinner. And then, of course, someone mentioned that we had agreed to go to Radost. Needless to say, we were all still there at about 2.00 am and, as was often the norm, I found myself propped up at the bar chatting, possibly even flirting, with Jeremy. And then, just as I was starting to waver and forget what I had planned for the following day, a little nagging voice reminded me and I pulled myself together, announced I was going home, and left; a bit drunk and disorderly and way later than I should have been, but on my own. Hallelujah.

Despite waking up easily enough when the alarm went off, I was feeling pretty shabby when I got a cab at 6.00 am to head to the airport to meet Katy. She, of course, was half an hour late – imagine my surprise – so I was already irritated from waiting when she arrived brandishing our tickets just before check-in was going to close, by which time my heart rate was through the roof. I know I go on about it, but I just don't get why some people are unable to be on time. And why they don't realise the effect their being late can have on people like me, especially when we are hungover and tired.

But there we are. Somehow, I managed to bite my lip and not say anything that would immediately spoil the day ahead, and soon we were hurtling through the airport as the plane was already boarding and heading straight to our seats as the last people got on, which is just what you want with a hangover and no breakfast.

Our descent into Stockholm was like arriving in the middle of a Christmas fairy tale: endless snow-capped pine forests, where you can imagine Santa and herds of reindeer hanging out, interspersed with a load of stand-alone painted wooden houses and not a lot else. The airport seemed to be almost in miniature, with just a short walk from getting off the plane to customs, where nearly everyone from our plane was being stopped and having their suitcases checked. It wasn't clear when they searched our bags what exactly they were looking for as the customs people were not at all friendly, but we later found out they were checking to see if we were smuggling in booze, which kind of made sense, since we were travelling from the land of alcoholics to the land of booze being way too expensive for anyone to buy.

Having said that, nearly everyone in Stockholm drinks even more than the Czechs, and that is really saying something. It's true that buying alcohol in the shops or bars is very expensive, but rumour has it that every household has a garage full of the stuff, which they either buy on duty free cruises between Sweden and Finland or have brought in from their own or their friends' travels. And because it is as cold there as it is in the Czech Republic in the winter, and even darker, everyone drinks vodka to 'warm up', since they make a lot of it themselves.

Katy's secretary had got us tickets for the bus to the city centre from the airport, which was way quicker and cheaper than any other method, and then, thankfully, had booked us two rooms in a small and modern boutique hotel right in the centre. Once we had checked in and dumped our stuff, we were off and out to get our bearings and consider how we were going to approach Bjørn and Lennart.

213

Stockholm itself was a surprise, although I'm not really sure what I had expected. It was nice to find that most people spoke English, and the shops were, after Prague, extremely tempting. I thought that, if nothing else, it would have been worth coming just to be able to buy a few bits and pieces for my flat. Small things, I mean, I wasn't planning to lug an IKEA armchair or two on the plane. The areas around the Old Town and along the waterfront were lovely and just so different to other cities that I had visited; pretty, tall and narrow old buildings facing out over the harbour area, the sea and the canals that wove around and through the majority of the central streets, and then the super modern cafes, shops and office blocks that were in stark contrast to the historic areas; it was like nowhere else I had been to in Europe. Even Katy, who is way more travelled than me, agreed. And then it was kind of cute to hear 'Mamma Mia', 'Dancing Queen' and all the other Abba tracks blaring out just about everywhere we went. I may be a former rock chick, so not always one for 'popular' music, but I do love Abba, even though I don't often admit it. But once we had spent a couple of hours walking around, and then sat down in a very modern café right on the water for a snack, the reason why we were there started to nag at us.

Luckily, the café had a phone booth in its reception area so, once we had ordered a few sandwiches and some coffee, we took it in turns to go and try and call our respective targets. Katy made three separate attempts. Her first had no answer, the second was Bjørn's wife, so she put the phone down, the third was a success.

Coming back from the phone booth with a big smile on her face she said, "Finally, I got him. He is at home now, but he will meet us for dinner in a restaurant not far from here, I've written it down. So, we could go back to the hotel soon, get changed and then head back there in plenty of time."

"Okay, good," I said. "Was he surprised to hear from you?"

"Oh no, not really," she responded. "From my experience of Bjørn, I doubt he gets surprised by anything! I think he was happy. We will find out later I guess!"

214

"Okay, I'll keep trying Lennart." Which I did, three times. The first two times I hung up before the answering machine clicked on. The third I worked up the courage to leave a message. "Hi Lennart, it's Joanna. I'm here in Stockholm, as I mentioned before, staying at the Radisson Hotel in the centre. I'll be there early this evening and will try you again later in case we could meet up tonight or tomorrow." That was scary, and way more forward than I was used to being, but hey, what was the point of being there if I didn't at least try to see him.

Then we headed back to the hotel for a bit of a freshen-up before we turned around and headed out to dinner again. Katy was full of beans, but I felt a little bit fed up and was already thinking I should forget about my Lennart. But then, quite amazingly, just as I was getting out of the shower and pondering which of my two dresses to put on for the evening, the hotel phone rang and the receptionist told me that she had a call for me. Lennart was at the other end.

"I'm so sorry, Yo Hanna," he said. "I should have called you before, but I have been in hospital. I had my knee smashed in a game a few weeks ago and have only been out a few days. I've just woken up and seem to want to sleep all the time."

A sudden maternal urge washed over me. "No need to be sorry at all!" I said. "Poor you! How are you managing? Do you have anyone there to help you?" Of course, I was visualising some big blonde Swedish bird dressed up in a nurse's outfit. And that thought, in itself, made me realise maybe I did like him a bit more than I was admitting to myself.

"No, no," he said. "I'm fine. I've got crutches and can move about. My club is sending food and stuff over every day with my physio. So why don't you come over in the morning? Or do you have to work?"

"Work finishes tonight," I said, crossing my fingers. "So yes, that would be great. Tell me how to find you. What time? 11.00 am?"

"11.00 am is perfect." He gave me the address, adding, "You will find it easily. Just ring the bell and I will buzz you in."

215

Dinner with Bjørn and Katy was a lot more fun than I had expected after that, since I was happy to sit back and watch the two of them 'sparring', as that is what they were like; two very clever people trying to outdo each other while, at the same time, obviously finding each other attractive. But the situation was difficult. I, on the other hand, drank a couple of glasses of wine and never did find out what it cost, as the menus didn't have prices and Bjørn insisted on paying. I had some amazing seafood, since the whole city is literally awash with it, and just kind of relaxed into being an onlooker whilst pondering what the morning would bring. Bjørn, though, did ask whether I was going to see Lennart while we were there, which proved that we had clearly played it all way too cool as even he didn't realise that the sole purpose of our trip was to see the two of them, or maybe he was just being a man.

"Yes, I'm seeing him tomorrow," I said. "I'm going to his apartment as he is on crutches."

"Yes, I know. He had a terrible accident a few weeks ago," said Bjørn. "It has been in all the papers."

"It has? I didn't know!" *Thanks for telling me*, I thought a bit crossly.

"I think you maybe don't realise just who he is," replied Bjørn. "He's Stockholm's golden boy. That's probably why he likes you, you just treat him like a normal person." *Of course, that must be it*, I thought. *It has nothing to do with my being gorgeous, witty and almost successful. Oh well.*

The funny thing about hockey players, I soon realised with Lennart, and again on many occasions later, is that while they are completely idolised by their respective team's supporters, especially if they play for the national team, when they become super-heroes, no-one other than the real fanatics recognises them off of the rink. When they are playing, of course, there is very little part of their body on show, so to speak, as their faces are more or less covered and they look about ten times their actual size, due to all the padding. And that means that, unless they actively hunt down publicity, or are caught with supermodels or similar at parties, they can generally

216

move around mostly ignored, which is good for some but not so good for others.

That reminds me of a conversation I had with another very famous ice hockey player in the Czech Republic a lot later on. He was bemoaning the fact that he had rarely had a serious girlfriend since he hung out at all the 'in' places and all the girls chased him because he was an ice hockey player and earned millions of dollars. He told me once that he could never imagine meeting someone who was nice and who wanted to be with him just for being him.

"You should move to the UK," I said. "No-one will recognise you there as we don't understand the first thing about ice hockey and never really watch it." He never did though.

Anyway, Lennart was very 'un-celebrity-esque'. He was dead sexy, in a dark, non-Swedish way, obviously very fit, but not as huge as he appeared on the rink, and very 'calm' and laid back, which was a nice change from my maniacal friends in Prague. Plus, as I had found out when I met him, he was newly divorced, partly due to having been very young when he had met his wife, and partly due to the lifestyle, which I had yet to really find out about. And that meant, apparently, that he wasn't really into the womanising, parties and public life that many of the other players were enjoying.

The next morning, I found Lennart's flat easily, as it was in a great location, right bang in the centre of the city. From the outside, the building looked quite ordinary, but he was on the top floor and the apartment was lovely, with a wrap-around terrace and amazing views out across the sea. It wasn't flashy and over the top, though. In fact, I could almost imagine myself living there, but only almost, since there was the small matter of it being in another country to the one that I was working in. But I wasn't going to think about that just then.

He was, though, in a lot of pain. After sitting and chatting to him for a couple of hours and thinking how nice it was that we just continued where we had left off in Prague, he started to fade a bit. And since Katy had taken herself off to do a bit of sightseeing but had agreed to meet back at the hotel at around lunchtime, I thought I should get back to see her and leave him in peace. And no, I didn't try to jump him as I'm sure that wouldn't have been welcome! In fact, we only kissed each other on both cheeks as I was leaving. But then, just before he closed the door, he said, "I'll keep in touch this time. I promise. And then, why don't you come back for a weekend in two or three weeks' time? I should be better by then and we can do it all properly."

And, as I walked out to the elevator, I thought, *Yes, I definitely will.*

One Step Forward, One Step Back

BACK TO PRAGUE and reality hit on Tuesday morning when I was early in the office to see what I had missed. Even after just a week with Annie there the atmosphere was already a lot calmer than before, and with Simon's wedding just under two weeks' away, we were all involved in last-minute preparations for that. I had spoken to Simon on a more or less daily basis the past few weeks and he seemed to be holding up, which was a surprise. And even Ewan and Jonathan said he was behaving okay, so we were all hoping it would stay that way. The stress of his family coming and the wedding itself, we felt, could be enough to send him off on a never-ending bender if we weren't careful, so we were all monitoring him closely.

Once the wedding was over, I had made up my mind that I would take up Lennart's invitation and go back to Stockholm for another weekend, so I headed off later that day to get my flight tickets before I lost my bottle, due to the huge amount of work that we had ahead of us. The week after the wedding we had the opening of Pavilon, plus, just a few days later, we planned to take a coachload of 50 friends and clients who had all bought tickets for our boxes, to the first Pardubice race day, with the hope of finally making a bit of profit on it all. If it worked, and we could do the same every race day throughout the summer we could, potentially, make a reasonable amount of money. Then I had an appointment booked with Maurice at Bass the week after *that* to discuss the ice hockey project that I had been 'researching' – if only he knew – and another, as yet unknown, project, as well as some regular promotional materials to prepare for Kumar and a couple of others.

The next two weeks went by in a haze of very long days, not enough sleep and a minimal amount of food and drink; not because I was being so disciplined, although the fear (excuse me for this) of taking my clothes off in front of an elite athlete in a few weeks' time was pretty motivational, but more that there just didn't seem to be any time available for eating much! I was up at 6.30 am most mornings, jumping into a taxi to go to the gym and either run on the running machine or train with Vladimir, and I must say, he really earned his money as some days I felt way too tired to do anything much and he always knew just how much he could push me without being punched in the face. I'd then have a quick shower, jump into another taxi to go to the office and arrive at about 8.30 am, just as the ladies were arriving. And then, most mornings, we would gather around the meeting room table, run quickly through everything that needed doing, and then work pretty much non-stop until they all headed off early evening and I would stay until everything that had to be done 'was' done. And quite often, that was pretty damn late.

By the time I walked home, or took the tram if the weather was bad, it was usually so late I could barely be bothered to eat a thing. My favourite 'easy dish' was cooking up some pasta, mixing in some baked beans, then grating some cheese over it and eating the whole lot from the saucepan. I know, it sounds disgusting, but also great as the whole process only took about 12 minutes!

With just a week to go before the wedding, everything seemed to be under control and I was starting to count the days until my Stockholm trip, when yet another bombshell landed on my desk. In all the time Jana had worked for me she had been the size of a house, but she didn't seem that bothered about it, or at least she never said she was, and, if there was any food around she was usually the first to grab it. But just recently, her belly had been expanding every day, while she appeared not to be eating. And that was ringing all sorts of bells in my head which I promised myself I would address soon, but not now, when we were all so busy. That wasn't to be, however, as, just as the other ladies were getting ready to leave for the evening, Jana appeared at my door and asked if she could speak to me. As soon as I told her to come in and sit down, she started crying into a pile of tissues. After a few gulps and false starts, the cause of her upset was revealed. She was pregnant. So many thoughts ran through my head, *Did that mean she had had sex? How was that possible? With who? I hope not with him. How will she possibly cope?* And so on. But I really didn't have a good enough relationship with Jana to feel that I could ask any of these questions. In fact, all I managed was, "Oh dear." And then realised that that probably wasn't the right reaction. Then I said, "How many months? When do you need to leave?"

The crux of the matter was that not only was she six months gone but the doctors regarded her as a 'problem pregnancy'. I could understand that, although I later found out that most doctors in the Czech Republic offer to give pregnant girls a letter to say that they are 'problem pregnancies' if they would like one in order for them to finish work straightaway. Then the penny dropped. Jana would have to finish work there and then in order to rest up. That day. Immediately. *God help us.* Literally.

In a matter of hours, therefore, funny old Jana, who had driven us all mad on so many different occasions, who was so complex and peculiar, but just occasionally funny and clever, had packed her stuff and left us, right in the middle of all our chaos, and without even a minute for us to wish her well or to say, 'keep in touch', or anything really. Which meant that within just a handful of days, we were back to three again. And since I couldn't even imagine how we could possibly cope at such a difficult time, there was only one thing for it, and that was to shut up shop and head to The Joyce to drink as much as possible.

The worst thing about Jana being gone during the week of the wedding was that poor Petra had to do everything that required a Czech speaker, even though, strictly speaking, she wasn't one. That meant that following up with all the different people involved in the event to check that they were still ready and willing was putting a huge stress on her, notwithstanding the fact that she would be the only one on the day itself that could deal with whatever was slung at us by non-English speakers.

My job in the lead-up to the wedding was to run about and try to ensure that Simon, Francesca and the two families were happy, which wasn't that easy since some of the groom's older relatives didn't do 'happy' very readily. Plus, I needed to be in the office to field the endless questions from the guests, as well as anything relating to the other clients, while Annie was concentrating solely on Stewart Morris, since he was starting to flap again as the Pavilon opening was just around the corner. As usual, and as is always the case, it never happens that Monday is *x* client, Tuesday is *y* and Wednesday is *z*. *If only.* Usually, Monday was all our clients wanting everything straightaway, Tuesday was similar, and then Wednesday, Thursday and Friday, up until about lunchtime, everything was relatively calm. But then Friday afternoon they usually all kicked off again, usually with urgent requests for certain things to be done by Monday morning. It would all be so much easier if clients could just take it in turns!

The Wedding

I HAD BOUGHT a very nice suit for the wedding in the UK a few weeks previously. It was from a one-off new boutique, was very cheap but looked expensive. It was pale green and fitted, with lovely gold buttons in the shape of daisies. Since I had managed to get rid of a couple of kilos over the past two or three weeks, I thought I looked pretty good when I did my 'dress rehearsal' earlier in the week. That was always necessary, since, at most of the events we organised, we usually ended up getting dressed in a cupboard, or worse, as we never wanted to do the set up in all of our finery, and there was never time to go home and get changed properly once it all was ready. My main worry, therefore, wasn't the lack of something nice to wear, nor was it the actual work. It was that Jonathan was obviously going to be coming to the wedding and that meant that he would probably be bringing Lucie. And, as this would be the first time I had seen her since she left, and I was still feeling bruised and hurt, how was I going to behave towards her?

The morning of the wedding was one of those lovely Prague spring days when the sun is shining, the sky is blue and you can feel that summer is just around the corner, which means that everyone's mood immediately improves. Even though the wedding itself wasn't until 2.00 pm and it was only across the road from our office, I was awake early, as usual, worrying about what I would have to worry about. But since, by that time, everything was in place, there was very little to actually do. I decided, therefore, that the best way to keep calm was to go to the gym and do a good workout and then come back home to shower and so on, with a view to getting properly dressed up in the office later on. By the time I got there, Annie and Petra had already been working the phone and checking there were no last-minute hitches and, when I arrived, they were already changing into their own 'wedding clothes', which for them, as 'workers', we had decided would be navy suits and white shirts, as they both had something suitable that fitted that mould. Soon after they headed out the door to the main hotel where all the guests would be gathered from 1.00 pm onwards, in order to make sure that everyone got onto the buses and arrived on time. Which left me pacing around on my own.

Rather than hang around in the office though, I decided to walk down to the venue and do a last check before I changed into my outfit. Simon's mother and grandmother had eventually chosen a very lovely old and historic building for the wedding and reception, and by the time I got there our amazing florist, Mr Dvořak, had already finished the decoration, using white, pink and red roses combined with silver and gold ribbons, with two large displays either side of the area of the small 'official room' where the actual ceremony would be held. The upstairs room, where the after-wedding party would be held, already looked amazing, and would look even more so in the evening when it was dark outside and would be full of candles. It was pretty big, but with the buffet tables along one side, lots of different seating areas and a 'dance floor' sectioned off at one end, it looked much smaller and really spectacular.

The best bit for me was the table in the corner where the three-tier wedding cake that was my own 'gift' to Simon and Francesca was on display and looking spectacular. I had had the cake made in the UK and, a few weeks previously, had flown over to see Mum and brought it back. What I hadn't thought about, of course, was how that would work in practice, and when I had gone to collect it, it was in three big boxes, each weighing a ton and all needing transportation back to Prague. I obviously couldn't check them in as luggage, so I figured I would have to try to persuade the guys on the boarding gate to allow me to take them on the plane, which was not as much of a challenge as it might sound, as in those days most of us regulars had got to know the UK managers of Czech Airlines and, if we had 'gold cards', as frequent flyers, they always looked after us. I had therefore pitched up at the airport, gone to customs, put my bag and three boxes through the X-ray machine and then been immediately pulled over.

"What've you got in those boxes, love?" said the customs person as I walked through.

"It's a wedding cake. I'm taking it back to Prague for a friend's wedding," I answered.

"Well, we're going to have to take a look," he said, feeling around the edge to see if he could open one of the boxes easily.

"You can look, but you can't cut into it!" I said, smiling in what I hoped was a 'melt his heart' kind of way.

Duly opened, he stared into the box. "I see. Hmm. Looks lovely," he said. We looked at each other for a while. "Okay, you had better take them through." Off I went, boxes on the trolley, thinking that for someone so inclined, that would have been a very easy and clever way to smuggle in just about anything. As expected, too, the gate manager was fine with me taking the cake on the plane. Since I was sitting in Club Class – a new benefit that we gold card holders received being an automatic upgrade – I was able to sit all three boxes in the middle seat, enabling them to travel back to Prague in comfort.

Anyway, I digress. The two different groups of musicians, a traditional folk band and a Czech group that specialised in old Jewish songs, were already setting up their instruments, and by the time I had walked downstairs again the officials for the ceremony had arrived and were getting prepared and the photographer had just turned up. Unusually, and thankfully, all seemed to be in place. By the time I got back to the office to get changed, therefore, I was ready, almost, to look forward to the day ahead.

One of the things about having done a huge amount of sport for an awful long time, especially having worn leather riding boots for most of my early years, was that my feet are a mess. I therefore always ask myself, *How are my feet feeling today?* before deciding what to wear, and the answer is usually *awful.* That had been my main concern when I had bought my wedding suit as the only shoes I could wear with it were proper high heeled 'court' types and that meant that within about two minutes of being ready, I was already feeling the pain. I really would have rather worn trainers. The five-minute walk back down to the venue didn't help and so, by the time

I was waiting in the reception area, the biggest thing on my mind was how I would get through the rest of the day and evening without being crippled. However, being the good PR girl that I was gradually turning into, I had plastered a smile on my face and was ready to greet the guests as they arrived, bang on time at 1.30 pm, with Annie and Petra leading the way off each of the buses and straight inside.

I don't know what it is about weddings, but I always find them emotional, even when I don't know the people involved very well. This was no exception, especially as I loved Simon who, after all, was the main reason I had even stayed in Prague after my first few weeks of hideousness. I also love seeing everyone in all their 'finery'. Penelope was one of the first to get off the bus in a beautiful suit and hat, followed by her husband Alex, who I had only ever seen in jeans and a T-shirt before and who looked dashing in a dark grey suit. Then came Katy, looking lovely in a bright green silk dress with tiny pink flowers embroidered all over it, followed by Jeremy, Ewan and Jonathan, who, I hate to say it, are all head-turningly good looking, even on a normal day, and ridiculously so in their morning suits. I was an emotional wreck within about 20 minutes. That wasn't helped by the fact that Jeremy and Jonathan walked in together and I wasn't able to assess who was accompanying either of them. Once everyone had left the buses, though, it was clear that Lucie wasn't there. And that, I have to say, was a relief.

What was also clear was that Jonathan was not attending on his own. One of the last people to get off the first coach was a stunning, blonde model-type that Petra later told me was last year's 'Miss Vice Czech Republic'. She appeared to be Jonathan's date for the day (and night, by all accounts). I must say, I have always found the title hilarious, since for a long time I thought it was a separate competition to the regular Miss Czech Republic annual event; 'Miss Vice' being a competition for the most beautiful sex workers or something. Which, of course, it is not. Just one of those fairly regular bloopers that come from translating titles into English to make them seem more 'international'. Anyway, it was a bit shocking

226

to see that so soon after all the drama with Lucie, Jonathan was already openly flaunting someone else on his arm, but there we are. Leopards, spots, etc…

Once the buses had departed, and with everyone inside the main reception area, the two cars turned up with the bride and groom and their respective close families, and what a picture they made. Simon looked his usual dark and dashing self, and Francesca was looking even more beautiful than ever. Then there was Simon's mother, who made my day by greeting me with, "Jo, dear, you look absolutely gorgeous. I love the suit. Is it Chanel?"

Of course I said it was, having been taught by the master, my mum, who used to buy all her clothes in charity shops, but who could carry them off since she definitely *was* gorgeous and would never tell where she had bought them if anyone asked.

At 2.00 pm on the dot, the usher came out to tell everyone to file into the official room where the ceremony was to take place. As there were so many of us, it was standing room only by the time I nipped inside, having left Annie and Petra upstairs to ensure the caterers were ready to go with glasses of champagne as everyone returned from the ceremonial room. At least I got to see the whole thing, which was very simple and non-religious and actually quite moving. Only the end bit was a nod to the Jewish faith, when Simon was supposed to smash a glass on the ground – something he has had years of practice at – but, for some reason, even though he walloped it onto the floor, it didn't break. In the end, he had to stamp all over it, muttering, "Break, you fucker," under his breath, before everyone shouted 'mazel tov' to bring the official part to a finish.

After that, the whole crowd streamed out for photographs in the lobby area while waiters handed out glasses of champagne and then we all went upstairs to the main reception room for the wedding lunch, which was quite an informal affair, before the music started, the drink began flowing, and everyone got up to dance.

I always feel a bit awkward when wearing two hats, so to speak, and, for Simon's wedding, it was particularly difficult. Being the organiser, I had to be professional and not eat or drink too much (and definitely not get roaring drunk). But then, as one of the groom's best friends, I was almost obliged to eat and drink everything in sight, just like everyone else. I was aiming, therefore, at doing something in between and, since the actual party itself started at around 4.00 pm, and went on right up until midnight, it was quite an achievement for me to finish the evening in a reasonably sober, albeit unable to walk, state.

Part of the reason for that, unfortunately, was that there was a lot going on behind the scenes. The caterers, despite us ordering millions of bottles of wine for the evening, told us that we were close to running out quite early on. Sadly, I didn't really believe them and suspected they hadn't brought anywhere near as many as we had ordered and were therefore cheating us, but it was a difficult one to prove without completely falling out with them and having them 'down tools' there and then. Instead, the only immediate solution we could come up with was for two of the waiters to run off to the nearest 24-hour Vietnamese corner store – these were a relatively new phenomena in Prague and a godsend in many different ways – and buy every bottle of wine they could lay their hands on. They came back with two huge boxes full of bottles, many of which had wine so foul that no sane person would normally touch them but, in the state that most people were in by then, they never noticed.

Then the musicians had a bit of a falling-out as we had agreed they would take it in turns to play; the first hour would be Czech folk songs, and then that group would have a break and the Jewish group would play for an hour, and then they would have a break, and so on. But, as I had found out during the agency's earliest days, when dealing with musicians, things never work out quite as they are supposed to. For some reason, they cannot always anticipate when they will be ready for a break, presumably due to them being 'artists', and generally they seem to want to eat or drink something about every ten minutes. That meant we kept having long gaps with no music as all the musicians were huddled together in the back room, stuffing their faces and, possibly, drinking a great deal of our wine!

Each time we were without music though, one of the family came to chase me to sort it out and I had to go and find one of the groups, urge them to finish eating and get back out to play. It was all very stressful.

Plus, of course, there was also quite a lot going on in the main room itself. Simon's family clearly weren't happy with the amount of time being spent on Czech folk songs and dances, since they didn't know the words or the steps and kept going over to the band and asking them to play Jewish songs, which they couldn't. But then, when the Jewish band came out to play, Francesca's Czech family, who had drunk so much by that time that they could barely stand up, were determined to get involved and kept on jumping about and getting in the way as the English family tried to do their usual tried and tested dance routines. By the time the band started on the traditional Jewish wedding dance, 'Hava Nagila', and everyone linked arms and formed a circle in order to dance along with the music, half the Czechs were in drunken heaps in the middle of the floor and having hysterics.

In the meantime, those guests that didn't fit into the Czech folksong or Jewish dance group sector were continuing to drink and get more and more raucous. Ewan was begging to be given the microphone so that he could sing, which he later managed to do to the huge delight of all of us expats, while Jonathan smooched about with Miss Vice, his smugness at having pulled her over-riding the slight embarrassment he must have been feeling about not being with Lucie. He even came over to me at one point, saying, "Jo, darling, I presume I can trust you not to breath a word about my bringing another woman to the wedding?"

To which I responded, "If you are suggesting there is any chance of me saying something to Lucie, you must be crazy. I haven't seen or heard from her since she walked out on me. Thanks to you!"

It wasn't very friendly of me, it's true, but with everything that was going on, it was a bit ridiculous to think that what Jonathan was or wasn't doing was top of my list of priorities (even if it had been a cause of some stress in the lead up to the wedding, but he didn't need to know that). Generally, anyway, I didn't get too much of a chance to talk to many people for any length of time as, if I wasn't rushing about behind the scenes, or checking that Petra and Annie were okay, I was either sitting with Katy discussing all things Swedish (I got the feeling that her stint with Bjørn was now over – if it had even started – but she is such a dark horse that it was difficult to be sure), or with Jeremy, who came over and joined us on several occasions, since he was on his own for the day, much to my surprise. I couldn't help but ask why he hadn't brought along one of his lady friends, to which he replied, "Why would I want to bring anyone with me when some of my best lady friends are already here?" *Smooth.*

But then, he rather spoiled it by continuing with, "Katy tells me you picked up some Swedish hockey player when the two of you were in Stockholm. Is that why you have lost all that weight? Trying to impress him, are you?"

To which I answered, "No, the weight has come off due to all the fantastic sex." I was rather proud of myself for that one.

In the end, I got home at about 2.00 am, having shoved Petra and Annie out the door just before that and told them to take the next day off. Then I went to bed, straight to sleep and woke up in the morning thinking, *just two more days and Stockholm, here I come.* Which pleased me enormously.

Gimme! Gimme! Gimme! (A Man After Midnight)

DESPITE GIVING THE other two the day after the wedding off, I myself had a normal day in the office. What a relief it was to have everything done and dusted with Simon before running through our timeline for the Pavilon opening, which seemed to look okay. I also decided I would bite the bullet and suggest to Stewart Morris that we meet the morning of my departure and that way, hopefully, he wouldn't notice that I had gone AWOL for the weekend, since generally Stewart thought nothing of calling the office or my flat phone in the evening, over the weekend, or whenever really.

I had warmed to him a lot since our initial falling out. After one of our most recent meetings he had given me a bit of a 'lost boy' look and said, "Did you know, Jo, that everyone living within about a 20 kilometre radius of the building signed a petition saying that they didn't want it to open at all. Of course, they would all much prefer to have a dilapidated old wreck standing there, instead of a beautifully reconstructed and attractive shopping mall."

I was shocked and said as much. I had no idea.

"No," he went on, "no-one really knew what was going on. The media were supporting the local council in its delaying of the permits and in the end, I had no choice but to go and do a bit of 'persuasion' of some of the councillors. Even then, there was no guarantee that it would go ahead. Sorry if I have been a bit brutal with you over the past few weeks, but honestly, I have been near to giving up on so many occasions." *Poor thing.* I wanted to hug him.

What I *did* know was that the fantastic advertising campaign that Penelope's people had come up with had been absolutely slated, with some of the billboards being smeared with red paint around the town. I loved it, as did many of the international advertising awards people, as it won all the big ones that year. But clearly, the locals didn't. Each advert followed a theme, which was an item of clothing. My favourite was a beautiful court shoe (typical me, I love to look at shoes, just can't wear them) in orange and bright pink, against a background of a contrasting block of colour, with simple wording saying, in Czech, words to the effect of, 'At last, you can buy this here,' and the word 'Pavilon' underneath. Despite the awards, many of the Czech media described the campaign as terrible, since it showed, or so they said, that whatever was going to be sold in the mall would be too expensive for the locals, which wasn't really true, but was a fairly standard reaction to most things new and/ or foreign.

Because of all the bad publicity – and we really tried hard to manage it but were backed-up against a wall – poor Jeremy, who was in charge of the letting, had a lot of the bigger brands that had shown interest in having stores there, cancelling at the very last minute. That meant his team were now under huge pressure to fill the stores up with whoever they could find, which they managed by dropping the rent significantly and by signing up just about anyone they could lay their hands on. This proved to be a bit of a kiss of death for Pavilon in the long run, but at the time everyone was so relieved to have all the shops occupied for the opening that they didn't really care.

As I said, I understood why Stewart had been so demanding, and since I was still the 'blue-eyed girl' (yes, I know my eyes are green), he was relatively happy when I went to see him Friday morning to assure him that everything was looking good for the launch the following week.

Friday afternoon I was off to the airport again. Without going into too much detail about it, it all went so well that my weekends for the rest of the year mostly involved my hopping on a plane to Stockholm whenever I could. Sometimes, obviously, I wanted to go to the UK to see my mum and sometimes I had to work, but Lennart and I made a deal that we would try to alternate the weekends and that he would come to Prague as much as he could. The reality, however, was that that was impossible, since most Saturdays in the winter he was playing, and in the summer, he was either on duty for the national team, with all sorts of championships and so on, going off on training camps, or being required to attend some sort of publicity for the club. In the end, it was me who became the frequent flyer between Stockholm and Prague, not him.

The first weekend I went, special as it was, and in spite of what I had said to Jeremy, I was pretty damned nervous, as we hadn't actually done much besides kiss each other on the cheek. Safe to say, that soon changed. And, as Lennart was still recuperating from his knee injury, he still wasn't back on the team, which meant that when we weren't 'getting to know each other' in the flat, we wandered about Stockholm which, in the spring, is gorgeous, and hung out at various lovely outside cafés in and around the Old Town, talking pretty much non-stop. I tried not to be, but of course I was kind of impressed that people kept on coming up to him. Not to ask for autographs – that wouldn't be cool enough for the Swedes – but to shake his hand or say something nice. And then, imagine, on Saturday afternoon, while we were sitting outside yet another café, one of the Abba guys, the one with the beard, shuffled past us – I say 'shuffled' as, at first glance, he looked like the local *houmlesák* (homeless person, as the Czechs would say). Maybe it was just a sophisticated disguise? Anyway, not only did he shuffle past, but Bjørn or Benny, whichever one it was, actually came right over to say hello. I nearly exploded.

That weekend I thought I would happily give up work and move over to Stockholm straightaway, but Sunday evening, when I left, reality hit me like a ton of bricks. I had a business to run, clients to work for and people I paid who depended on me to bring in the work. Stockholm on a full-time basis, at least for the time being, would have to wait!

Monday morning, then, was full-on back to the 'real world', as we were straight into the last-minute preparations for the opening of Pavilon. In the end, despite all of my misgivings, it went really well. The whole event started with a formal 'ribbon cutting' ceremony and, since we had the Prague mayor coming to do that – he was quite a draw at that time, although he was later found out to have been just about the most corrupt politician in the Czech Republic in the early years – there was a huge amount of media waiting around to take photos and get the chance to talk to him.

The only hitch was the huge pair of silver scissors we'd had engraved with the date, time and place, and that were to be used for the cutting of the ribbon, went missing. No-one could find them. And we never did, so we ended up running over to my flat to grab a pair of kitchen scissors to do the job. That wasn't quite the photo opportunity we had hoped for!

But, other than that, the place looked amazing when it was finally unveiled. On each floor were different food and drink stations, along with buskers (who were actually professional musicians, but were dressed busker-like for the occasion), barrow boys running around handing out drinks and nibbles from their carts, and amazingly, we had found a 'circus school' that was able to supply us with an unlimited number of acrobats, trapeze artists and men on giant stilts; you name it, we had it, and more.

On top of that, the whole place was full of flowers, candles, plants and special lighting, all supplied by our lovely Mr Dvořák, which ensured a wonderful atmosphere, especially when combined with the big jazz band we had put in the centre of the ground floor to play later in the evening. When those trumpets started to get going, the sound as it echoed around the whole central atrium made the hairs on the back of your neck stand on end. Even though I say it myself, we put on one hell of a show, which is what Stewart kept telling everyone as he walked around with a huge smile on his face. I think I can safely say that it was the first event we had organised that I really enjoyed.

In fact, I enjoyed it all so much I didn't want the evening to end, hence why, when the doors were finally closed at around 11.00 pm, me and my ladies, together with Penelope, Alex and Katy – who had come along to lend moral support – plus Jeremy, who was there as the boss of the letting agency, as well as a couple of others, ended up back in my flat with whatever leftover booze we could gather to continue the 'celebration'. Incidentally, I should say here that by that time I had a few more bits of furniture, so it wasn't quite as embarrassing as it might have been! By 2.00 am, most people had gone home and that left Katy calling a taxi and telling Jeremy that she would give him a lift home and him saying that wasn't necessary. She, being a good girl though, refused to leave without him, so they eventually went, leaving me to check my answering machine and to hear three messages from Lennart, who, by the time of the third one, sounded extremely peeved, saying, "It's now 1.30 am and I'm going to bed. Sorry that you are not there to answer the phone."

"These guys are really bad and I really have to pay them or Nenad will tell Nico to kill them to keep me safe. He wasn't joking!"

Goodbye to Rhys

WITH OUR TWO big events over with, I was really hoping we could start to get some normality going in the Žitná offices. It felt like we had been there for years, but in fact it was just a few months, and now we were getting into summer, I thought everything would start to feel a lot better. We had money in the bank, we had lovely Annie and a lot less drama. Plus, I had a much more stable personal life and we had plenty of work to keep us going. But Žitná hadn't been named Shitna by me for nothing. I don't know what it was, I just had bad vibes about the place.

Before moving to Prague and starting my new life, I would never have said I was a worrier. Even then, life had already hit me with various trucks over the years and, due to that, I was always banging on about living life to the full, as you never know what's around the proverbial corner, and trying to be that happy person with what people would call a 'sunny personality'. Once I started my own business, I realised there were so many things to worry about that I soon worried about what I would have to worry about if there was nothing at that moment that was particularly concerning, if you see what I mean. Usually, I woke up in the night with whatever was niggling me at the forefront of my mind, and I would keep a notepad and pencil by the bed to write down whatever I had figured out during those early hours when it all seemed so bleak. That particular morning, I had woken up at 3.00 am with a feeling that something was about to go horribly wrong and, having analysed the various things that it could be, my gut said that there was something not quite right about Rhys.

Again, I can't say exactly what it was, but I definitely worried that I hadn't seen him very much recently and when I did, he just ran into the office briefly, chatted in his usual way, then legged it out again. And since I hadn't had a chance to visit any of our usual haunts the last few weeks as it had all been so hectic, I hadn't been able to ask any of the others if they had seen him. The only thing to do once the whole Pavilon thing was over, I decided, was to spend an evening on a mission to track him down.

I grabbed Annie late one afternoon and suggested we head down to Molly's to meet some people since she had barely had a chance to do anything other than work flat out since she started. We left the office in bright sunshine and, as we walked across the Old Town, I was reminded why living in Prague could sometimes be very nice.

"It's funny," I said to Annie as we strolled down the main avenue of the big Wenceslas Square towards the Old Town. "Every winter I think I can't bear another one as I so hate the cold, but then the spring comes and I realise that I do, actually, like it here. All the flowers and greenery, the amazing light, and then the endless warm evenings. I love it that we can sit outside the cafes and restaurants as they come out of hibernation and open up the terraces and gardens. It's almost like being on one constant holiday."

As we neared Molly's, I showed her the doors that led to our old cottage – sorely missed by me – but tried not to dwell on it. And then we walked up the steps and into the pub, where we were greeted first by Gary, who was, as usual, propping up the bar and who hailed me as if he hadn't seen me for years – it felt like that – and then by Ewan, who was sitting in the corner with a strikingly handsome but rather effeminate-looking boy who he introduced to us as Piers, a new property baron who had just arrived in Prague.

No sooner had we sat down than Jacob the accountant walked in and joined us. Jacob and Piers immediately hit it off. What was clear, though, from subsequent conversations was that Piers, contrary to his angelic appearance, could probably match Simon in the nutcase stakes and soon, both he and Jacob were seeing who could outdo the other with outrageous stories. While they were falling about laughing and trying to impress Annie, I grabbed the opportunity to ask Ewan if he had seen Rhys recently. To which he replied, "Yes, a few times, but he is a bit distracted at the moment."

"Distracted? What do you mean? Has he got a new woman? What's going on?"

"No woman, as far as I know," said Ewan, looking a bit evasive. "I think he just has a few business issues that he's trying to sort out and doesn't want you to get dragged into them."

"Okay, so now you really have me worried. What sort of 'business issues?' Is he in trouble?"

"I'm not really sure. You'll have to ask him yourself."

"Well, I will, if I can just find him." *Oof.* My nice mood was fast disappearing. "Is he likely to come in here, do you think? Or shall we go to the Joyce? Or pop into U Zlatá Ulička and ask Nenad?"

"I think you need to ask Nenad. I know he has been going there a bit to get food."

"Okay, I'm going to do that."

I thought it would be best to go on my own, so I asked Annie if she wouldn't mind staying put a while as I needed to just pop around the corner. Leaving her to be entertained by the three of them, which she, being the coolest girl in town, was absolutely fine with, I walked around to U Zlatá Ulička to talk to Nenad. I felt a bit guilty about him too, since I hadn't been to see him for weeks, but needn't have worried since I was engulfed in a huge hug as soon as I walked through the door and, seconds later, was sitting at my old table with a glass of my favourite Yugoslavian red wine in my hand.

"I have big news," he said. "I've taken on a new place, just across town. We're calling it 'U Zlatá Ulička Two' and it's about ten times bigger than this place."

"That's fantastic! Are you going to keep this one on as well? Or giving it up?"

"We're not keeping it, no." He made a bit of a face. "The landlord just came in a couple of weeks ago and told us he was terminating our lease. I couldn't believe it. When we signed it, he insisted on it being for a minimum of two years before it could be broken by either side, and now he has broken it himself. Typical Czech."

"Bloody hell! How is that possible? Couldn't you fight him about it?"

"Well, we could have fought him, yes. I have some friends here that could have persuaded him to change his mind. But, you know, maybe it is the hand of God. I knew we would need to leave one of these days as this place is not big enough for us. It's a bit sooner than expected. But good, it's good."

And then I remembered why I was there.

"Nenad, I don't want you to think I'm only here because I need something. I'm so happy to see you and feel so guilty I haven't been here for such a long time. But I'm trying to find Rhys. I heard he's been coming here a bit."

"Ah, Rhys, yes. He's not doing so well. I've put him in touch with my friend Nico. Do you remember him? He's that big Serbian guy that used to sit in the corner here."

"Not really," I said, although I did vaguely remember a great big beast who never spoke to anyone and who we suspected should never be asked what he was doing here in Prague, nor what he had been doing back in Yugoslavia. "But why would Rhys want to be in touch with him?"

"You need to ask him yourself," said Nenad. "I know he doesn't want you involved, so I can't really say anything more."

For God's sake. Typical blokes, all sticking together. "Okay," I said. "If you do see him, will you please, *please,* ask him to come to the office, or to the flat. I need to find out what is happening."

"I will," said Nenad. "But I'm not sure I'll see him. I can only tell you, and I am not really supposed to do that either, that he has been talking about going somewhere else for a while. It may be that he has already. I really don't know."

On that note, I walked back to Molly's to find Annie and to try and enjoy a bit more of the evening. But I couldn't. Of all the people I had met in Prague and of all my friends, Rhys was a bit special. I loved him, mostly in a brotherly way, but we had had our moments and the whole reason I even went looking for him that evening was down to my gut sending out warning signals. Now, those warning signals had turned into bloody great siren calls.

The evening drifted along, we drank a lot more, the others were in great form and Annie was enjoying herself. Piers was flirting outrageously with her and failing to get anywhere and, along the way, various of the other boys came and went. I tried not to be a party pooper but just couldn't get into the usual sparring and, in the end, made my apologies and took myself home. I made my late-night call to Lennart and tried to act normally, then went to bed and tried to sleep, before working my way through the next two days on 'automatic pilot'. From the outside everything seemed normal, while, inside, my stomach was churning continually and my heart racing.

Then, just two days after my visit to Nenad, we were sitting in the office in the afternoon, all working away as usual, when the door opened and in walked Rhys. Looking white as a sheet and unshaven but still putting on his usual 'big personality' face.

"Where the bloody hell have you been?" I shouted at him. "I've been worrying myself stupid!" The other two, having welcomed him in happily, put their heads down and pretended to be oblivious to what was going on.

"Let's go into the meeting room, J'ver," he said and led the way through. "I can't tell you too much, but I had to come and see you before I left."

"Left? What do you mean 'left'? Where are you going?"

"I'm in big trouble. I've run up a load of bills with some of the printers here as the clients haven't been paying me. Then I had to borrow some money off some dodgy guy, as one of the big guys was getting threatening. Now I can't pay him back either. Nenad told his Nico that he should look after me, but he says these guys are really bad and that I really have to pay them or Nenad will tell Nico to kill them to keep me safe. He wasn't joking! I can't pay them. I've got to go, J'ver."

I felt sick. "How much do you owe? Why didn't you tell me? Can I give you the money?"

"It's too much, J'ver. I can't stay here. I'm going to Poland. I'm sorry. I'll let you know where when I can, you look after yourself." And with that he was gone. Never to return to Prague again. My heart was nearly broken.

"anyone who thinks these great big
ice hockey players are sex maniacs
has got it all wrong!"

Hockey Here, Hockey There

THE NEXT FEW WEEKS I was a right old misery. I went to Stockholm again the Friday after Rhys had gone and tried to be cheerful. That wasn't very easy since, when I arrived, it still felt a bit wintry, whereas it was already lovely and warm in Prague. And then, when I got to Lennart's flat and rang the doorbell, no-one answered. He knew what time I was arriving, so I didn't want to move away from there on the basis that I assumed he would turn up any minute but, after half an hour, there was still no sign of him, and I was freezing to death and not at all happy. Plus, in my usual catastrophist way, I had started to imagine that all sorts of things had happened to him and then started wondering what I would do if they had!

But then, just as I was about to go into mad panic mode, he came running around the corner full of apologies for having been delayed at the rink and, as usual, my stomach lurched on seeing him, particularly once he had promised to warm me up as soon as we got inside. However, he had mentioned on the phone earlier in the week that he would be getting up at the crack of dawn Saturday morning as his club was travelling to another part of the country for a match and he was finally going to get on the ice competitively, albeit maybe only for a few minutes. I hadn't really taken it all on board as my head was still full of Rhys. But then, over dinner on Friday evening, he explained that as he was going to be off playing somewhere else in the morning, I would either have to go with him and watch or stay behind and be on my own. Since I didn't yet know anyone else on the team, I just couldn't imagine myself travelling there on the coach with them and then sitting as a spare part in the stands. Which meant that staying behind seemed to be a much better option and, since he was up and out while I was still barely awake, I had a whole day in Stockholm on my own to look forward to.

That might sound quite nice in theory and, as I pottered about in the flat gazing out the windows at the streets below and considering what I might do, I thought that it 'could be fun'. But then, once I had wrapped myself up and headed out, I started to realise it really wasn't going to be fun at all! I already knew my way around the centre quite well so, unless I got really adventurous and went further afield, there wasn't a lot I wanted to go and see. Plus, the weather was damp, grey and dreary, so sitting outside a café and watching the world go by wasn't that appealing. And while the shops had all sorts of temptations on offer, I didn't really want to blow a load of money I didn't have on clothes I didn't need. So, what to do? In the end, I decided to go to one of the fish markets, buy a load of stuff for my own lunch and possibly dinner later, and, can you believe it, go back to the flat and watch the bloody match on TV!

The problem with all of that was that, being on my own, I had too much time to worry about Rhys and what I was going to do without him, to the point I even felt a little bit tearful and sorry for myself, which I clearly had to get over before Lennart got back, since I was supposed to be this bright and dynamic tough girl. And besides, explaining to one man why I was crying over another one was clearly not going to be easy. However much I might say that Rhys was my friend and partner in crime and that nothing naughty had ever gone on between us, I doubted I would be believed. A woman would understand; a man, well, probably not..

By about 7.00 pm, though, I was feeling better (partly as I had made a good start on one of the bottles of wine I had brought from Prague airport) and decided to put some food together and then see what other entertainment I could find to watch on the TV. If you are reading this and are Swedish, please forgive me, but Swedish TV is even worse than Czech. It seemed the highlight of Swedish Saturday night TV was a quiz show where each of the moderators/hostesses, or whatever they are called, take off one piece of clothing each time their respective team gets a question wrong; the winning team is the one whose moderator manages to keep at least one bit of clothing on for the longest. Then they do the same thing all over again and everyone cheers and loves it. Honestly!

I watched that wondering why it should be that people from very cold countries are so obsessed with getting naked, since surely they should be more interested in keeping their kit on, and as much of it as possible? Then I drank a bit more wine, ate a bit of food, and waited for Lennart to arrive back, which he duly did at around 10.00 pm, completely and utterly knackered, barely able to walk, and really only interested in eating as much food as possible, before heading straight to bed and falling asleep before his head hit the pillow. Let me tell you, anyone who thinks these great big ice hockey players are sex maniacs has got it all wrong! They are all way too tired to do a thing, unless it is more that they have been shagged stupid by one or more of the cheerleaders during the breaks. I somehow doubt it.

By the time I headed back to the airport on Sunday evening, I have to say I was sort of relieved to be leaving. We had had a nice day pottering about, had some lunch out and chatted as normal – we always found a lot to talk about – but I realised as I was sitting on the plane back to Prague that this relationship was not going to be easy unless something gave. And I wasn't really sure what that might be.

Monday morning, then, I was back in the office and still feeling miserable about Rhys and a bit worn out from the travelling, the damp in Sweden, and generally not having done very much. But, as usual, once we all sat down for our Monday morning meeting and realised how much we had to do that week, we were soon back in full-on work mode, which left very little time to think about anything on the man front; Rhys, Lennart, or anyone else.

As we were getting into the summer, there were a few new things taking us over. First was the ice hockey sponsorship I had been discussing with Maurice, and on which basis I had to prepare a presentation for later in the week. Originally, we had been discussing that Bass would sponsor one of the top Czech teams, or the national team, if that was even possible, since the primary purpose of sponsorship at that time was to promote the various Bass-owned Czech beers to as many people as possible. But then, having reflected on this quite a lot over the past few weeks I had started to question my original standpoint: who are the main drinkers of beer? Yes, men aged about 18-45, according to the research, although personally, I would say that in the Czech Republic, the ages are probably nearer to about 10-100! And what do Czech men of that age like to do most, apart from the obvious? Watch ice hockey. But the thing was, the majority of Czech men in that age group already knew of and drank Bass-owned beers. So the big question was whether the cost of the sponsorship would actually drive such a huge increase in sales to make it all worthwhile.

Two things had happened since Maurice and I had first started discussing all of this though. First was that one of Bass's main and newest focuses was the export of their premium Staropramen beer to the UK. And the second was my starting to date Lennart and him telling me that he had met various people from the UK over the past year or so who had been out in Sweden collecting information and investigating the possibility of bringing some of their top players – including Lennart, for God's sake – to the UK, as they wanted to really up the profile of ice hockey there. Gradually, therefore, due to my being a 'clever clogs', I had come up with the idea of turning the whole sponsorship idea upside down and, instead of Bass sponsoring a team in the Czech Republic, its main Czech beer, Staropramen, could sponsor a team, even the national team, in the UK. Smart, eh?

Then, as mentioned previously, we were taking a coach load of people down to Pardubice the following weekend for the first race day of the season. We had already sold our 50 tickets, had the coach lined up and had organised the catering and, if all went according to plan, we were on target to make a reasonable amount of cash. Added to that, the Tomašes had mentioned they were going to hold a party in a restaurant close by immediately after the races to which we were all invited, so our guests were getting a pretty good deal. And since I couldn't really face going back to Stockholm in just five days, and Lennart wasn't able to come to Prague, due to his game schedule, I was faced with nearly three weeks before I would see him again – the weekend after the races. But that, I figured, was probably okay.

By this time, Annie was already settled in as part of our team and Petra was happier than ever. I think that even though she never said anything bad about her, Jana's departure, and the removal of her constant sniping, had cheered her up immensely. Certainly, the idea

246

that 'two is company and three is a crowd' was not in any way the case with us three, as we all seemed to get on very well. And with the weather getting warmer and the evenings staying lighter, we started to head out after work more often together, something that was made even easier by the advent of a new 'taxi' service that had just appeared in town. The taxis were, in fact, a group of young guys on regular bicycles, and each one had a kind of wooden seat attached to the front of it; you could flag them down or find them parked up waiting for a customer in various areas of the town. One group used to hang out at the top of Wenceslas Square, which was just a few minutes' walk from our office, so we would walk down there, grab one of the boys and then the three of us would sit in the wooden seat at the front and be propelled through Prague, swinging our legs and bouncing around as the bikes skidded on the cobbles. It was completely hilarious, especially as we would often see people that we knew as we flew past, waving at the crowds. One evening we saw Maurice and some senior Bass guys walking along near The Joyce and, as we swept past, and he saw us, we heard his, "Oh, for God's sake, ladies," as he jumped out of the way, all of us shrieking at the top of our voices. Our usual route was from the top of the square down to Molly's, where the bikes would drop us off and hang around, waiting to see who was leaving and whether they would need to be biked off somewhere else.

With the advent of summer, too, everyone had started to come out of hibernation. Simon, who was now a 'happily married' man had calmed down a bit, but he was still out and about several evenings a week and on that basis, I had kept to my rule of never answering the door at home in the evenings. Ewan, though, was becoming a lot more serious as he was on the brink of leaving corporate life and launching his new company, Eagle Property Services, on the Prague world, with the aim of offering a range of management services to the constant stream of developers that were descending on the city. For now, though, he could still be found in The Joyce in the evenings, chatting up the girls and competing with his new best friend Piers as to who could behave the worst. And Piers, despite our first meeting where he flirted outrageously with

Annie, had taken a bit of a shine to Petra, who we were watching like a hawk, since first, she had a very nice Slovak boyfriend that she lived with in Prague and, second, as Piers, despite his humour and sweet boy looks, was clearly 'bad news'. Of course, we also crossed paths with many of the others on a regular basis, including Jonathan, who had an ever-changing group of young Czech ladies in attendance but never, as far as I could see, Lucie; the rumour being that she had been well and truly dumped.

However, always at the back of my mind at that time was the thought, *Where's Rhys and is he okay?* I found it difficult to shake the worry off. Most nights I left the others to continue their rampaging without me and headed across the square to see Nenad, who was working out his last couple of weeks in the old restaurant before moving to the new one, and we would sit in the corner, drinking lots of wine, listening to old, sad Bosnian songs and talk about Rhys. Or I would just go home and make my late-night call to Lennart who, I have to say, was mostly at home and always cheered me up, even though I didn't let on exactly why that was necessary.

Then the night before our trip to Pardubice, when I was just arriving home from the pub and getting ready to make my nightly call to Stockholm, the phone pretty much rang in my hand and, without even thinking, I answered.

"Ah, there you are, J'ver. How the devil are you?"

Rhys. Full of beans, settled in in Warsaw and wanting to know when I was going to hop on a plane and visit him; a huge black dog had been lifted from my back.

Pardubice Part II

I WAS UP very early the morning of the next race day in Pardubice, partly in order to organise what I would be wearing, and partly as I had arranged to meet the others at the office, as that was where we would meet the bus that would take us all to the races. As is usual in late spring in Prague, it was difficult to know what to wear, but in the end, I decided on a shirt, trousers and boots, with a sort of summer coat on the top, figuring that the coat could be discarded if it was too warm. I had bought it in the UK on one of my 'comfort buying' days, which usually resulted in my returning to Prague and wondering why on earth I had bought whatever it was. This coat was no exception. It had big black and white checks, was three-quarter-length and absolutely not me at all. But maybe I had a premonition…

Petra and Annie were waiting for me when I got to the office, as was the bus, which had pulled up on the kerb outside so that we could load it up with booze for the journey down. Once that was done, we all hopped on for the drive to our agreed meeting point, which was just by the bus station in the centre of Prague, where everyone expected quickly boarded and we headed out of town.

The trip down to Pardubice was uneventful. The bus was full, and while I knew most of the people attending, there were some new faces as well, one being a very grand guy called Michael Rippon, who was about 40 and spoke like Prince Charles (and even looked a bit like him). He was going to be in Jonathan's box, but since Jonathan had set off the day before to do some shooting down there – I presumed it was pheasant or boar, but never actually asked – he had pitched up on his own. Since I was the 'host' for the day, or at least for the trip down, I told Michael to come and sit with me as he didn't know anyone else on the bus so, for the whole drive to the racecourse, I heard his life story. That included the fact that he had arrived in Prague just a few weeks earlier and was in the process of setting up what he called 'the first proper PR agency in Prague'.

Apparently, he and his partner already had a successful company in London, and this was going to be their first foray abroad.

"I actually run a PR and marketing agency myself," I told him, slightly affronted.

"Yes, I know. Jonathan mentioned to me that I should meet you since he said you do a bit of event management and so on. We should definitely talk as it may be that we can sub-contract a few bits and bobs to you once we get going."

"Well, that would be great," I responded, thinking I might punch him in the face. "But, actually, we're pretty busy and not really looking for any new work at the moment."

"Oh really," he responded, sounding a bit bored. "Well, let's have a chat when we get back and see what we can do."

Arrogant bastard.

Later on I found out that the idea for Michael opening the agency in Prague had come about due to his best friend Nick having arrived a few months earlier to be the new marketing director for one of the spirits companies I had actually been involved with before I had gone out on my own. Clive, at the time, was heading up a team that was investigating the huge amount of counterfeit whisky that had been hitting the Czech market immediately after the revolution, and we were trying to establish where it was coming from, where it was being sold and how much damage it was causing the company that sold the real thing, in other words, Nick's company.

In fact, I remember one particular evening when the fraud police had delivered a whole load of supposedly counterfeit whisky to us as part of the investigation, and Clive had got it into his head that we should have a competition to see who was best at telling the difference between the fake stuff and the real whisky. Michael, the most boring man in the world, was tasked with setting it all up in the main room, since he didn't drink.

Once it was ready, Clive rushed out, shouting, "Josefina, you go first!" He pointed to the table where a row of glasses was lined up next to various bottles and giggled away to himself. "Put this bag on your head," he said, handing me a DHL bag with holes cut in the

250

nose and mouth area. Oh yes, he was loving this. "Now, take a sip," he said, handing me a glass of what tasted like whisky. He did this four times. "Now then, which two do you think are real?"

"Well," I said, completely clueless. "I think two and four."

"Okay. Michael, write that down. Josefina, you leave and tell Eva to come in." And so it went. And not one of us got it right! Clearly the fake stuff was pretty good. And knowing what I know now, which is just how vile and dangerous it actually was, it was a miracle we survived the evening!

Anyway, I digress. Nick, the new marketing director of the company, was thinking he would need an agency to support them in Prague and elsewhere, once they got going properly and he had suggested to Michael (the PR one, not Clive's) that if he were to set up shop there, he could work for them. And the rest, as they say, is history. Not only that, but Nick, having been to school with Jonathan – and hadn't they all – had introduced Michael to him with the suggestion that Jonathan might need some PR one day too, so Michael wasted no time in getting a plane over, finding an office in Jonathan's nice building (not the 'Shitna' one we were in, though) and getting started. My blood was boiling.

I had met Nick just a few weeks earlier in The Joyce and found out he was a very nice guy and not at all like the usual 'Jonathan's friend from the UK' type, and so, despite everything, we soon became friends. He had only been in Prague a short time then and even though he was young and good looking, he hadn't yet fully discovered its attractions. Jonathan, though, was determined to put that right by bringing him down to Pardubice the day before the races, and they had clearly enjoyed their first night. Apparently, they had spent the day shooting and then, having got cleaned up, had hit the Pardubice nightspots, which basically meant the one pub and one small and very dodgy nightclub, where, while packed with locals, it appeared that nearly everyone was a couple. Jonathan's solution from a 'girl-pulling' point of view was to put a load of money behind the bar and then ask the club to announce that all drinks that evening were on the house. At which point, all the Czech guys rushed to drink as much as they possibly could as quickly as possible before being pushed by their girlfriends into taxis to take them home in a near paralytic state, the girls then returning to the club to make themselves available to Jonathan and Nick. Good plan, huh?

It seemed, judging from the interesting mix of people in Jonathan's box that day, that one or two of the 'chosen ones' had been brought along for the races too, although that might not have been in the original plan but, with the rest of the guests being mostly guys, those girls probably thought it was Christmas all over again.

During what generally seemed to be turning out to be a successful afternoon, I got the chance to catch up with Katy, who was the guest of a company I had never heard of but who had booked the box some time ago and it now turned out were one of Katy's clients. I assumed, therefore, that I had her to thank for that one. She, like most of the others, was moving between the boxes, since everyone knew everyone, and, of course, we needed to talk about all things Swedish, since it seemed she was still hoping that Bjørn would turn up in Prague again and they might yet make something happen together. I was happy for her to chat away as I didn't want to go into too much detail about Lennart with all the regular guys about. I especially didn't want to talk about him in front of Jeremy, who had spotted Katy and I sitting together and headed over to us whistling 'Dancing Queen' to himself and looking as if he had had a few (drinks, not dancing queens, although he had probably had a few of those too!)

I stood up to kiss him on his cheek but then, when he got right up to us, he grabbed hold of both front pockets of my coat, which were square and on either side of the buttons, and ripped them both downwards, leaving a great big hole where each pocket had been.

"Hope you didn't like that coat," he said, smirking, while Katy gasped and everyone around us looked shocked. I just smiled and said nothing, since I didn't really like the coat anyway. What wasn't funny, though, was that, by that time, it was getting a bit chilly, so I couldn't really be without it, and obviously not everyone knew about our 'coat history'. Which meant that as the day wore on, I was continually being asked, 'Whatever happened to your coat?' and,

252

when Jeremy overheard that, he whispered to me, "I suppose I could ask the same of you about mine!"

Generally, though, the afternoon went along without too many hitches and soon we were all back on the coach and heading to the restaurant where the party organised by the Tomašes was taking place. For a Czech restaurant, in those days, it was a really upmarket affair in a stand-alone old cottage with a lovely interior full of beams and antiques and a big garden wrapped around it, where a barbeque had been set up and a small stage for the band had been placed. Obviously, everyone from our side had been drinking all day, so we were quite a boisterous group but, for the most part, all were reasonably well behaved. That is, until the band started up and the dancing began, at which point one of the girls that had been brought along by Gary, and was clearly very much the worse for wear, demanded the band played 'Like a Virgin' by Madonna, got on the stage, grabbed the microphone and started singing along. The only trouble was that, instead of singing 'Like a Virgin' she had changed the words to, 'I'm not a fucking virgin,' which, of course, the English speakers understood and mostly found very funny. The Czech dignitaries, however, having had the words translated for them, were extremely unamused, and it wasn't much later that I decided that we should probably round everyone up and head for home, feeling a bit shameful of our behaviour.

"Mum, who, after all, had been a spy in the war and wasn't rattled easily, jumped in."

Czechs and Crooks

WITH SO MANY of our big projects coming to fruition in the spring and early summer, our lives in Shitna started to settle into a reasonable routine, which involved very long hours during the week and then, when I was in town on the weekend, I would spend at least half of both Saturday and Sunday in the office trying to catch up for the weekends I was away. My dislike for Shitna only grew at that time, since the offices were completely characterless and, walking down from my flat on the weekend when the street was deserted, save for some dodgy looking characters ambling about, only emphasised how ugly that particularly area was.

The work, though, kept coming in and we had enough to keep us very busy right through the summer, to the point that we started to look around again for another person to join our team. Meanwhile, I was still commuting to Stockholm as many weekends as possible. I had so much to do though that I tended to leave on the Friday night flight and return on the very late Sunday one, which was expensive and a bit tiring. And, even though I had assumed that the ice hockey would have slowed down by then, Lennart was still having to stay put for matches, training camps and publicity type things, which meant he only made it to Prague once in our first six months together. The whole situation was becoming a bit of a problem, with no conceivable solution.

It also meant I had very few spare weekends to go to the UK and see Mum so, instead, she took it on herself to come to me. That was great as she was as hopeless as I was at sitting about doing nothing and so, while I was out at work, she was either pottering about in the flat doing bits of housework (she even more OCD about tidiness than me), cooking, or taking herself off to see Prague, which she loved. She also acted as a bit of a calming influence on me since I couldn't really go out and about the evenings she was staying as she had been on her own all day. I think she would have been very happy if I had offered her a job in the agency and, being just about the cleverest person I knew, I'm sure she would have been very good

255

at it, but, much as I loved my mum, that would have been pushing it a bit!

One day in early summer, when she was over for one of her regular visits in order to help out, we met at the office late in the afternoon for a cup of tea – as I say, she was a calming influence on me – then we strolled back to the flat for dinner. As we got to my floor, we found the guy that had been living for the last couple of months in the flat across the landing from me sitting on the top step and crying.

"Whatever has happened?" I asked him. I had never actually spoken to him before as the few times I had seen him, he seemed very unfriendly.

"I'm waiting for the police," he said, between sobs. "I've been burgled and they've taken absolutely everything."

Mum, who, after all, had been a spy in the war and wasn't rattled easily, jumped in.

"Come with us," she said, opening the door to my flat. "Let's get you a cup of tea while you wait here for the police; you can't sit out there."

Half an hour after that, two heavy-looking police pitched up, dressed head-to-toe in black, with guns and batons strapped to their waists, and took him over to the flat to see what had been going on. We hovered in the background and snooped. It was shocking. They had indeed taken everything, not just the furniture, but the pictures from the walls, the magazines from the tables, even the loo rolls. Everything. It looked like an unfurnished flat ready for rental. Surely something strange was going on and I, ever the catastrophist, started to visualise mafia shoot-outs, drug barons, all sorts. But since we didn't have a legitimate reason to hang about, we went back into my flat and got on with our evening.

Having taken ourselves off to bed at a reasonable time, I woke up what felt like a few hours later with a start and looked at my clock. 2.00 am. That, in itself, wasn't unusual, but what *was* was the sound of drilling coming from downstairs. I crept out of the bedroom to see if I could hear anything more from the front door and met Mum in the hall, doing the same.

"Did you hear that?" I asked her. "It sounds like someone is drilling into a door or something. Do you think it could be the burglars? Should we call the police again?"

We decided we probably should, but then realised that we didn't actually know how to do that. What to do?

"I know who will know," I said. "Ewan." Ewan, now the head of 'Eagle Services', prided himself in knowing just about everything about anything. I dialled his number. 2.00 am was still early for him, but I hoped he might be home by then and sure enough, he answered immediately.

"Hey, what's up?" he asked.

I explained what had been going on and asked him how we might call the police.

"Don't worry," he said. "I'll call them myself. You stay inside." He hung up.

The drilling noises continued, and we sat in the kitchen listening and wondering if we were the only ones in the whole building that could hear what was happening. But then, suddenly, all sorts of things happened at once. First, we heard a car screeching up outside with sirens blaring. We looked out the window to see two young police guys jump out, guns holstered and dash up the steps to the entrance. Next, a taxi pulled up and parked right behind the police car, out of which came Ewan, who also ran up the steps in pursuit of the police. Then we heard a load of shouting from the floor below.

"I have to see what is going on," I said to Mum and so, in my dressing gown, I opened the door, went out to the landing and looked down to the first floor, where I could see that one of the policemen had hold of an elderly man who was standing by the door to flat 1B with a drill in his hand, while the other one was hanging onto Ewan, who was gesticulating wildly and trying to avoid having handcuffs put onto him. Watching all this was the girl from the first floor flat who was slumped against the wall, head lolling to one side, completely paralytic.

Thankfully, the police let Ewan go once they realised that he had nothing to do with what was going on and he soon joined us and reported that the whole situation was completely unrelated to the earlier burglary. Apparently, from what Ewan could make out – he was a relatively good Czech speaker – the usually 'quiet' girl from downstairs had come home late and drunk and couldn't find her keys. She had rung the old boy, who was some sort of relative, and he, being a decent sort of bloke had toddled over with his drill in order to bust open the girl's front door, as you do at 2.00 am in the morning. And because the police had got there at the same time as Ewan, they somehow got the wrong end of the stick and thought he was the cause of it all. In the end, it all got sorted out; the girl got into her flat, never to be seen again, the old boy went home, and the police soon left, while Ewan came upstairs and got to know Mum. Finally.

She had, of course, heard a lot about him, but hadn't yet met him and, as I said before, she always warned me about short men and Welsh men, so now she was meeting a combination of both in the flesh. And, of course, they immediately hit it off. I knew they would since they both have such a great sense of humour. Plus, Mum always did have a penchant for good looking men, which overrode everything. Ewan spent the next two hours flirting outrageously with her and she cooed and played up to him as if she was a teenager. Meantime, I sat there like a gooseberry wishing they would both shut up and leave as the next day was a busy one and I needed to get to bed!

I found out later that there had been a spate of burglaries around the Prague 2 area, and particularly flats that were rented out to foreigners had been targeted. It seemed, although I was shocked to think it could be the case in our building, that a gang of burglars offered money to various different locals living in buildings that housed foreigners, in return for being given a tip-off when one of them left for some sort of trip. When the tip came through, the burglars turned up in a proper branded removal van, dressed accordingly, and were let in the main doors by the local. Then, all they had to do was force the lock on the inside door and load up everything from the flat – without anyone else taking the blind bit of notice, since foreigners were often moving in and out and, besides which, the locals wouldn't care – and then drive off.

Another rumour was that the tip-offs often came from the main radio taxi firm, who were often called to take people to the airport. I thought that was less likely as it wouldn't explain how the burglars managed to get into the main house, but it wasn't beyond the realms of possibility. Whichever way it worked, though, it was just one more reason for my still not being completely happy living in Prague. But that didn't mean I could leave.

"Drunk again, Jo?"

260

Party Time

THAT JULY THERE were two parties all of us were looking forward to. First up was a party in Lávka that was being thrown by the investment bank that Clive's old friend Diana had been working for. The party was to say goodbye to her as she was heading back to the UK for good and, since she knew nearly everyone in Prague, it was sure to be a big one. It was a Thursday evening, and I was heading to Stockholm on the late flight the next day, so I had it in my mind I wouldn't stay too late.

As usual, I didn't want to turn up there on my own – pathetic, I know – so I arranged to meet Katy beforehand, and then the two of us went along together. The bank had taken over the whole of the inside of Lávka, but the garden at the back that overlooks the river remained open to anyone, and sure enough, we all eventually ended up outside anyway. Incidentally, earlier in the evening, a rumour had gone around that Bjørn Borg was sitting at one of the far tables overlooking the water. Since everyone knew who he was, but no-one was sure they would recognise him (come on!), I was sent to check if it was true, and sure enough, there he was, surrounded by various young ladies and his team. Thrilling as it was, it is irrelevant to this story. I just felt the need to share.

The party was full-on. I soon realised there was no way I was going to be leaving early, since so many of my old friends were there. They included, of course, Eva, who had flown out especially and was completely over-excited. Clive was also there, who Diana seemed to be having one last try at getting off with (and failing), as well as her boss, a grand Czech guy called Jiři, as so many men are over here, if they are not called Jan. I had only met him a few times before, and every time he was completely pissed. Jeremy, Jonathan, Simon, Ewan and the others were being boisterous and over the top and looking to see what was cooking for the evening in the 'girl stakes'. Then, there among them was Michael Rippon, who was busy introducing everyone he knew to a young, portly guy who went by

261

the name of Callum and who, Michael had told me previously, he had head-hunted in the UK to come and be his right-hand man.

Callum was a bit odd looking, with a head that seemed to be way too big for his body, a huge mouth that stretched for miles and a rather wild mop of reddish-brown hair. Plus, he was a bit rotund for someone who was probably 25 if that. I didn't really like him as you have probably realised. He was what I regarded to be a typical 'PR lovey'; awfully posh, smarmy and determined to climb up the bottom of anyone he thought could be in any way useful to him, particularly Jiři the banker. Clearly, I was way beneath him, and he barely looked at me when Michael brought him over, which was fine, since I didn't like looking at him either.

Once the party got going properly, I decided to head to the dance floor to find Ewan and ignore the others. I could see Simon was off on a kamikaze lunatic evening and didn't feel like talking to Jonathan, so a bit of wild dancing seemed in order, particularly as Katy and Jeremy remained upstairs being corporate. Eventually, we headed outside to the garden, propping up the bar with Michael's friend Nick, the booze man, while keeping an eye out for Bjørn (Borg that is). We were soon joined by another guy Nick seemed to know and who I talked to for about an hour without having any idea who he was nor what he looked like since he was wearing a mask that appeared to be made of a whole deer's head, complete with antlers, and which covered his whole face. He was completely charming, and I found out a few days later that he was a famous actor who the boys all knew and was regularly in the gutter press. That wasn't the reason for him coming to Lávka in disguise, though. He had been at a fancy-dress party earlier, Jeremy had mentioned, in case we thought that it was his usual attire. Duh.

Soon, various others came from the dancefloor and joined us at the bar, including Clive, with Diana in close pursuit, and the rather obnoxious Callum, who had clearly given up on Jiři since he was in a near paralytic state and had decided that Jeremy was now the person he most needed to meet. Since the only people that were vaguely interesting to me were Bjørn (Borg) and the man dressed as a deer, I decided that it was probably time for me to leave so I made my excuses and headed off.

I later heard that Jeremy had taken Diana off for a 'one-night-only' goodbye shag, although she did, apparently, pitch up again some months later in the hopes of a re-run, which even shocked Katy, who always seemed to me to be unshockable. I don't mean to sound like a bitch – nor, God forbid, jealous – but Diana really was no oil painting and was decidedly 'odd'. What I also heard later was that Callum had spent a good part of the evening plotting the demise of poor old Michael, but that had not yet made the news.

Earlier in the year, Jeremy had moved into a new apartment very close to the centre of town, having given up his splendid villa in the middle of nowhere. The apartment was on the ground floor of a huge house that belonged to Jiři the banker, Diana's old boss. Perhaps the goodbye shag had been part of the deal that got Jeremy the flat. I never got around to asking him. The house had been given back to Jiři's family by the new government after the demise of communism, along with several other buildings around the Old Town, under what was known as the 'restitution process'. What that meant was that if a person or family could prove that they had originally owned a property that had been taken away from them by the communists, they could go through a lengthy and complicated 'restitution process' to get the property back into their ownership. Sometimes, that turned into a bit of a poisoned chalice as many of the buildings had gotten into a horrible state of disrepair, and since the families that received them back often didn't have the money to do the necessary reconstruction, they would find themselves left with a bit of a white elephant on their hands.

That wasn't the case with the house where Jeremy had his apartment. It was palatial and had been used to house various diplomats and other dignitaries during the years since it had been taken from Jiři's family. Jiři himself lived on the upper floors, while Jeremy's flat took over the whole of the lower ground floor and opened out onto its own beautiful garden.

Once he moved in and had instructed the latest interior designer to arrive in Prague to make it completely gorgeous, Jeremy obviously wanted to show the flat off to the world in general. To do that, he decided to host a summer party that would soon become an annual event on the Prague social calendar. At the time, of course, hosting such a party wasn't as straightforward as it might sound, but Jeremy, being good friends with the owner of the Joyce, an Irish ex-banker named Tom, had discussed the party with him and Tom had offered to put on a huge barbeque for the day, something he had been a dab hand at back in Ireland.

Needless to say, Jeremy's view on the rest of the organisation was that it was a 'girly' sort of thing. I was therefore roped in to add a bit of support, which in this case was mainly to help in sourcing enough decent sausages, bacon, and other typical English foods in time for the party. This I did during one of my very few recent trips to the UK to see my mum and yet again, I made the 'food run' back on Czech Airlines, only this time, instead of having a wedding cake on the seat next to me, I had a massive box of Marks and Spencer's best sausages, which had, again, caused a bit of a stir when going through customs.

I had discussed the party with Lennart some time previously and agreed that if I went to him the weekend before, he would fly to Prague for this one. As the party got closer, I got more and more nervous about how it would all go. He had only visited me in Prague once before, as mentioned, and that was in our early days, when we had had plenty of things to keep us occupied – if you know what I mean – so he hadn't really met anyone other than Katy. This time, though, he was coming to be visible as my 'boyfriend' and to attend an event where he would meet just about all of my closest friends. That would have been scary enough, even if they had been normal. But with people like Simon, who referred to Lennart as the 'invisible man', Ewan, who might do or say anything at any time, and, of course, Jeremy, around, I was pretty terrified.

On that basis, when I was on the sausage run to the UK, I had dragged my mum to London to help me look for a dress I could wear to the party that would be 'wow' enough to give me that additional bit of confidence I would need. We had gone to Harrods, as one does, and strolled around the ladies' dress department, which was ablaze with colour and had so many designer clothes in lots of different and gorgeous materials that I was too scared to touch a thing. Plus, the girls who worked there were terrifying. Apart from being thin, stunning and immaculately dressed and made up, they were, I felt, looking down their noses at me and Mum, as if we had been dragged in there on the sole of someone's shoe. In the end, I forced myself to pick up a pretty pink silk dress which came to just above the knee, was sleeveless with a round neck, and had a kind of transparent lacy overlay with flowers sketched onto it. It was also quite sexy as it had a zip up the middle of both the front and the back.

"Could I try this on, please?" I asked the snooty cow that had been shadowing us as we walked around.

"Are you sure it's your size?" she had asked. I had checked and it was, but since she seemed to think I required the elephant department, I suspected I wouldn't even get it on.

"Yes, thank you," I said and marched to the changing room, where not only did I get it on – those zips had many benefits – but I actually thought I looked pretty damned hot. So hot that I didn't even bother to check the price tag until I went outside and said to the snoot, "I'll take it."

She looked at me aghast and then took it over to the till, wrapped it up in nice tissue paper and said, "That will be 800 pounds please."

At that point, I nearly collapsed. But I didn't want her to see that and add to my earlier humiliation. So, keeping all my fingers and toes crossed that my credit card wouldn't bounce, I said, "That's fine," and handed it over. Five minutes later, we left with the dress in the bag. I felt like I might be sick at any moment!

"How much was it?" asked Mum, who, out of her usual 'English politeness' hadn't liked to listen in to the final transaction.

"You don't even want to know," I responded.

So anyway, the dress was ready. The party was under control, and all that was needed was for Lennart to fly in on the Friday afternoon flight and then I could look forward to the whole event. Except he didn't. As usual, 'something had come up' and he had to stay in Stockholm. So, the dress and I would have to go to the party on our own.

I was furious. Of course, I got it that he had this huge career that he had to make sacrifices for, and I did trust that he wasn't off gallivanting with other ladies – although I couldn't guarantee it, since there were many evenings when I tried to call him at the regular 11.00 pm slot and he didn't answer – but I did feel that, just for one weekend, he could have put me first. So, Saturday morning, instead of getting ready at home and turning up later with a great big ice hockey star on my arm, I was up and out early to help the girls with the set-up, determined to behave dreadfully the whole day, in order to pay Lennart back and make myself feel better. Although, of course, it didn't.

By the time of the 2.00 pm kick-off, everything was in place. Jeremy's flat was beautiful and designed in such a way that each room flowed through to the next, although, for a tearaway like him, I couldn't help feeling it was all a bit too perfect and, dare I say it, slightly feminine. But maybe that's just me being a bit of a sour-faced old bag, since my own flat, while being a bit more furnished than it had been in the early days, was so far from being interior designed it was almost an embarrassment.

The garden, too, was in full bloom and looked like something from a magazine. Once the barbeque was set up along the long wall that ran parallel to the road, and the various wooden tables and chairs that we had hired had been scattered around among the old oak trees and the flowerbeds that were full of colour, you could almost imagine yourself in an English country garden. By the time people started arriving, Tom had the barbeque fired up, the students we had brought in to serve the drinks were lined up at the entrance, and everything looked perfect.

As usual, all that remained was for the three of us to go and get changed, at least in a bathroom this time, and then we were ready. The dress, I felt, was a big hit. Certainly, Annie and Petra made all the right noises, although I wondered what they would say if they

266

knew that I had spent more than their monthly wage on it, which was a bit of an awful thought. Even Jeremy managed a 'you look gorgeous' comment as we came out to the garden and changed our personas from workers into guests, which all of us were now very well used to doing!

As expected, the party was great. The weather was hot and sunny, which was a relief since everyone had worried about what we would do if it rained, and just about all of my friends were there, as well as a lot of new people as the flood of companies entering the Czech market had still not slowed down and Jeremy generally met all of them before anyone else.

I spent a good part of the early afternoon sitting at a table with Simon and Francesca, which was nice as I had seen so little of Simon recently and Francesca had always been a bit standoffish with me. I always thought that she suspected something had gone on between me and Simon, which it most definitely had not, but that afternoon she was less frosty than usual. We were soon joined by Penelope and Alex, who had finally made the decision to move out to Prague and take his chances on getting some form of work, while Penelope and I were about to start on a new project for Stewart Morris, so we mulled that over for a while. At some point mid-afternoon Jeremy brought a very nice guy called Doug over to introduce to all of us and I chatted to him for quite a long time as he had only arrived in Prague a couple of days ago. It transpired that he was to head up the new British Airways office in Prague and once *that* news got out lots of other people came to join us since everyone clearly wanted to be his new best friend.

Eventually, the music that had been playing in the sitting room was turned up loud and the terrace area became a makeshift dance floor. By that time many of us – and by that, I mean myself, in particular – had had just about enough to drink to want to get up and make a complete and utter tit of themselves by dancing and flirting outrageously with just about anyone that came within reach. First, that meant Ewan – Ewan and I always ended up dancing together and it's all completely harmless – then I dragged poor old

Jiři the banker up for a bit of a jig about. I think I terrified him as he headed off as soon as he possibly could, never to be seen again, and then it was pretty much anyone that was brave enough to get out on the floor with me.

At one point, I even managed to trip over, due to the gold sandals I was wearing being a bit slippery, and landed on my bum right in front of Maurice from Bass, who had arrived earlier in the evening with his wife and who looked at me on the floor and said, "Drunk again, Jo?" Not something I am at all proud of.

It gets worse. Stewart Morris had shown his face briefly and had brought with him a very good-looking American guy called Charles, who everyone around seemed to be sucking up to. He was, apparently, one of Stewart's big investors and very important to him, so I was chuffed when Stewart introduced me to him as, "The head of his PR agency." Anyway, Charles had been wandering about chatting to various people – and yes, I had noticed – but had eventually turned up near the dance area to watch everyone's antics. He seemed particular interested in mine though, to the point that, shortly after I had had my collision with Maurice, he came over, took my arm and said, "Come and sit with me over there," in a sort of bossy manner that I quite liked, and guided me over to a chair under the tree where we then sat and chatted for hours. About what, I have no idea. And then, as the party was winding down, he suggested he drop me home, since he was staying near to where I lived – which I must have told him – and then I was getting into the taxi with him…

But then as we pulled up outside my building, I went to get out and suddenly felt – thank the Lord – quite sober. "Aren't you going to invite me in?" he said, starting to get out himself.

I responded, "No, I'm terribly sorry. I'm not going to," at the same time trying to leap out of the car, but he sort of yanked me back in.

"If you don't want to invite me in, then come back to my hotel," he said, still holding onto my arm and pulling the door closed by leaning right across me. And then, just when I thought things were going to get nasty, they did. For him. The taxi driver suddenly turned around with a gun in his hand, which he waved vaguely in Charles's face, saying words to the effect of 'let her go'. At which point my arm was released and I opened the door, jumped out and ran indoors, thinking, and who would ever have thought it, *Thank God for Czech taxi drivers.* That was a first. I got inside just as the phone was ringing for what I then found out from listening to the answering machine was about the tenth time that night. *Lennart.* And no, I didn't answer it.

The following day, I met up with Katy for a coffee, as I usually do when I have a load on my chest to unburden and was pleased to hear that I wasn't the only person that had behaved atrociously. Apparently, Simon had taken Francesca home and then snuck back out to the party again and gone completely nuts drinking everything in sight before leaving to go who knows where. He eventually pitched up about a week later, having gone for his first proper bender since getting married. Sadly, not his last.

Then there was the lovely Doug, who had told me his wife was joining him in Prague within just days, and who, I had felt, had come across as a bit prim and proper. Obviously not, since he was later seen snogging in the garden with one of Jeremy's secretaries, as, too, was Tom the Barbecue Man, who was doing the same, but with her sister. The worst bit of all, though, was that bloody Piers had managed, finally, to get off with Petra. That bit had a very funny side story to it, although it didn't stay funny for long. My lovely Petra had recently moved out of her flat in Prague as her boyfriend Milan had had to go back to Slovakia for a few months and she couldn't afford to stay there on her own. For now, she was staying in Matthew's spare room in the basement. Piers had very kindly escorted Petra home after the party, where he had then stayed, only to get up in the morning, go upstairs and come face to face with Matthew in his dressing gown, who then asked him who he was, having not met him previously, and slung him out on his ear.

There was some positive news too. Katy had sat for a while with one of the guys she works with, and he had brought along his very nice girlfriend, Magdalena. According to her, Magdalena (or Magda as everyone called her) had been in the UK for a year as a nanny, as usual, and spoke fluent English. She was also very pretty and smiley and, while she hadn't yet had any proper work experience, was looking for an office job. So, Katy, bless her, had told her to report to me on Monday morning for an interview, which she duly did. One day later, we had our next new member of the team!

Hotels and Maltesers

The weather in Prague, as I keep saying, is tricky. Despite us all saying that the spring and summer is gorgeous in the Czech Republic, sometimes it feels as if we just go straight from winter into summer, and then back to winter again at some point from September onwards. So, after the heat of the summer and all the partying and gallivanting, we woke up one morning to find it was basically winter, and suddenly everything got a bit serious.

We had a new project for Bass, even though the ice hockey sponsorship had been put on hold for now, as, while they liked the idea of getting involved with a UK team, exporting beer from the Czech Republic was turning out to be way more complicated than at first expected and there was no real point in promoting it heavily if it wasn't possible to get enough beer onto the supermarket shelves. On the other hand, someone in the Bass hierarchy had decided it would be worth trying to launch a new alcoholic lemonade called Hooch on the Czech market, and so we were playing around with all sorts of ideas for that as they wanted it out there before Christmas.

We also had a new project for Stewart Morris, which I figured could get a bit complicated if Charles the investor was going to show his face. I had debated mentioning what had happened between me and Charles to Stewart, but just couldn't imagine it. I then thought about asking Penelope for advice before we got properly into it but felt that that would need to be over a drink. So, as usual, I just parked it with a view to 'seeing what would happen'. Then we had the big race in Pardubice in October, plus other bits and pieces that would keep us busy, even without these bigger projects. Added to all of that, a new and very exciting piece of work turned up out of the blue.

On the weekends I stayed in Prague, I often used to head off with Katy to a hotel just outside the city centre called The Forex, which was on the edge of a lovely area of Prague called Vyšehrad. Vyšehrad itself is up in the hills above the Vltava river and is full of architectural treasures that we sometimes went to have a look at, or we would just sit on a bench and look across at the amazing views of the city. But mostly, we hung out in the hotel's very nice coffee shop on the first floor. Not only did they have good coffee – cakes too, which Katy loved but I tried to avoid – but they also had a selection of English newspapers which we would sit and read, having been starved of English news for weeks on end.

One thing we noticed though, while sitting in the coffee shop and 'chilling' one day was the number of young girls that would wander through. Not to do anything in particular it seemed, they would just stroll into the coffee shop at one end and out again at the other. And then we realised they were working the hotel. In fact, it seemed there was some sort of booking system in place, as the girls would walk through at intervals and then one of the men sitting around the coffee shop would go to the counter, say something, and be given what appeared to be a raffle ticket. Shortly afterwards, one of the girls would walk through again, come up to whichever man had last been at the counter, take the ticket off him and then the two of them would disappear off together.

One Saturday, I kid you not, we were watching the girls walking through, as usual, and among them was a face that looked very familiar. I couldn't quite place her but then I realised that she was the new trainee working for Clive. It turned out that she was studying and working for him during the week and then moonlighting in the hotel on the weekend in order to make a bit of extra cash. I decided to keep my mouth shut as who knew how Clive would react to that piece of news.

While I had spent quite a few Saturday mornings in the hotel, I had never at that point been there on a weekday or evening. But then I was invited to meet a group of Maltese businessmen who were in town to look at a few different hotels, with a view to buying one, and were staying at The Forex. They were clearly interested in buying it and wanted to discuss how we might handle the PR campaign around a potential purchase.

"We understand it has a bit of a murky reputation, we even heard rumours that there are a few working girls doing business in the bars and restaurants," one of them said, which was the understatement of the week.

We had met in the lobby bar, which was a huge open space with sofas, tables and chairs placed randomly into seating areas that were marked out by huge round white pillars. Halfway through the meeting, as the sun went down behind the windows, and just as I was in the middle of telling them all very seriously about my lengthy experience of doing business in the Czech Republic, how I knew everyone in the media and politics that they would need to know and so on, the lights came on, and what were once innocent white pillars turned into colourful and rather 'erect', so to speak, penis-lookalikes. I am pretty sure my mouth literally dropped open mid-sentence, but the Maltese, bless them, continued to sit quietly, listening intently to what I had to say, and appeared to take absolutely no notice, even when the pillars/ penises changed colour at regular intervals and became almost hypnotic.

Fast forward to late summer, when I received a call from an English guy called Will, an old friend of Jacob, the accountant, who had given him my name. Will had already been in Prague for some time, although I had never come across him as he lived outside the city and was one of the few foreigners that had already mastered the language and was able to live much less of an 'expat life' than the rest of us.

Will ran his own small design agency and was one of the best designers ever. Okay, I hadn't worked with many at that time – so I didn't know that for a fact – but I found it out as we went along and, because of it, he brought in a lot of big clients. He had called me as he had been appointed to handle the complete re-branding and re-launch campaign for, what would soon be known as, the Revolution Tower Hotel. And, since Will focused on pure and simple design, he was looking for an agency to sub-contract some of the marketing and PR to, and that meant us!

My first meeting with him was in the kitchen of his office, in one of the most run-down areas of Prague. When I was trying to find it, I kept thinking I must be in the wrong place as most of the buildings were completely dilapidated; the shops were either closed and abandoned or had a weird and wonderful selection of second-hand clothes and strange knickknacks in their dusty windows, and the air was thick with smoke and smog. Needless to say, there were a lot of dusky characters hanging about that, had I been as prejudiced as the locals, I might have been a bit wary of. Either way, it definitely wasn't an area where you would expect to find a leading advertising agency. Eventually, I found the door to his office, went inside and into what was a very smart reception, and out came this shortish, chubby, grey-haired and bearded English guy who beckoned me into the kitchen, asking, "Do you fancy a cuppa?" as we walked in and sat down.

I immediately liked him as he was so creative and had so many ideas. Plus, he talked all the time, barely drawing breath, his blue eyes twinkling as he went along while he fired out swear word after swear word. All I could really do was nod and agree to pretty much everything he said. But the plan for the coming months did sound very exciting, and with the hotel being refurbished throughout the winter and then launched sometime in the New Year, it was sure to give us a lot of good-paying work on an ongoing basis. The only snag – which I didn't say to Will, of course – was that I couldn't imagine in a million years how we would ever manage all of it on top of everything else that was going on at the moment, even with our new Magda.

As more and more work appeared, I was continually worrying about having enough people to do it all, but then, finding good new people was so difficult, if not impossible. And even if I could find them, what if the work then slowed down and left me with lots of additional costs and no income to match? The Czech Republic makes it very difficult and expensive to get rid of people, so you couldn't just take someone on and then dismiss them if the work ran out. It was a conundrum I just had to live with until I found an answer.

Despite that ongoing worry, I should have been happy that the business seemed to be booming. But there was still that one big shadow, which was my ongoing situation with Lennart, as things between us had been a bit strained after Jeremy's party. I had flown over for a weekend after that when he hadn't had to play and all was bright and rosy again, at least for now. But with the winter coming, I could see that there was no way he would be able to come to Prague if he had matches every weekend, and I doubted that I would get to Sweden on a regular basis with so much work to do. And that was a stress that didn't seem to have any workable solution.

"It was bad enough having to pay them Kč 1,500 in cash, but to have to give them both a blow job too would have been too much."

Harry Honda

ONE MORNING I got a call from Jeremy, which was not something I was very used to, to tell me that one of his senior people was leaving and, since he had only just had a new company car bought for him, he wondered if I would like to buy it – his idea being I would just take over the monthly instalments and the money already spent would be written off. That seemed like a very good deal and I was definitely tempted, as it was getting more and more difficult to ask if I could borrow a car from Simon, or someone else, every time we needed to go outside of Prague. Plus, I could see that it could be very useful to have a nice big car that we could take all of our gear around in when we were doing events and so on, rather than having to manage with hiring taxis.

So, having pondered if I could even afford to buy a car at this stage, since it would involve fairly hefty monthly repayments, off I went to see it. I was thinking I would only go for it if it was big enough and cheap enough and if the deal really was as good as Jeremy had said. But then, when I got to Jeremy's company's garage, I had one of those 'love at first sight' moments as I looked at this beautiful Honda sports car sitting there, almost purring. I loved its bright red metallic finish, the black leather seats inside – just two, bucket-style – and its great big exhaust. And, while my head was telling me it was completely impractical and I shouldn't do it, my heart forced the words out of my mouth, "Yes, I'll have it."

As usual in the Czech Republic, nothing was as simple as it looked. Not long after I signed all the papers, the lease company advised Jeremy it wouldn't be possible for me to just take over the monthly instalments – which would have been manageable – but that, instead, I would have to buy the car outright, which would clear out the 'rainy day fund' I had been gradually squireling away, and a bit more. And, despite my saying that this new deal would really kill me, Jeremy, bless him, insisted that the deal had been done and there was no going back. Me being me, I was unable to resist the

277

car anyway. Which meant that it was only a matter of days before 'Harry the Honda' joined our team.

Bearing all of that in mind, you can imagine how angry I was when, shortly after I had first turned up at Molly's with Harry and parked him right outside so that everyone could see him, Gary told me that there was a rumour going around that Harry had been bought for me by my Swedish ice hockey player boyfriend. Obviously, I couldn't possibly have bought the car myself. I could have said 'if only', but I wouldn't really have meant it. I did wonder, though, and for only about the millionth time, if the same type of comment would have been levied at a guy in such a situation. It would have been funny if it wasn't so bloody annoying.

But, anyway, we loved Harry, and, despite him being completely impractical – we could just about get Magda and Petra into the 'back seat' area if they more or less sat on top of each other and Annie sat in the front –what we lacked in space, we made up for in style, since every time we turned up somewhere in him everyone stopped to look, especially when they saw all the pretty girls falling out of the door as it was more or less impossible to get out in any sort of dignified way.

Harry made life easier for me in so many ways. Getting up early and heading to train with Vladimir, or just going to the gym on my own was so much easier by car, and that meant I started to get back to a much more regular training routine. Most mornings, I headed out at the crack of dawn, barely awake, and then, just a few minutes later, I was parked next to the gym and ready to go. Then, after a quick shower, I was back in the car and off to the office, where I could park in the courtyard just below us and was often there before the others even arrived.

Most evenings, too, I would be off again – often with Annie, and sometimes the other two as well – down to Molly's, and sometimes continuing onto the new U Zlata Ulicka Two, and therefore able to start seeing Nenad and the others more often again, and still get home at a reasonable hour. It was almost as easy as when we were back in our cottage.

The only downside was that Harry was a police magnet, and since those were the days when drinking and driving was the norm and I, while not liking myself for it, did sometimes get behind the wheel a bit the worse for wear, we would often get stopped. In fact, I probably hold some sort of Czech record for having been stopped three times in one evening and getting away scot-free every time! The thing was, though, the police at that time – and apologies to any police reading this now – were mostly stopping cars in order to make money, and since Harry was so flashy and looked expensive, we were always a target since they figured we could afford to pay more money than if we were driving, say, a regular Škoda.

The key to getting away with paying as little as possible, I had found, was to pretend not to understand a word of Czech, since the majority of the police didn't speak English. Plus, when faced with two or more young ladies who acted completely innocently, they often just gave up and let us go. One evening, though, Annie and I had been out and about on the town, and I was giving her a lift home (she rented a flat with Christie quite near to Shitna at that time) when, sure enough, a police car appeared out of nowhere, the siren came on and we were pulled over.

Two young tough guys got out. They were dressed in tight black commando uniforms that showed off their rippling muscles rather fetchingly and had pistols, handcuffs and other bits and pieces nicely on display. One stood behind Harry, looking him over, while the other rapped on my window.

"Get out of the car and show me your papers," he said in Czech.

I put on my big eyed, pretty girl lost look and said, "I'm sorry, I don't speak Czech. Do you speak English?" I was thinking he wouldn't.

He gave me a look, walked to the back of the car, said something to his colleague and then the two of them returned together. His colleague leant down and spoke through the window.

"Get out of the car and show me your papers," he said in fairly reasonable English.

It was unheard of. *Bugger.* I got out with a bit of difficulty, as usual, not helped by the alcohol in my blood and the fact I was already beginning to feel rather nervous, and handed my papers over.

"Okay, these are fine." He flicked through my license and passport. But then, instead of telling us to go, as I expected, or giving us a fine for whatever reason he could come up with, he whipped out a breathalyser kit and said, "Now, I need you to take this test."

I had never taken a breathalyser test before and got into a right old muddle with it, which only convinced them I was even more pissed than they first expected. And, of course, they were right. It showed positive. *Now what?* They deliberated together.

"You'll need to pay us 1,500 crowns [about £50]," said the English speaker. He started to write on a piece of paper. I didn't actually have Kč 1,500 on me, nor did Annie. Mild panic started to set in.

"I'm afraid we don't have 1,500 crowns," I said. "We only have about 700. Will that do?"

"Well, no," he said, with a bit of a smirk. "You're driving under the influence of alcohol, and this is the minimum amount we can accept. Where do you live?"

By this time, Annie had got out of the car and joined me. "Don't tell them," she whispered. But then added, "Don't we have some cash in the office?"

"Okay," I said. "I live in Prague 5." A lie. "But our office is just around the corner and we have some money there."

"We'll drive with you to your office and you can give us the money, and then you can leave the car there and take a taxi home."

We got back in the car and drove to the office with the police car following. But instead of just the two of us going upstairs to get the cash, the police boys joined us and we all walked up together. Something felt a bit off, but we weren't in any position to argue, so in we all went. They sat themselves down at Petra's desk while I went and found the petty cash box, which, thankfully, had enough cash for me to be able to hand over the Kč 1,500 they wanted.

"Do we get a receipt?" I asked.

"Not this time," said the English speaker.

"So, are we done here now?"

They both continued to sit there, looking a little bit nervous and giggling slightly. Despite them having the cash, they didn't look as if they were planning on going anywhere soon. I wondered if I should offer them a cup of coffee or something and make it into a jolly social occasion.

"If you want us to be done now?" he answered.

I looked at Annie and wondered if they were suggesting what I thought they were suggesting. "I think so," I said, trying to look cool. And then, thankfully, they both got up and left, with no further mention of leaving the car behind or getting a taxi home. But we did that anyway as we were both a bit shaken up. As Annie said the next day when we were regaling the story to the other two, "It was bad enough having to pay them Kč 1,500 in cash, but to have to give them both a blow job too would have been too much."

"Who is that in my bed?
It looks like Simon?"

Autumn

IT WASN'T JUST ME that was flat-out busy. Gone were the days of heading down to one of the Irish pubs at about 6.00 pm on a working day, as no-one would be there. Most of us old-timers were still stuck in our offices well into the evening and then, with more decent restaurants opening up all over town, 'dining out with clients' was much more likely than any form of nightclubbing or partying. Friday nights, though, everyone that was staying put would head to The Joyce to let their hair down and then finish the evening in Lávka, just like in the 'old' days. In my case, having spent most of my summer weekends in Sweden, I felt I had missed out a bit and so it was quite nice to be staying in Prague a bit more often and to have the chance to catch up with everyone.

Jonathan, having bought several big residential properties over the past year had now decided to 'go big' and had become involved in a battle with some very unsavoury characters in order to try to buy the Kotva department store, which was still the only place in Prague where you could, in theory, buy most things. The building, as I have mentioned previously, was a huge eyesore but its size and location made it the most sought-after potential development project in town, so when it became known that it could be bought, there were a lot of potential buyers and developers in the running. Some were not averse to scaring people off competing with them and, since Jonathan was not one to shirk a battle, things had begun to get quite nasty, to the point that he now employed a full-time driver, as well as a bodyguard.

The driver, Matej, was a former crack soldier and a raving lunatic. Jonathan had bought a bloody great blue Range Rover to move around the town, probably bullet-proofed and so on – who knows – and we all assumed that Matej must have contacts at the very highest level, as he never got stopped or fined, despite the fact he believed that the quickest way to get anywhere was as the crow flies, flat out and ignoring all relevant street directions. After my first experience of being in the car with Matej at the wheel, I decided the best way to travel with him was to lie on the floor in the back and pray. Once, Jonathan gave me a lift to the airport with Matej driving and, as we were late leaving, Jonathan told him we needed to do the usual half an hour or so journey in fifteen minutes, or we would miss the plane. *Piece of cake.* We even had time to have a drink at the bar before we went to board. I, for one, needed it.

The bodyguard was more sinister. According to Jonathan, since the bodyguard himself never seemed to speak, he was a former Israeli agent, and you'd always know if Jonathan was in a bar or restaurant because he would be lurking about outside. Despite all of that security, however, one day someone actually did get to the Range Rover and tamper with the brakes (not that they were used very often) but somehow – I'm not quite sure what exactly happened – Matej managed to get them all out of what was, apparently, a near death experience.

Jonathan was never very popular with the other guys, for various reasons, not least the fact that he was one of the richest people in the country and all the girls loved him, partly for his money and partly because he was a handsome devil, just a bit lacking in charm! Even when he had what appeared to be a 'regular' girlfriend (or wife, in the past), there were always others hanging about him, usually models. Despite all these distractions, however, when he was focused on a project, he was a complete workaholic. I liked him for that, and a lot of other things too. It would have been so easy for him just to spend his life as a rich playboy, dabbling with whatever took his fancy, but that wasn't his way. Eventually, I forgave him for Lucie as he was, underneath it all, a very good friend.

Simon, though, didn't handle the stress of working with Jonathan very well, even though they were the best of friends, and Jonathan had saved him many times over, literally. When the Kotva project got going, Simon started to go off the rails he had managed to more or less stay on since his wedding, and we were back to the days of finding him asleep in the gym or having him pitch up at the office for a lie down after having disappeared for days on end. My ladies were so used to it they took very little notice when he turned up at the office in Shitna in the mornings and just opened the door,

284

led him to the meeting room and gave him a blanket. Sooner or later, he would wake up and take himself off with a slightly sheepish, "Bye, darlings," and we would wait until the next time.

One time, when Mum was staying for a few days, I had left her in the flat to have an early night and, with her permission, had headed off for one of my dinners with Katy. It was a while since we had been out together, and once we had finished dinner we headed to The Joyce for a quick nightcap. Unfortunately, it was one of those nights when everyone we knew had descended on the pub, and since Tom, the owner, had brought in an Irish band to play – God knows where from – everyone was getting up to dance or, in Ewan's case, to join in with the singing. Somehow it was midnight and I found myself being swept along on a wave of people leaving to go to Lávka for what might be the last evening we could spend outside before the winter set in properly.

Off we went, me and Ewan to dance, as usual, and then to prop up the bar, also as usual, and then to chat with Jeremy and cross-examine him about the new girlfriend that Katy had mentioned over dinner and who, he said, wasn't really a proper girlfriend (but then he would say that). And then, somewhere in my warped brain, I decided I needed to see if I could still 'pull him' – I know, it's a huge character flaw of mine – so I was being a little bit flirtatious and felt pleased to find out I probably could. Then it was 3.00 am and, thankfully, Katy appeared just as I may or may not have gone off and done the dirty deed, shovelled me into a taxi and sent me home to bed.

Except when I got into the flat and opened my bedroom door, I found that that might be a bit difficult as there appeared to be someone already in my bed and, judging by the thick black hair that was poking out above the duvet, that person appeared to be Simon. Since he was out for the count and I didn't want to disturb Mum, I ended up curled up on the sofa, under the only blanket I could find, until the light and cold woke me up shortly before she pottered out to the kitchen to make her first cuppa of the day.

I called out to her, "Mum, I'm in here," as she passed the sitting room doors and shortly after she appeared with two cups in her hand, one for me.

"Who is that in my bed? It looks like Simon?"

"Ah yes," she answered. "I was just getting ready for bed myself last night when the doorbell rang. Not the door downstairs, but your door. I figured it was either a neighbour or someone else with a key, so I opened up. And standing there was Simon, dressed only in his underpants. Anyway, he barged past me saying that it was bloody cold out there and that he needed to get to bed. And then he helped himself to your room. Not much I could do about it. I am so sorry, though, that I didn't leave you out more blankets."

It turned out later that Simon had been out on the rampage in town and, rather than going home, had let himself into what was now Jonathan's flat at the top of our building, Jonathan having taken it back off Annabel after the divorce. He had then sleep-walked, ending up outside the building, and eventually waking up to find himself asleep on the doorstep, nearly naked. Of course. Why didn't I think of that.

Anyway, there were many days Jonathan and I – and others – would sit and wonder what we could do to help Simon but, in the end, as with so many other things, it was one of those problems that was impossible to solve, but that, one day, we hoped, would work themselves out.

Ewan, too, was working 24 hours a day, seven days a week, to get his property management company, Eagle Services (after the song 'Fly Like an Eagle'), off the ground, and it seemed that the work was flying in. But Ewan's problem, just the same as everyone else's in the Czech 'service industry', was finding good people to do the work. Especially as he needed to be in his office to field the calls that came in all day long. But then, if he was in the office answering the telephone he wasn't watching over his 'maintenance people' when they went out on a job, which meant that anything could happen, or, more likely, not happen! And since a lot of the clients were Ewan's friends, most of the time he was in a state of near nervous breakdown.

That winter, however, life in the Czech Republic got a whole lot better. The lack of telephone lines had been everyone's biggest bugbear since the day we all arrived, and even though the situation had been slowly improving, it was still a big subject for discussion. What we knew, too, was that back home in the UK, the US, or wherever we came from, the mobile phone was now changing people's lives, and we were therefore desperate to know when such things would become available here. Finally, the news broke that a new Czech company was about to launch its own mobile phone on the market and the race was on to be the first person to get one. Ewan was so ecstatic that he stood outside the shop where the phones were going to be on sale all night in order not to miss out, and soon after he was calling everyone and shouting, "I've got one!" in near hysteria down the line.

I'm not sure what we expected when he told us all about it but don't think we imagined it would be a 'nearly-non mobile' phone, since it was the size of a suitcase and weighed a ton. But it could be carried about and that was all that mattered. For Ewan it was a lifesaver. For me, I wasn't so sure. The first version was hugely expensive, something like £2,000, and even though I'm not exactly a frail wallflower, I couldn't really see myself lugging such a great big beast about every time I left the office, especially with a handbag in my other hand. But, of course, as we all now know, it wasn't long before new and more practical versions came on the market. Then I understood what all the fuss was about.

"Oh, that won't be possible
in the Czech Republic."

Tyre Slashers, Cheaters and Dead Cows

I SPENT THE FIRST WEEKEND in October, just before the ice hockey season kicked off in earnest, with Lennart in Stockholm, during which time, in addition to visiting Bjørn out in the countryside, we went to see the band Roxette in concert. At that time, they were huge in Sweden, and their songs and the atmosphere ensured that I spent most of the evening trying not to cry (not unusual with me and music!) and mostly failing. That kind of set the tone for the rest of the weekend, when we spent a good part of what was left of it trying figure out what we would both do over Christmas, and how often we might see each other in between. By the time I landed back in Prague, the reality of our impossible situation was weighing me down heavily and I was looking forward to getting home and having a relaxing and sober evening, in order to mull everything over. Unfortunately, it wasn't to be.

As usual, I had left Harry parked in the road just around the corner from the house when I left for Sweden and had taken a taxi to the airport. On arriving home, therefore, the first thing I did was to walk around to where he was parked to check he was okay. Thankfully, there he was, all red and gorgeous, but something didn't look quite right. And then, after doing a double-take, I realised what it was. Some absolute bastard had slashed all four tyres, which were now completely flat, meaning Harry was slumped down on the road looking very much the worse for wear. My heart completely sank. Talk about adding to the misery! It was not just because I now had to figure out how to get him repaired, and the cost of that, but also that someone that may be living in the same building, or nearby, had so much 'hate' inside them that they would actually do such a thing. And not just that, that it might even be personal.

Amongst ourselves, we often talked about the Czechs' envy of other people, explaining it like this: 'Mrs Jones, in the UK, had a cow that she kept as a pet in her garden. One day, the cow died, and all the neighbours rallied around to bake her a cake and try to cheer her up. Meantime, Mrs Součková in the Czech Republic, also had a cow that she kept as a pet in her garden. One day the cow died, and all of her neighbours gathered around to celebrate.'

There were a lot of affluent Czechs, and plenty of foreigners living around my Prague 2 area, and it was common to hear about cars being damaged or stolen, especially if they were German and/or expensive. But while Harry was flashy, I couldn't really see why someone would be so jealous of me that they would do that amount of damage to him. It was a scary thought, but it was eminently possible.

Since it was early evening when I found Harry, there was nothing much I could do there and then, and besides, the damage was already done. I just left him there and first thing the next morning, I put Petra onto sorting it all out, which is the kind of thing she was very good at. I also raged about the situation to Jonathan, since I lived in his building, and he told me about a new 'car alarm' he had just heard about, and which he thought I should have installed. I added that to Petra's list and, within a couple of days, Harry returned home with new tyres – at a huge and unrecoverable cost – and an alarm system that was triggered by any sort of movement within a certain amount of space from the car. What that meant was that if anyone got close enough, the alarm was triggered, and suddenly a loud man's voice would shout, 'Get away from the car,' over and over again, until whoever it was moved away, and then it would switch off. It was great fun testing it. It wasn't so much fun sitting at home in the evening and having my ears stretched out to hear if the alarm was going to be triggered, then wondering what I would do if it was! Some months later, the Czech government banned the use of such alarms, presumably because they had given too many innocent people a near heart attack, but, by then, the job of frightening people away had been more or less done, in my case at least.

One of the positive things about this story, though, was that Lennart was so enraged by both the damage to the car and my feeling that someone might have it in for me, that he cancelled everything and came to Prague the following weekend, spending a great deal of time sitting by the window waiting to see if the alarm would go off and hoping it would! I had mixed feelings. If it did, then God help whoever might have caused it as Lennart was just itching to get hold of them, and if it didn't, then we had wasted a lot of time that could have been put to better use than just sitting about waiting! Hopefully, anyway, word got out that my rather large and fearsome ice hockey-playing boyfriend was around, and that would be enough to scare any tyre slashers off for a while.

What we also did that weekend was pay a visit, of course, to a match between two Czech ice hockey teams and, since the manager of one was an old friend of Lennart's, having played together with him in the US, word got out that he was in Prague, and we ended up joining half the team for dinner that evening. During dinner, not only did a conversation brew that there could be an opportunity for Lennart to come and play for the team, but also, that I could maybe help them with some of their marketing. Well, just goes to show that something good often comes from something bad.

Life after Lennart's visit soon got back into its usual routine. Annie continued to be a star and by now she was, I felt, nearly irreplaceable. Magda had slotted in really well and was doing fine, although every time I mentioned something new that we might consider doing, she came back with, "Oh, that won't be possible in the Czech Republic." It was a bit irritating, to say the least, and enough for me to decide one day to put a great big notice up on the wall with the words, 'We never say that anything is impossible,' on it, suggesting to everyone that we keep it in mind when talking to clients. I'm not sure if Magda realised the notice was directed at her, but when I mentioned it to the boys one evening in the pub, they all rolled their eyes and said, "God, why do the Czechs always say that?" That reminded me I wasn't the only one who still struggled with working with the locals.

Since, as already mentioned, I make it a habit to worry about what I'm going to have to worry about, I was mildly concerned that life was running a bit too smoothly and, sure enough, just a few days later, I realised Petra wasn't her usual bubbly self. Soon after, the cause of it became clear. One morning, we heard a load of yelling from the road outside our office and she rushed to the window, looked out, and said, "It's Milan [her 'former' boyfriend]. He's returned to Prague and is stalking me. He's found out I have been seeing Piers," which was news to me, "and now he won't leave me alone."

"Oh dear," I said, imaginatively. "What can we do? Do you want to tell him to come in and then you can discuss everything with him?"

"No, I've tried already. He'll go away eventually."

Of course, he did, since he couldn't really stand outside on Shitna all day shouting at the windows. But then he returned the following morning, and the one after that, and did exactly the same thing. Meanwhile, Piers, the main cause of the problem, from what I could understand, wanted nothing more to do with her since what had started as a fling had got way too heavy for him and he was not one for anything too serious. The result of all of that, in a very fast-forwarded version, was that within just a very few days, Petra was persuaded to go back to Milan. And since he didn't trust her to stay in Prague if he was in Bratislava, she made what seemed to me to be a huge decision, and that was to move back to Slovakia. Which meant that, in the middle of October, our lovely Petra handed in her notice, and, while not quite 'doing a Lucie' on me, left soon after, having made it quite clear that she really wanted to be gone sooner rather than later and not get pushed into working through her notice period. And me being me – too nice for my own good – agreed that at the end of the week, she could go.

By this time, I felt I could be forgiven for not ever wanting to employ a woman again, and this feeling was reinforced when I got a letter from Jana telling me that she had just had the baby, and that she had spoken to her lawyer who had confirmed that she was entitled to a chunk of holiday pay for the time that she had worked that year, and by working, that included being on maternity leave. I was clueless about all these sorts of things at that time and immediately called Ondrej, our accountant, and he confirmed that not only was that true, but that I should be aware I would have to keep her job open the following three years, due to the Czech Republic's unbelievably antiquated maternity laws. For God's sake.

Now you can see what I mean about worrying about what I would have to worry about! I pondered where I was going to find another person in such a hurry during the following few sleepless nights and endless pounding on the treadmill early in the mornings. I also wondered whether I could murder Jana and get away with it, and then whether I could say no to any of the projects we were already working on. Clearly, Pardubice had to continue as usual, and I wouldn't want to give up on Bass or Stewart Morris, as they were our 'big clients' who gave us continued and ongoing work. I also couldn't tell Will we wouldn't be able to do the hotel job, as that was likely to be another very lucrative and interesting project. But, that said, the other, smaller projects we had on were much more doable, and besides, stopping any one of them wouldn't make a huge difference to our daily workload. As usual, I figured, we had to just keep going and see what happened!

Eventually, at 3.00 am one morning, as usual, my brain woke me up with a possible solution, and that was to ask Michael Rippon if he would be interested in us sub-contracting some of our work to him on a temporary basis, on the understanding that once we could manage it ourselves, we would take it back. That seemed to be worth a shot (and would be an amusing conversation at the very least). So, the following morning, I called Michael's company and asked to speak to him but was told that he was not available but that the receptionist could put me through to Ewan instead.

"I don't want to speak to Ewan," I said. "When will Michael be available?"

"I'm afraid I don't know," she responded. "You need to speak to Ewan."

Well, I wasn't going to do that. Instead, I called Simon.

"I'm trying to get hold of Michael Rippon," I said. "Do you have any idea where he is? The receptionist in his office didn't seem to know where he was."

"Ah," he responded. "I suppose it will come out sooner or later. Michael has left. Actually, he had a bit of a nervous breakdown and is in Switzerland in some sort of clinic, recovering."

"What?" I couldn't believe it. It wasn't so long since I had spoken to him and he had sounded fine. "Whatever has happened?"

"It's a long story. But it seems that Callum has done the dirty on him and nicked the business."

Basically, with funding from Jiří the banker and a couple of others, Callum had found himself an office, set up a new company, and had gradually been persuading all of Michael's clients and employees to desert what he said was a 'sinking ship' and instead come and work for him. And, since Michael was so often out of the office, the relationships the clients had with the employees were such that they mostly agreed to go with Callum, leaving Michael with just a few small contracts and a very expensive and unbreakable lease. Callum, in the meantime, became the big PR man about town. And someone that I, for one, would have nothing more to do with.

# Winter Creeps in

I HADN'T BEEN that close to Michael and had disliked Callum from the moment I met him so shouldn't have been too surprised that he would do something dirty but, despite that, I found the whole situation depressing. There were so many times it felt as if we were working in a place where normal laws and morals didn't count, and that made me feel uneasy.

Despite that, and while I felt very sorry for Michael, we, ourselves, benefited in a couple of different ways from his demise, the most immediate one being that not all his former employees wanted to desert Michael and work for Callum but, with no real business left, those that had wanted to stay found themselves without a job. And that meant that soon after the whole mess went public, I got a call from a Czech girl called Stepanka who had been working for Michael and was now looking for a job.

"Can you come over now?" I asked her and, after a short interview and a quick introduction to the team, Stepanka became the latest JWA girl.

Stepanka, or 'Stefi', as we called her, was a bit different to the other girls in that she was older and married, which meant, I hoped, that she wouldn't end up shagging the clients and/ or friends – although that wasn't necessarily guaranteed – with all the resulting problems that brought. Her husband worked for Jeremy, although I didn't find that out until a few months later, strangely, when she came for a drink at the Joyce with me and Annie, and Jeremy and the hubby pitched up soon after we arrived. Very odd, but also, again, very Czech. She was also the first person I had employed that had had some relevant experience, and even though I found out later that that wasn't always a good thing, in Stefi's case, it helped a lot.

Back to reasonably full strength, we went into the winter with barely a moment to spare. The races at Pardubice came and went pretty much without any major drama for a change, and, with two of the top jockeys from the UK coming over to ride English horses in the Velká Pardubická, our boxes sold out very quickly and the publicity around the event was huge. Of course, there was a lot of stress in the lead-up to the big day, not least because the lorry bringing the horses from the UK got stuck on the border with Germany for 18 hours and, somewhere along the line, the Tomašes decided it must be my responsibility to sort that out. That was fun. And then, one of the jockeys missed his planned flight and could only get to the racecourse in time for the main race if we could somehow get him from Prague to Pardubice in about half an hour (it usually took about two). I debated asking Jonathan if I could borrow Mirek to do the necessary, as that timing would be a piece of cake for him, but then decided it would be easier and safer to hire a helicopter. I kid you not. The helicopter was duly sorted, since, as I keep saying, one of the good things about working in the Czech Republic is that we can often access things that we could only dream about in 'real' life. I just regretted I hadn't gone to the airport and had a lift down on the 'heli' myself, as that would have been quite the entrance.

By this time, we were also busy working on Stewart Morris' new project, which was the reconstruction of a really beautiful Art Deco building in a tree-lined avenue in the same area as my flat, Prague 2, but in the even posher part. The building was due to be finished in the New Year and we were planning yet another big launch party, similar to the one for Pavilon, but with a very different target audience, namely, the richest people in Prague. Before getting started, though, I wanted to talk to Penelope about what had happened with Charles the investor after Jeremy's party. Unfortunately, however, before I got a chance to do that, I had a very embarrassing conversation with Stewart himself when we all turned up for our first briefing on the project.

As soon as I walked through the door of his building, I was told to go through to Stewart's office which, in itself, was unusual, as we were normally all sent straight to the meeting room, plus he always liked to keep everyone waiting for as long as possible.

"Come in, Jo," he said, waving me to a seat by his desk. "Before we meet with the others, I want to just ask you something." He looked a bit shifty. "You know that Charles is the main investor in this project?"

"Yes, I think he mentioned it," I answered, carefully.

"That means he's going to be involved in a lot of our meetings and discussions."

"Okay."

"How do you feel about it? I mean, you won't feel conflicted in any way about working for him?"

"Um, no," I responded. "Why should I be?"

"Well," he wriggled about a bit. "Charles mentioned to me that you had slept together after the party where we all met. I just wanted to make sure there wouldn't be any awkwardness between you."

"Ah, okay. Well, that's not actually true." I paused, unsure as to whether I should say anything more and decided maybe it was best not to. "But never mind, I won't have a problem working with him, don't worry."

"Good, well, sorry to bring it up. I just wanted to make sure. Let's go and meet the others and say no more about it."

That was it. To say I was furious would be an understatement, but what could I do? If I had told Stewart what had actually happened, he would either not believe me and think badly of me for making it up. Or believe it and then worry about Charles as a business partner. Neither outcome was ideal. So, for now, anyway, I figured it was best just to pretend that nothing had happened and to stay 'professional' whenever Charles and I crossed paths, which was quite often and quite difficult!

We then had the launch of Hooch on the Czech market to think about, and that turned out to be a lot of fun. One of the best things about working for Bass was that Maurice, once I got to know him, was actually very nice, and, since he was so experienced in all things marketing, he became almost a mentor for me. Whatever it was we were asked to do, he always had millions of suggestions as, when it came to promoting alcohol, he had pretty much 'been there and done that', and, while it sometimes felt as if we were simply carrying out instructions rather than being in anyway creative ourselves, we learned a huge amount. In fact, at that time, I had a bit of a 'crush' on him, as I suppose is often the case with mentor-type people, even though nothing would ever come of it. He was married and I was with Lennart. But still, it made me look forward to our meetings more than I might have done normally.

For the launch of Hooch, in addition to a pretty full-on advertising campaign that was being organised by Bass' own UK advertising agency, we were carrying out a lot of different promotional and media related activities that required a huge amount of organisation, something Magda had proved to be very good at. That meant I was able to leave her pretty much to it and only get involved when a meeting at the brewery was required or I just needed to oversee what she was doing. That was a good thing, since the combination of Stewart's property, the hotel launch in the New Year, and a few other things, meant that, as usual, I was pretty much flat out.

By November, the weather in Prague was already getting very difficult to cope with. The UK has always, of course, been notorious for the way it manages (or most often, doesn't) the snow, ice and cold, and the consequent disruption to traveling and life in general that that causes. The Czech Republic is nowhere near in the same league, but it has its own issues, which sometimes makes getting about very difficult.

What is very good in the Czech Republic (and actually Sweden too) is that cars have to get their tyres changed from summer to winter every October, and the winter tyres, especially for cars such as Harry, are incredible; you can pretty much drive about in snow and ice as if it doesn't exist, unlike in the UK, where cars have the same tyres all the year round and the only way that people can manage to drive in the snow is if they attempt to use the special snow chains that are both expensive and pretty much ineffective. Then, unlike in the UK, the gritters are in constant use in the Czech Republic, so that the main roads, especially, are kept pretty clear.

What is not so good is that the law requires that homeowners (or managers of apartment buildings), as well as shop owners/renters, keep the pavements outside their doors clear of snow at all times, which, if you ask me, is completely stupid. The consequence of that is that, while everyone goes out to shovel the snow away early in the morning, the resulting melted leftovers on the pavements often turn quickly into black ice due to the freezing conditions. There are many mornings when I walk outside the house and, the minute I step on the pavement, I fall straight down on my bum, and then slide along, colliding with others who have done the same thing, eventually skidding to a halt shortly before the entrance to the National Museum. Okay, maybe I slightly exaggerate this bit, but you get the drift, pardon the pun. In any event, it bloody hurts!

Then there is the airport, which, whilst having the very best snow-clearing equipment, in the days before it had the necessary technology had a huge problem with fog, which meant that every winter we all had stories of being diverted from landing in Prague and ending up in Vienna or Ostrava (then the armpit of the Czech Republic), or some other far-flung place.

When you take all the above into consideration, moving around more than from home to the office and back was quite a challenge, and any sort of long-distance travelling had to be considered very carefully! With Christmas just around the corner, therefore, I was getting quite stressed about how I was going to factor in a trip to the UK, either before or during, as well as one or two trips to Stockholm. I also needed to give the ladies some much-needed time off and, at the same time, manage all the work that needed to be kept moving along in readiness for the New Year. Something, I felt, was going to have to give.

"when the pilots went for their training at the Boeing head office, they forgot to show them how to land the damn thing."

Flying Here, Flying There

In the end, I decided to forego one of my planned Stockholm trips in mid-November in order to go to the UK and see my mum, and then, at the same time, to do some necessary Christmas shopping, since that still wasn't something that was easy to do in the Czech Republic. Then I planned to go to Stockholm for a few days before Christmas, fly from there to the UK on Christmas Eve, when Lennart would go to his parents, then fly back from the UK to Stockholm the day after Boxing Day, when he would be playing, and finally fly back from Stockholm to Prague after the New Year. Easy, eh? Not really!

One Friday morning in mid-November saw me setting off in Harry to the airport, in order to fly to the UK for a couple of days. Despite Harry's alarm, I didn't want to leave him outside the whole weekend, especially with the amount of snow that was being chucked down. That bit was easy enough and, having parked him in the covered carpark, I made my way very tentatively across the road to the terminal and check-in. As was usual on a Friday, I knew just about everyone in the queue and, having said my hellos and got myself upgraded, I made my way through to the duty free, with a view to stocking up on a few bits and pieces to take to the UK and leave there in readiness for Christmas. Leaving duty free with four bottles of Czech sparkling wine and two tins of Russian caviar (we did live in those days!), as well as some perfumy bits for presents, I bumped straight into Clive, who was on one of his regular trips to London and who I hadn't seen for an age.

"Josefina, you off to London? Where are you sitting?" We compared our boarding passes and realised there was something a bit odd about them as, while we had both been upgraded to business class, as usual, we appeared to be sitting in rows nine and ten, and the 'flying pub' business class section only went up to row three. Girding ourselves up for an argument, since it looked like we had been downgraded, we cheered up once we got to the boarding gate and saw parked outside one of the brand-new Boeing airplanes that had just been delivered to Czech Airlines. It was a great deal bigger than the flying pub, obviously, and, therefore, there was much more space in business class, so our little panic was over. Plus, not only was it parked, but it was dressed up with balloons and ribbons floating about from its wings, since this was going to be its inaugural flight to London. But what a day to choose! It was pouring with snow, there was ice on the runway, and it was freezing cold.

Once we got on board, jigging along to the tune of 'Jingle Bells', which was being piped through the intercom as we walked through the door, we were greeted by a stewardess who handed us a bag of goodies that included a Christmas bobble hat, which Clive immediately put on to cover his bald patch. I didn't put mine on as it would mess up my hair. We also got a Czech Airlines branded key ring and whistle – not entirely sure what that was for, but, of course, we tried it out a few times once we took off – and two mini mince pies, which we both scoffed immediately. Then we trundled off to have the wings de-iced, which burst all the balloons, before we were eventually airborne. By that time, Clive had asked various people to change seats so the two of us were able to sit together and we settled down for what we expected to be a very comfortable journey.

Our flight was made a lot more pleasant by the fact the drinks trolley was in constant use, with the stewardesses offering free sparkling wine to anyone that wanted it, and, since we were getting into the Christmas spirit, we did! Plus, what a difference there was between bumping along on the flying pub and gliding silently in a spanking new, pristine Boeing. As usual, Clive was on top form, regaling everyone around us with stories of the good old days, and some of his internal flights in Russia, where, apparently, he was once attacked by a promiscuous cockerel that had gotten out of its container on the floor next to its owner, and was, as he put it, trying to 'mount' anyone within reach, before one of the stewards managed to catch it and get it back in its cage. And then, another time, when a goat appeared on board, apparently on its own, stood in the gangway the whole journey, and then left with everyone else on landing. I have to say, you never quite know with Clive how much of anything he says is true but, after a few glasses of wine, everyone wanted to believe that it all was and was encouraging him to get more and more outrageous.

That is, until we started to near Heathrow and the pilot announced we were going to be held 'indefinitely', due to the extreme bad weather, and the whole plane went a bit quiet.

"Of course," said Clive loudly into the silence, rolling his eyes as he spoke, "It's nothing to do with the weather. It's just that when the pilots went for their training at the Boeing head office, they forgot to show them how to land the damn thing."

Round and round we went in the bright blue sky, with who-knew-what underneath the blanket of white fluffy clouds. And then, after about an hour – by which time I was desperate to go to the loo, as, I am sure, were many others, and was holding my breath, and everything else, while concentrating like mad – the pilot announced that we had now been cleared to land and we made our way downwards, bumping and lurching about as we got lower, until we broke through the now dark grey clouds and saw the tarmac straight underneath us. At which point, the wheels touched down and then, suddenly, the plane accelerated and up we started to climb again.

"Ah, you see, that was just a test run," said Clive, again guffawing away with a mad look about him, then giving a few blasts on his whistle. I'm afraid that no-one, not even me, found him amusing by that point. Thankfully, my own source of concern – the need to pee – was alleviated by the stewardess saying we could leave our seats momentarily, as we were going to be held again until the weather calmed down and we could attempt another landing, so that was something. Shortly after that, round we went again, and this time, once we touched down, we stayed down – skidding about a bit – but landed, nonetheless.

Unfortunately, by the time we got off and through customs we were three hours later than we should have been. Which meant that, by the time I got to Mum's place – needless to say, in the pouring rain – the day was over with and all there was time for was a chat, a bit of dinner, then bed. Saturday, then, was full-on with shopping, before I headed back to the bloody airport again for the flight out on Sunday afternoon. And since, from what I had heard, the weather was still vile in Prague, it was no surprise to find the flight out was delayed. *Bugger*.

We eventually took off at 5.00 pm UK time, instead of 2.00 pm, and this time the atmosphere on the plane was subdued, even though there were many of the same people on board as the flight out on Friday. Thankfully, Clive was due to fly the next day – I wasn't feeling very chatty – and he would definitely have led me astray on the booze front! That said, there were a few others I knew, including Maurice from Bass, who was skulking at the back with, he said, a humungous hangover, having been to a press do in London the previous night.

The flight was uneventful, and it wasn't until we started our descent towards Prague that I started to become apprehensive, having overheard one of the stewardesses saying something about Vienna. And, sure enough, just minutes away from landing, or so it seemed, the pilot came on the intercom to announce that the weather in Prague was getting worse and worse and, guess what, we were heading to Vienna.

One hour later, pretty much on the dot of 8.30 pm, we landed in Vienna and were shunted off and told to wait in the transfer lounge while they decided what to do with us. Shortly after that, and thankfully, given the circumstances, rather than being put onto a coach to take us straight home, we were taken by an airport bus to a very shabby hotel just outside the airport, where we would stay overnight and then be sent back to Prague on the first flight out the next morning.

There was only one thing for it, as usual. Once I had hooked up with Maurice and we had sorted out our rooms – mine was a horrible little box with just a single bed, a small wardrobe and a desk with a very sad looking tube of peanuts displayed nicely in the middle – the only way to deal with the whole situation was to go to the bar and get very drunk. And then, after about the fifth glass of vile red wine on my part, and about a bottle of scotch on his, something very weird and worrying happened. We were in the middle of a discussion about relationships. I was telling him about the impossible situation that Lennart and I were in and he was

304

telling me that his wife didn't like living in Prague and was heading back to the UK soon. He thought, probably, that that would be it between them as they had been heading that way for a while. Suddenly, the air about us crackled a bit and we both started to get a bit twitchy, and then he was leaning towards me looking as if he was going in for a kiss. And I was thinking I wouldn't mind that one bit. But then, thank God – and everyone else – at the very last minute I saw sense and called a halt to the proceedings in a very indelicate way, basically just turning my head away, lurching to my feet and saying, "Sorry, Maurice, I have to go now," and rushed off to my room.

Then, in the morning, after just three hours sleep, and on a very silent trip back to Prague when the two of us barely spoke, I played the game Jeremy had taught me once, which is to mutter as many swear words to myself for as long as possible without drawing breath. I did that for a good while, all the time wondering whatever was going to happen next.

"Not everyone wants to get their jigger out in public, let alone in the freezing cold and on skis!"

Thank God for Christmas

It MUST BE SAID this was definitely one of those years when I said many times, 'Thank God for Christmas,' even though it's not a time of year I usually look forward to. The whole lead up to the holidays was full-on, particularly as I was spending a lot of time with Will putting together the PR strategy to support his advertising campaign for the newly branded hotel, which would kick off straight after Christmas. The reconstruction was well underway and so far, everything was going smoothly. All we were waiting for was confirmation from the owner that the date for our planned press conference to launch the whole thing worked for him, and then we would be off and running.

In addition to that, we were in and out of Stewart Morris' offices on an almost weekly basis, as his residential building was due to be completed in the spring but was still looking like a construction site, as was most of Prague, to be fair. At that time, you could barely walk down the street without coming across a building in the process of either being pulled down or rebuilt, since, with all of the restitutions taking place, and the number of developers and investors flooding into the country, just about every decent property was on the market, or changing hands fast. Stewart's work itself was going okay, but the meetings were always a bit tricky, especially as Charles the investor liked to make me feel uncomfortable at every opportunity. And then, along similar lines, Maurice, who has always had his difficult moments, had become even more demanding since our Vienna experience. I'm not sure if that was because of my behaviour that night or his marital situation but, either way, I was apprehensive every time I headed to a meeting at the brewery, and since the work for Bass was piling up, that was pretty often.

Added to all of that, it being December there were parties most evenings, kicking off with the annual British Embassy bash, where just about everyone that was anyone turned out. That was swiftly followed by Clive hosting another of his annual parties in the same venue as previous years. I flirted outrageously with Jeremy – for old-times' sake – danced like a lunatic with Ewan – also for old times' sake – and then managed to persuade myself to leave alone and make the requisite call to Lennart, who, even though it was way later than usual, was also home alone and awake. Then there was what I regarded as the highlight of the party season – if nothing else, because it was so bizarre – which was the do that was organised by Jonathan in the new Italian restaurant across the road from his flat.

The restaurant itself was nothing special; a big square room with white walls lined with shelves of Italian wines and memorabilia, and wooden floorboards that, for some reason, made the whole place echo horribly. The food was amazing though, and since opening, it had become one of *the* new places to eat. It's possible – I never knew for sure, though – that Jonathan had invested in the restaurant as it was all to his taste, and he was good friends with the owner. Either way, it was a great place for him to host a Christmas bash. What was strange, though, was that the invitation stated that the dress code was formal and that we should all arrive for drinks at 7.00 pm, but that we should also bring warm outdoor clothing with us.

That was easy enough for me since the restaurant wasn't just across the road from Jonathan's flat, but mine too, both of us being in the same building. So, having got done up in my favourite little black dress and high heeled black court shoes – I wouldn't have to walk far, so could actually suffer decent shoes for one evening – I slung on my (fake) fur coat and gathered together my woolly boots, gloves and scarf for whatever we were going to need them for later, and tottered in the snow and ice across to the restaurant.

Jonathan, as mentioned previously, while not always being popular with everyone, knew a lot of people. However, as the restaurant wasn't so big, he had invited just his closest friends, which meant 'old timers', such as Katy, Ewan, Jeremy, Simon, Francesca and myself, and just a handful of business contacts that included Clive, Stewart Morris and his 'partner' – a very hard-looking Czech woman I later found out was his 'partner' in more ways than one – and my now good friend as well as client, Kumar, who I had been working for on and off ever since we started, and who it was rare to see anywhere out and about other than in one of his own restaurants. Drinks, then, were duly served, and, since it was Jonathan, that meant real champagne, as well as delicious red wine that was so easy to drink it was hard to stop, along with a lot of antipasti. Then, about an hour or so into the evening, a bell was rung and one of Jonathan's people announced we should all collect our warm clothes and make our way outside.

I have to say, no-one was overly keen on heading out, especially when we were led around the corner from the restaurant and started walking down the road that led to one of the pretty small parks that are dotted about throughout Prague 2. But who wants to visit a pretty park when it's freezing cold, snowing and pitch black? But, you know, no-one argues with Jonathan, so we all slithered and tottered along the road and down the path that led into the main open area, where two big flood lights lit up a space that had been set up with lines of chairs we were told to sit down on. Then, once everyone had taken their seats and, while we all muttered about what might or might not happen next, out of the darkness to the side of where we were sitting came a row of ethereal and shadowy figures which, as they got nearer and into the light, turned out to be about eight elderly men skiing in single file, all naked.

"Cover your eyes, girls," said Jeremy to Katy and me; we were sitting on either side of him. "This is not something you should be looking at."

What followed next is hard to describe. It was a kind of acrobatics show on skis that went on for about 15 minutes, with no accompaniment, just the silence of the snow and cold and the occasional muffled snort as one or other of us tried desperately not to collapse into laughter. You couldn't really see the faces of the skiers, since the light from the spots kind of reflected off the snow, so they could have been anyone, but I don't really want to think about the possibility of one or other of them, potentially, being someone I knew! And you couldn't really see anything else, if you get my drift, since it was way too cold for a normal guy to be outside waving his doodah around. But the kind of 'show' they put on was clearly quite skilful, bearing in mind they were balancing all their movements on thin cross-country skis. It was, however, utterly random. And when, at the end, they all formed a line and took a bow, before turning and skiing off into the darkness again, the light reflecting off the row of naked white buttocks, well, near hysteria broke out. Clive, of course, was nearly apoplectic.

"Good Lord," he spluttered. "I haven't seen so many white arses in a row since I was in the showers at Westminster. Hats off to them. Not everyone wants to get their jigger out in public, let alone in the freezing cold and on skis!"

"Presumably they were paid to do it," responded Jeremy wryly.

"Jeremy, my dear boy. I love to ski, as you know, and as you do yourself. But really, how much would I or you need to be paid to get our todgers out and put on a performance like that? In my own case, I'm sure even Jonny couldn't afford it!"

What Jonny could afford though, was a magnificent spread to warm us all up once we had gathered ourselves together and staggered back to the restaurant. And, from then on, the evening followed the more normal format of drinking as much as humanely possible, eating in between, and then dancing until the early hours. The only disappointing part was that the skiers never returned in their civvies so we could find out who they were and whatever gave them the idea for the performance. Maybe that was a good thing.

Snow, Ice and a Miserable Start to the New Year

I HEADED OFF to Sweden for the first part of the Christmas holiday shortly after. I was having mixed feelings as I packed everything up and got ready to go, mainly as I was feeling guilty that I wasn't going to be spending as much time with Mum as usual. But once I landed in Stockholm airport and headed into town on the bus, I was glad to be there. I was enjoying the Christmas decorations everywhere and tried to ignore the fact that it was already pitch black at 3.00 pm and really bloody cold.

Despite spending so much time apart, Lennart and I always got on very well when we were together and, even though I'm not a very trusting sort of woman when it comes to men – which is hardly surprising when you consider some of what had gone before – I never thought he was off gallivanting with other ladies when I wasn't there. If anything, I was more jealous of his ice hockey and the fact that always came first, so when he told me that the Prague team we had met when he was over had made him an offer to play for them, my initial reaction was maybe a bit less enthusiastic than he might have expected. On the one hand, it would be amazing for him to be living in the Czech Republic, presumably with me, but who knew how that might turn out. On the other hand, I still wouldn't see him that much as the hockey would still be claiming him at all hours. Plus, I would have the 'burden' of him living there with me and having to manage everything that would entail, as well as my own fairly manic life. This was not, we both agreed, something to rush into, but since the club needed an answer soon, we agreed we would think about it over the Christmas period and come to some kind of a conclusion before I headed back in the New Year.

The few days I spent in the UK were lovely. I saw lots of old friends, spent time with Mum and behaved impeccably (which is not something I can always say, since, in a normal mother and daughter way, we do seem to rub each other up the wrong way on a regular basis). Then I was back in Stockholm for New Year's Eve, which we spent with Bjørn and his family in their wonderful house out in the Swedish countryside. Surrounded by pine forests, and with a garden that slopes down to the beach and the sea (completely covered in ice at that time), the house was a big Swedish chalet painted light blue and white and with a lot of open plan space and huge windows that make it very light and airy. We had visited a few times in the summer and often spent our afternoons out on the water in Bjørn's boat, fishing for herring. I found this to be a bit of a barbaric experience as you basically just hang these little rods with wires and bait attached over the edge, jig them about a bit, and then wait for the herring to grab hold of the wires. Then you pull the rods back into the boat and kill all the herrings that are hanging from them by squeezing their heads as you pull them off the wires. *Yuck.* I couldn't bring myself to do it but was more than happy to eat them once they had been cleaned up and served with some special Swedish mustard. *Delicious.* You wouldn't, however, want to be out on a boat in the winter. Indeed, you can see some of the big ferries that sail between Sweden and Finland – booze cruises where all the Swedes go to buy enormous amounts of alcohol abroad to stash away – from Bjørn's house and, on New Year's Eve, they were literally ploughing their way through ice as we watched them plodding past.

New Year's Eve itself was fantastic. Some friends of Bjørn's joined us and loads of amazing food was served up by Bjørn's wife, Ritva, plus, of course, copious amounts of alcohol, until the early morning. And then, just a few hours after we had gone to bed, we were all woken up to go cross country skiing. Thankfully, not naked. Now, I am, of course, British (ish) and, as such, I've had only a limited amount of skiing experience. In fact, before I came to Prague, I had only tried it a few times on the artificial ski run that was built just outside Tunbridge Wells to accommodate all the luvvies that like to head off to Kitzbühel, or wherever, in the winter and need to train in advance. We were never part of that group, needless to say! And then, after that, I went on a couple of trips to Austria and had a few odd days here and there on the Czech mountains. The Scandinavians though, like the Czechs, are all more or less born on skis, and Lennart, while being a devil on skates,

312

managed skis just as well, and so the idea of all of us heading out with our hangovers at the crack of dawn was not quite my idea of fun.

I like to think I'm good at all sports though, and I definitely wasn't going to bottle out, so, having been given some slightly large ski boots to put on, and various other bits of ski wear, I joined up with the others as we skied straight out the back door, across the garden and out into the absolutely amazing pine forests where the trails ran for miles, and every few minutes we jumped out of our skins as a huge elk, or similar, crashed out of the trees and crossed the path right in front of us. It was just beautiful. The air was so crisp it killed off our hangovers as we breathed it in, and the snow dripped from the pine needles and muffled all sound as we whooshed across the pathways with just a dim early morning light peeping through the treetops. Like all sport, of course, cross country skiing, while looking relatively easy when you watch it on the telly, is a lot more difficult than it seems. I mentally took my hat off to Vladimir as all the squats and lunges I'd been doing for months on end paid off and I managed not to look like a complete and utter prat, even if I couldn't always keep up with the others. Running up hills is not my favourite thing at the best of times, but trying to do it on cross country skis? Is there anything as awful or as difficult?

Anyway, after about two hours out on the tracks, we headed back to the house, where, as per tradition – and God, these Scandinavians are as bad as the Czechs when it comes to getting their kit off – everyone had to strip off and get into the huge sauna that takes over half of Bjørn's basement (by 'everyone', I mean Bjørn, Lennart and Ritva, as their friends had headed off to do their own thing). But, despite us all knowing each other so well, I still felt uncomfortable relaxing naked in such a confined space with someone who was once a client sitting there in the buff; I doubt that that will ever change. I therefore wrapped myself in a sheet and sweated out the aches and pains just as effectively until, horror of horrors, Bjørn announced that we would all now leave the sauna, run through the garden, and jump in the swimming pool. Tradition required, apparently, that we do it naked and then dive through the thin sheet of ice that covered the pool. And that, I'm afraid, is when I said, 'enough is enough' and took myself off to the warmth of the kitchen, trying not to look as the three of them hurtled across the snow and disappeared into the pool. Raving lunatics, the lot of them!

Maybe they had a point, though, since the following morning I could barely walk, while the others announced they were completely fine. Whether it was the sauna, the ice bath, or just their years of skiing experience, I don't know, but I still cannot imagine a time when I will willingly cavort about naked in the snow and jump into a pool full of ice. I've had many opportunities since then but have always turned them down, plus I have had a few other rather hideous sauna experiences that I'm saving for later!

Having left Bjørn's house in the afternoon, the two of us then spent the evening having dinner and discussing what we might or might not do with our lives. I have to say I hadn't really thought it all through too much in the past week or so, and whenever I tried, I ran up against a bit of a brick wall. It seemed Lennart had though and, while I kind of agreed with what he had to say, it wasn't really what I expected.

"You know, Yo Hanna, I love being with you and I could see us making a great life for ourselves if you came to live here in Stockholm. But I just can't see myself in Prague. I don't speak the language, I won't earn anywhere near as much money, and I don't have so many more years that I will be playing. If I retired after that, and then stayed living in Prague, what would I do?"

"I understand," I responded. "But I can't see how I could move to Stockholm and still run my business. And I couldn't do what I do in Prague here. What would *I* do if I moved here? Wind my company up and start all over again? Or just wind the company up, move here and do nothing?"

"Well," he said. "You could. I mean, we don't need the money. And maybe you could help with our marketing here or something?"

The thing was, I completely got what he was saying, which is basically why I didn't want to give it all too much thought, even though I knew it needed to be discussed. Probably if I hadn't spent the last couple of years building up something that was starting to become really good and that I was very proud of, I might have agreed to give moving to Stockholm a go. But the idea of just throwing my Prague life away and then taking on a job or, worse, being a housewife? Well, I just couldn't see it. And if the two of us couldn't find a way to make our relationship work in the long term, then was it even worth us continuing? I wasn't sure.

Our last evening was sad. And by the time I had flown home, I knew what I had to do.

"A little bird told me you used to
be a very good tennis player."

 # January Blues

I LANDED BACK in Prague on the afternoon of January 2nd. It was bitterly cold. I thought Stockholm was bad, but the Czech Republic in January can be absolutely unbearable. I collected Harry from the carpark and checked, as I always did after the tyre slashing incident, that everything was still intact – thankfully, it was – and then drove to my flat, let myself in and sat staring out the window, wondering if the decision I had made was the right one. Did I really want to stay in this sometimes impossible and complicated country, battling with endless difficult clients, continuing with the problems I had with everyone I employed and the amount of work I had to do just to break even, let alone make any money? Wouldn't it be easier just to say yes to Lennart, that I would come and live in Stockholm and do whatever job I could find or, God forbid, start a family? That really wasn't on my agenda at that point, even though I was 'getting on a bit'? Okay, we would have plenty of money, and all that went along with that. But I needed to use my brain, I needed the stress, the challenges, the drama. I just couldn't see how I could have any of that there. And to continue commuting between the two countries, keeping the relationship going, even though we had no real plan for the future, and spending lots of money and time doing it whilst foregoing meeting anyone else in the meantime? What was the point?

Eventually, and with a heavy heart, I took a bit of a coward's way out and, instead of phoning Lennart, I wrote him a letter where I tried to explain all of this and told him that it would be better if we didn't speak or see each other again as that would be the only way to really break up. Then I went to the office and faxed it to his home fax machine before I could have second thoughts, and then spent most evenings for the next few weeks sitting by the phone and hoping he would ring. He never did.

To say I had the blues would be an understatement. I went to the gym every morning and trained very hard. Vladimir tried shouting at me to make me angry, being sympathetic to make me cry, all the while pushing me harder and harder. He even suggested I take part in a running race, or do a fitness competition, or just do something, anything, to snap me out of my depression. Simon took me out for lunch and tried to encourage me to drink, even though he himself was temporarily on the wagon. Ewan turned up at the office regularly to make me laugh, and even Jeremy popped around to the flat a couple of times, presumably to see if a shag would help (no, we didn't find out). Nothing really worked. Even the girls in the office tried hard to cheer me up and worked harder than ever, as did I, but I just couldn't snap out of what I can only call my misery.

And then, one morning in January, I bumped into Jacob the accountant as I was walking to a meeting and stopped for a quick chat. I later found out that he, like everyone else, knew I was in a black funk, and the reason for it.

"A little bird told me you used to be a very good tennis player," he said. "Do you ever play now?" It took me by surprise. I couldn't remember ever having mentioned that to anyone in this, my new life in Prague. "Well, no," I said. "I haven't played for years. It's so difficult to find good people to play with and over here, I wouldn't even know where to start."

"But this is the 'home of tennis'," he responded. "Everyone plays. I joined the club down by the Hilton a few months ago and started playing regularly. Why don't you join too?"

Well, I thought, *no harm in investigating*, and as soon as I got back to the office, I asked Magda to find the number and give them a call to find out what the membership terms were, and whether they might have a coach that could speak English. After some confusion, Magda came in to tell me the only club 'by the Hilton' she could find was the National Tennis Centre, and obviously, it couldn't be that one. But then I checked with Jacob, and he said yes, that was it (which was typical of him; only the best will ever do). In the end, and after I had lost my nerve for a few days, my first training was set up for that Saturday with someone called Václav Neuman. I remember thinking too that if I didn't join the club, I wouldn't keep it up, so my membership had also been sorted out for the princely sum of Kč 8,000 a year (about £160 at that time, imagine!).

That Saturday morning, therefore, instead of being in Stockholm, as was originally planned, and whilst trying not to think about that, I got myself dressed up in my warmest gym gear – I imagined it would be very cold inside the stadium, or wherever we were going to play – got into Harry, and drove down to the club in what can only be described as a state of sheer terror.

Having parked around the back, and noticing all the huge Mercedes, Range Rovers and sports cars that took up most of the carpark, I walked into the main reception area. Sitting at the desk was a tall, blonde woman with pretty much the biggest boobs I'd ever seen hanging out of her very tight white T-shirt, who stared at me as if I had crawled out of the nearest bushes and asked in a very rude way, in Czech, what I wanted. I explained I had come for a lesson with Václav Neuman and she told me I would find him sitting outside the restaurant. But, as I started to walk the way she pointed, she called me back, telling me I had to pay before I could go and play.

"I'm a member," I said in my best Czech.

"What?" she responded, in her worst.

"A member. Of the club?"

"Yes, so? You still have to pay."

"Ah, okay. How much?"

"200 crowns for the court. In cash." It was about four quid. Was the money really worth being that rude for? Probably not. I handed the cash over. "Can I go now?" I asked, thinking it would be really amusing to lean over and pour the bottle of very cold water I had brought with me down her cleavage. I refrained.

I walked outside, not really knowing what to expect, as I had jumped right into the tennis idea without giving it much thought. But the way the big clubs manage in the winter in the Czech Republic, and elsewhere in Europe – just not the UK, which is one of the reasons we are so crap at it, dare I say – is to cover all the tennis courts with big white tent-like structures called 'bubbles' that are lit and heated and allow everyone to continue playing on exactly the same courts all the year around; I was heading into one of those now. But first, I had to find Mr Neuman.

That wasn't difficult, since the restaurant was right there and sitting outside the main door smoking a cigarette, was a very fit looking and overly sun-tanned, even in the middle of winter, guy of about 40, dressed in tennis gear and holding a bag of rackets and a basket of balls, looking about as friendly as a Doberman Pinscher.

"Are you Václav?"

"Yes, you must be Mrs Weaver. Let's go." And up he got, striding off towards the row of bubbles ahead of us while I followed meekly about a metre behind.

To get into the 'bubble' itself, then, you had to go through one of those revolving door type structures, which Václav shot through, chucking his fag end into the grass behind him as he went. I followed, struggling to push the door around as it weighed a ton. Then we were inside this 'bubble', which was brightly lit, quite warm, and covering one of the red clay courts that are the norm in Europe. I, however, had never been on a red clay court before in my life.

To each side of the net were park-like benches, divided by a high-chair that would, presumably, accommodate an umpire, should such a thing be required. Václav marched to one of the benches and dumped his gear onto it. I realised I should probably put my stuff on the other one (I later found out it is really 'not on' to share a bench; I did that bit right, at least). Then he walked to the net and waited with the basket of balls while I took my various jackets off and took out my racket. Václav looked me up and down.

"Those are the wrong shoes," he said, looking down at my trainers. "You can play in them today, but you shouldn't really be wearing them, you need to buy new 'clay court' shoes before you come again."

Who knew?! Clay court shoes. I doubt anyone in the UK at that time had ever heard of such things!

"And that racket, you'll need to replace it. I'll get you a proper one for next time, but you can play with one of mine for now."

320

Bloody hell. Talk about putting someone at their ease! By this time, I was wondering whether I should just walk off the court and say, 'Forget it,' or burst into tears. Either way, I was pretty sure there was very little chance I would actually be able to hit a ball, if we even got that far.

If you've ever played tennis, you'll know that nerves have a very funny effect on your playing arm (well, your whole body really) and the reason today's tennis players do all sorts of weird and wonderful stretches, arm whirling and arse-scratching when they're about to start a match, or even an important point, is not to warm up, since they have already done that, but more to loosen their muscles and get rid of nerves. I'm sure you can imagine, therefore, just how badly I hit the first few balls that came flying over the net at me once Václav got going. It was as if I had never played tennis before, and I reflected on the big build up Magda had given the club about my level when I first registered and thought I may never live it down!

But then, after about half an hour, something weird happened. My body suddenly remembered how to play the damn game and my eyes began to work out how to see the ball when it bounced on the very peculiar surface that is clay. And just as Václav was starting to count the minutes before he could get off the court, the balls started to fly. In the right direction.

"Mrs Weaver," he said as we finished the hour, collected the balls and 'swept the court' (yes, clay courts are swept, something else no-one told me). "You can play. We have some things to work on, but you definitely have potential."

"Thank you!" I responded with a big grin on my face. "But just one thing. Please call me 'Jo'. Or 'Joanna' if you prefer. Everyone else does."

Then we walked off together; him to go back to the restaurant with barely a goodbye, and me to waltz off past the slapper in the reception without saying a word and to go home feeling like a new woman. Nothing like whacking a few balls to start the healing process!

At home that evening, I pondered why playing tennis should have been such a catalyst to making me feel so much better, which then turned into quite a bit of a self-assessment. I reflected on the person I had been when I first turned up in Prague and thought that, generally, I was not so different now. But my year with Lennart, and the resulting end of the relationship, had taught me quite a lot about myself. On one hand, I was a bit of a nutcase, and that hadn't really changed, although I could, I now knew, enjoy myself without getting completely wasted or dancing like a lunatic, or both. And while I was a terrible flirt, I knew I could be faithful to one guy, even when surrounded by temptation and given ample opportunity. That was a good thing, since I was always a bit hung up on my inability to commit, due, no doubt, to my dad dying young, and a few other connected things. And then there was work which, when I first arrived in Prague, I treated purely as a means to earning money, and which I worked bloody hard at. But now I knew I could work just as hard, or even harder, because I loved what I was doing and didn't want to give that up. And even though I grumbled about everything Czech, I realised that I must, in fact, like the place a lot more than I gave it credit for since, when the crunch came, I didn't want to leave. Was that just because of my company? Not really. I think it ran deeper than that; the amazing friends I had made had become family, something I was sorely lacking. And the fact I had Central Europe in my blood. Maybe I even felt at home there. *Strange*.

Hotel Libya

YOU MAY HAVE noticed by now that I don't really do things by halves. Once I get into something, I have to do it full-on, and then I want it all to fall into place straightaway. I suspect that my new thing for tennis had been amplified by my general sadness about Lennart, which meant I threw myself into it as if it was the 'new sex'. After getting my kit sorted out, I set up regular trainings with Václav – Tuesday and Thursday evenings at 7.00 pm and Sunday mornings at 11.00 am – and that was it. When I wasn't working, I was boring everyone about tennis, watching whichever tournaments I could find on Czech TV – which, actually, was a good thing, as they showed quite a lot and everything else they put out was absolute rubbish – thinking about tennis, and even keeping my tennis racket under the pillow. Okay, I wasn't actually doing that, I'm exaggerating. But I probably would have done if I wasn't such a bad sleeper!

The terrible cow in the club reception continued to be rude and unfriendly and had what was a bit of a bad Czech trait in those days, which was absolutely no power of recognition. It was pretty common for most waiters, receptionists, taxi drivers and so on, who you might have met many times before, to act as if you were a complete stranger every time you entered their restaurant or whatever, and she was an expert at it. Whenever I arrived at the club, I had a bit of a *Groundhog Day* moment when she asked me what I wanted, I said I was there to see Václav Neuman, and so on. And she always, of course, made sure I coughed up before I was allowed out to the courts. I eventually worked out that the problem was a combination of my being foreign and my being a woman, since she clearly wasn't quite as unfriendly (understatement of the day) to some of the guys I started to meet who also trained there. Need I say more…

Then there was Václav, who I was determined to eventually break; first by getting him to call me 'Jo' or 'Joanna' instead of 'Mrs Weaver' (which only took him about ten years) and second, by

323

making him laugh occasionally (which took longer). But that was okay, I kind of got used to him, and anyway, it didn't matter, since my tennis was getting better and better. I just loved it! And then there was the added bonus of this being *the* tennis club, and, as such, it was where many of the top players from around the country came to train. I became almost blasé about all the famous faces I would see in the restaurant – not that I ever went in there to eat or drink, that was way too scary, but I did occasionally use the loo – or sometimes, on the courts next to me. I even bumped into Martina Navratilova one day when she was on an unofficial trip to Prague and opened the door for her as I was leaving, without even realising who she was until I got into the car. Thrilling.

All of this meant, of course, that my heart started to heal, and I no longer mooned about at home late in the evening, waiting to see if the phone would ever ring again, or berating myself for making such a bad decision. Plus, all this tennis, combined with the training I was doing with Vladimir, meant I was getting even fitter. And fitter meant thinner! And who doesn't like that!

On the work front, too, I needed to be on good form since things were, as ever, getting a bit complicated. The first real drama of the year was the press conference to announce the opening of the newly refurbished former Forex Hotel, now the Revolution Tower Hotel, which we had worked on for months and which the owner was flying in for. In case you don't know, for a PR agency, organising a press conference is a very stressful thing in its own right. First of all, we put together a list of all the different media we would like to attend, from newspapers to magazines, radio, TV and so on. Then we send invitations to all the journalists, giving them the requisite information, particularly the fact that there will be free food and drink – which is generally the most important part, especially the drink – and add in a 'teaser' that one or two very interesting people will be speaking from the hosts' side (even when, as often happens, they are not at all interesting, and which can then be a problem that the agency is, apparently, responsible for).

Then, in the weeks leading up to the event, our job, in addition to the general organisation, is to call each of the journalists that have been invited and try to persuade them through things like blackmail, threats or offering them nights out with a member of our team of their choice, to actually attend. And that is the most important bit, since the success, or otherwise, of our work will be assessed based on how many journalists really do show up, at least in most cases. Some companies are more interested in the amount of actual press coverage the conference generates, but not many!

With this particular press conference, that was our first real problem. Once we started calling, we could tell that the media were not overly interested in this unknown foreign company buying an old communist hotel. They wanted more 'meat' to tempt them. And since, for them, 'meat' meant scandal, some of them thought they ought to do a bit of digging about before committing to attend; but we didn't know that at the time. And then there was the Maltese owner's ego, since he had told Will that if we didn't have at least one TV camera there, we would all be fired.

"The thing is, Will," I said when we discussed this latest problem, "from what I understand, Czech TV is nearly bankrupt and there is no way they are going to go to the expense of sending out a crew to televise this type of event, unless we offer them something earth-shattering to discuss."

"Could we offer to pay them?" he suggested, scratching his beard.

"But that would cost a fortune," I responded, "and even then, there would be no guarantee that they would come." We stared into our mugs of tea.

"How about this," he said, with a wicked smile. "Why don't we get Michel [his partner], to dress up as a TV journalist and then we find a man with a big camera that can come along and pretend to be filming. No-one will know any different!"

"Genius," I responded. And that is what we did.

By the day of the press conference, which we organised in a nice room in a hotel just around the corner from the Forex, we had a reasonable number of journalists confirmed, plus I had persuaded Ewan and some of his team to come along and act in a 'journalistic way'. That basically meant listening very intently, not saying a word, and then eating as much of the food as they wanted afterwards, although we restricted them from drinking too much as we felt they might then e accidentally give the game away. The room looked great, all the materials were translated and printed out ready, and we had a big pile of goodie bags to hand out that were full of Maltese gimmicks, including rather interestingly shaped small leather maracas (a set of which I planned to nick to give to Clive, since they would be right up his street!). As the journalists filed in and the speakers and their supporting people arrived and took their seats, it all looked as if it was going to go very well.

Pavel, a very nice young guy I had sat next to on the flying pub one day acted at a translator/ moderator and made a nice introductory speech to the hotel guys. His real job was to write about Czech rock music for an English music magazine. Can you imagine, Czech rock music? If there is one thing that the Czechs should never, ever do, it is to make that awful racket. He was followed by Manolo, a Maltese marketing guru I had met a few times in Prague by then, who gave an impressive explanation of why they had chosen to buy this particular hotel, why Prague, and so on. It was all very good and professional. Then the owner took over and gushed a bit more about how he had always wanted to buy a hotel in Prague – ever since he had visited in the 80s with his wife and they found it to be the most romantic place on earth – and now his dream was coming true. It all sounded great. Finally, after almost too long, Pavel invited the journalists to ask questions. The first hand went up and a middle-aged, sour-faced scruff of a man, who announced that he worked for the main daily newspaper said, "Can I ask you, Mr Morani, how you are financing the purchase of the hotel? There's a rumour you will be using Libyan money?"

Mr Morani's face turned a nasty colour of pink. "Well, that is a completely untrue rumour," he responded, scratching his moustache a bit nervously. "We are mostly financing the purchase ourselves from our own family company. Of course, we have a few other investors as well, but to say that we're using Libyan money is completely wrong."

"I have a print-out here of the investors that are listed as owning the operating company and, having checked them out, I think it would be safe to say they're Libyan nationals."

"Utter rubbish," Mr Morani responded, his face turning from pink to red. "That must be fake. Our investors are not listed anywhere publicly and, even if they were, there would be nothing available that would prove they were Libyan or Maltese, or anything else. Sorry, gentlemen, there will be no further questions."

And with that, Mr Morani, Manolo, and the supporting team gathered their things and stood up to leave, while Will and the rest of us sat wondering what on earth we should do next.

As it turned out, we didn't need to do a lot. The journalists helped themselves to the food, drink and goodie bags and hustled out. We cleared everything up. Then we went back to our respective offices and waited to see what the fallout would be. The good news was that Mr Morani and his merry men were reasonably okay about it all, saying it was all rubbish and the journalist had clearly been a trouble maker.

"My main concern," Mr Morani said on his call to me later that afternoon, "is that the TV was filming the whole event, and it would be very damaging to us to have something like this talked about at a national level. Can you try to stop it, Joanna?"

"Yes, of course. I will try to speak to them as soon as I get back to the office."

The bad news was that the following morning, most of the Czech newspapers led with the headline 'Forex Hotel bought by Libyans' and the statement that, due to their own embargo against any of their nationals doing any sort of business with anything Libyan, the American Embassy had immediately announced that they would be boycotting the hotel from the minute it opened its doors. Frankly, I was surprised there wasn't a photo of Colonel Gaddafi himself sitting at the bar. But there was time for that later.

"Unfortunately, Mr XX is unable to attend. He has been to a function this afternoon and is too drunk to even walk."

Fit for a Minister?

THE RUMBLING FROM the press conference and the fallout regarding the new 'Libyan Hotel' continued full-speed ahead, to the point I soon started to consider putting 'crisis queen' on my business cards, as it seemed that of the very few PR people there were in Prague at that time, I was fast gathering more experience than anyone else in the art of 'crisis management'. Something that stood me in very good stead for later!

I had earned a lot of brownie points from Mr Morani for 'stopping the TV from showing the press conference', although, if he is reading this now, he knows the truth! But, anyway, at that time he was very happy for me to continue managing what turned into an ongoing and difficult problem, especially when the hotel finally opened its doors, and the media went to town on the alleged Libyan connection. At one point, it got so bad I thought we might even have an embargo placed on us ourselves, since we were supposedly 'trading with a Libyan entity' but, as was common with these things, it was all very selective. On the one hand, whenever I told people I worked for the hotel, they came out with all sorts of, 'How could you work for a Libyan company?' rubbish, but then, when we invited them to events there – and we did, a lot, in order to encourage people to come and see just how fantastic the restaurants, the spa and so on were – they all turned out in force. It's that free food and drink thing again! Works every time.

One evening we organised a 'black tie' concert in the hotel's amazing high-tech – for those days – conference room, where we had a well-known violinist performing with a string quartet for an hour, and then a gala dinner to follow for the 'select few'. Through the violinist, we were able to get to a senior politician and soon to be Czech President – here I go again with the 'anything is possible in the Czech Republic' stories – who had promised to attend. Once that news came out, the media were all onto us begging for tickets, so we carefully selected those that could come on the basis that they had to promise us that they would write something positive about the hotel and not mention Libya. And then, in addition to Will and some of my friends, we had a few of the European ambassadors, including the British one, booked to turn up. He was clearly in two minds as to whether he should show up on the basis that, if the company was Maltese, they deserved his full support, but if they were Libyan, then the same probably applied, but he should be a bit less visible about it!

Everything was set up and ready well in advance of the politician arriving. The conference room looked amazing, plus it had the kind of technology that no-one had ever even seen before in the Czech Republic: large TV screens showing what was happening on the stage and amazing lighting that could stream different colours and patterns onto the walls. Plus, the tables were dressed with gorgeous flowers and candles that, once lit, made the room look almost magical. The whole place really looked 'fit for a queen' – or a politician – and so, once we were set, and the musicians were doing a last sound check, my ladies headed off and I hurried to get ready in the room I had been given to use for the night. And then, ten minutes before the politician was due to arrive, I met with the new GM, a very charismatic German – aren't they all (the GMs, I mean, not necessarily the Germans) – called Franz, who told me to go outside and wait to greet him.

Except, in the middle of all the different dignitaries and guests arriving, and being swept upstairs by members of the hotel staff for drinks in the room adjoining the main conference hall, and at about the time when the cars should have been arriving with the politician and his entourage, just one big Audi came hurtling down the drive, screeching to a halt in the middle of everything. Out jumped two smartly dressed young guys, presumably bodyguards, who rushed up to us and said, "Unfortunately, Mr XX is unable to attend. He has been to a function this afternoon and is too drunk to even walk."

Well, we all knew that this particular politician had a bit of a drink problem, since that was always being talked about in the media. But no wonder it was so well-known if this was how his minions reported on his behaviour! Could this even be an

330

opportunity for me, I wondered; you know, a bit of training for his staff in 'reputation management'?

"But anyway," they went onto explain, "Mrs XX has offered to turn up instead and is now on her way. But she will be about 20 minutes late."

"Okay, thank you," said Franz, beckoning the doorman over to attend to the bodyguards' car and take them inside. Meanwhile, I headed upstairs to tell the waiting audience and musicians there would be a delay while we waited for Mrs XX to arrive, and, since everyone was tucking into the champagne and nibbles, no-one batted an eyelid. In the end, it was probably a good thing she turned up instead of him; the journalists were happy to talk to her as they didn't often get the chance, and she was very nice and 'normal'. Plus, I fell in love with the violinist. Well, I didn't quite fall in love with him, but there is something about a man being up on a stage and 'commanding the audience' that gets me every time. Plus, the food – as we now knew was the norm at this hotel – was fantastic. The best bit of all though was that the following morning the reviews were gushing and, as I headed off to my weekly meeting with Franz later that week, I felt sure he would be very happy with the outcome.

Unfortunately, in the days between the concert and our meeting, various new things had come to light at the hotel, which meant he was in a very bad mood. And Franz, when he was in a bad mood, wasn't very easy to deal with. The main problem became clear as soon as I sat down.

"I know I have only been here a short time, and maybe I am wrong, but I think that for now I would like you to concentrate on what is going on inside the hotel, rather than telling the world outside what we are up to." He was sitting up in his chair looking menacing.

I just sat, waiting for him to go on.

"What I want you to do is to arrange for some of your friends to visit the hotel on a regular and 'incognito' basis and see what the staff are up to, report back to you, and then you report back to me. Can you do that? Do you have enough friends?"

Bloody rude.

331

Basically, when the Maltese bought the hotel, they bought all the staff that went with it too and Franz very quickly found out that an awful lot of them were 'on the take'. Unfortunately, I wasn't that surprised, since stealing from your employer was the norm at that time. Consider that one of the most popular Czech sayings of communist times translates as, 'If you don't steal from the state, you're stealing from your family,' and you will understand better why this was and why most Czechs, especially the older ones, saw nothing much wrong with it.

I had had some experience of this myself when I was working for Clive and found out that my cleaner was stealing from me; a bottle of perfume, half a box of 200 cigarettes, even, once, one of my best dresses! I had laid a kind of trap for her when I realised what was happening and she, sadly, fell straight into it. When challenged, though, she responded that she had, indeed, been taking things, but she showed no feeling of guilt or the need to apologise, since, she said, "she [i.e. me] can afford it!"

Anyway, back at the hotel, I had to agree I would gather some people together to do a bit of spying, as requested. What the client wanted, the client got, and all that. And, since my ladies were a bit against it, as this kind of spying smacked of the old regime, some of my friends agreed to do the occasional 'mystery shopping trips', since it meant they could hang around the bar and get all their drinks reimbursed afterwards and/ or get free membership in the gym, and so on. Sadly, it was soon clear that pretty much everyone was up to no good, as Franz had expected.

The worst part of that whole story, though, was that when I asked Franz why he hadn't sacked the barman, the waiter, or whoever the latest one to be caught out was, Franz's response was, "If I sack everyone that is stealing in this hotel, I'll be the only person working here! I can only do it stage by stage." Such was the life of a hotel manager in those days.

The other thing that had got him cross though, and which then got me cross too, was the press coverage we had received from the concert.

"I thought it was very good," I said, starting to bristle at the pissed-off look Franz had on his face, "Particularly when you think about the rubbish they were writing after the press conference. Most of the main papers and magazines covered it and there was no mention of Libya or Colonel Gaddafi."

"But I'm not happy about it," he responded, going a bit red in the face at my arguing with him.

"Okay, so can you let me know which bits you're not happy about so we know what to aim for in the future?"

"That's easy," he said. "From now on I want all the coverage that we get to include a photo of me, and to quote 'me', not one of the Maltese. And if you can't get a photo then I want an interview at the very least. I don't want pictures of the hotel or talk about the head office. If you get me that, I will be happy."

Another lesson learned, and who would have thought? I always thought that the purpose of PR was to promote the company with a view to building its brand and increasing sales. For the future, I made a mental note, I must always ask the clients in advance what they will regard to be a successful campaign before we even start. It may not be what we expect!

"I don't think I have ever had a 'gay moment' before, but watching this lot, I could almost be persuaded."

Bringing out my 'Crisis Queen' Hat

A VERY COLD FEBRUARY turned into an even colder and snowier March, which meant that, most days, once the work was done, we all headed home to hibernate. This was especially true in my case, since it was usually about 8.00 pm before I had finished and, after training at the crack of dawn, I had had enough by then. As ever, I had my hands full with various different projects, but what was taking up most of my time just then was the delayed launch of Hooch on the Czech market for Bass.

For various reasons, the launch had been pushed back from the originally planned date before Christmas until the end of February, and that meant that, with our hotel now open, we could suggest using the big conference room there, since it was pretty much ideal for what we had planned. This was, of course, a double whammy, since we got the room for free, which made Bass very happy, and the hotel boys were able to host a high-profile event full of lots of good people and journalists, without even lifting a finger.

To kick off the launch activities, we organised a Hooch-themed event to which as many pub and restaurant owners as we could track down had been invited to try what was, essentially, fizzy lemonade with about 20% alcohol. The room was decked out with yellow and black bunting and lighting, the tables were full of branded glasses and bottles of Hooch, we had waiters in yellow and gold outfits handing out a variety of colour-themed snacks, and then a small stage at the end of the room for the main presentation. The highlight though, at least for us ladies, was the group of small podiums we had scattered about the room, on each of which would be a yellow-painted male dancer who would be gyrating to the disco music that would be playing that evening. The dancers had originally been Maurice's idea, but I think he had imagined that we would have nubile young ladies dressed in skimpy yellow bikinis, or similar. In fact, once we started hunting about for dancers to hire, it was difficult to find girls at all and eventually, we hit on a group of

335

Angolan boys who could dance amazingly. The worst bit of course was that we had to do the necessary painting of the dancers before the event, which required them to stand very still dressed in just a thong, while we rubbed them all over with yellow paint. It was a drag, but someone had to do it. Clearly it was worthwhile though, as once they all began dancing, even the macho Maurice was mesmerised, at one point turning to me and saying, "I don't think I have ever had a 'gay moment' before, but watching this lot, I could almost be persuaded."

Needless to say there were a lot of very drunk people flopping about at the end of the evening as the innocent-looking Hooch packed a huge punch. So much so, that it soon became the subject of a media campaign to get it banned due to so many people buying it for their kids, not realising how alcoholic it was. Up until that point, I had always felt that we had more of an administrative role with Bass than anything strictly to do with marketing, since Maurice always had a concise plan for each activity and he had so much experience that any additional creativeness always came from him. But once the 'shit hit the fan' with Hooch, the launch plan changed completely and, with all the negative media attention it was getting, I was able to whip out my crisis management queen hat and go into battle, yet again. The difference, though, with the Hooch situation, as compared to the hotel, was that, in the end, it wasn't actually a crisis. You know the old saying, 'There is no such thing as negative publicity'? Well, with the papers full of talk about the excessively high alcohol rating of Hooch, the sales were going up and up. This proved my theory that the Czechs, being mostly alcoholics anyway, thought that giving their kids Hooch was an easier way to get them started on boozing than beer. That is probably not a politically correct comment to make, hence why I'm only saying it out loud now!

The Hooch event was followed by the opening of Stewart Morris's residential building, which was a success, but nothing very exciting to write home about, particularly as, by the time we formally 'cut the ribbon' and opened the doors, all the apartments had already been sold. They were probably the first reconstructed apartments in Prague that were put up for sale, as opposed to being rented, and they had all been sold 'off-plan', something I had never heard of before, and which, in case you don't know, means being sold based on the planned design and specs before a brick has even been laid. On that basis, the opening event was a bit pointless, but a good PR stunt for Stewart, nonetheless. This would be the last project we would work on for him, although I didn't know it at the time. What I did know, though, was that Charles, the investor, was unlikely to come to Prague again and I pondered, on that basis, the idea of poking him in the eye with a sharp stick, but decided it wasn't worth it. Probably a good thing.

By the time all of that was over, I was finally starting to think that I was no longer a fraud when it came to the PR and marketing game. If I compared myself to the very few other similar people around town, I had way more experience on the Czech market than anyone else, and it was clear that companies were happy to pay for my knowledge of doing business in such a tricky market. I also realised that, as long as either work or home was going well, I could be quite happy, although, of course, it would be nice to be happy with both. And without all of the travelling to Sweden, not only was I less tired, but I had so much more time to enjoy my friends. I had missed out on so many parties and activities with the old gang by being gone half of the time and, as the winter started to turn into spring, I began to enjoy living it up a bit at the weekends again, which meant long nights in Radost or Lávka, and even longer brunches in Zátiši. Life without Lennart was not, after all, such a terrible thing.

I also realised how much I had missed Katy, since she never had that much time to meet, especially during the week, and soon we were back to our regular weekend coffees and dinners, plus I had only spoken to Rhys a few times on the phone and had not had the chance to actually go and see him in Warsaw. I made a mental note to myself that I would make a trip there as soon as the weather was properly into summer. And then I couldn't remember when I had last been down to see Gary, who had now opened his own bar,

337

O'Boy's, and was fast becoming the richest man in Prague, nor had I seen much of Nenad in his new and bigger restaurant. All of that I planned to change.

Look out! Here Come the Stags!

WHILE MOLLY MALONE'S and The James Joyce held special places in our hearts, having been the first decent pubs to open in Prague and, as such, turning into our main meeting points, the influx of the Irish into Prague, generally, meant that more and more similar pubs were opening up all across town. However, there was another influx that was driving new bars and restaurants to open, and that was the infamous groups of 'stagnighters' that gradually started to see Prague as the place to go to for, as they would say, very cheap beer and very cheap women.

Gary was one of the smartest guys in town, even though a lot of the snooty accountants and lawyers looked down their noses at him due to his being a bit of a rough diamond, rather than your average British public-school boy. He was, though, the first to spot the opportunity that the stag-nighters would offer. As soon as he could find a suitable place, he'd opened O'Che's, with the aim of offering the huge groups of British 'stags' arriving every weekend everything they could want. Opening directly onto the cobbled street outside, the pub was quite small, with a bar running the length of the wall opposite the entrance and a few tables and chairs spread randomly around the rest of the space. During the daytime there were TV screens at either end of the bar showing various different sports, since it was now possible for bars with a special license to get some matches via satellite, while at night, especially on the weekend, the tables were pushed together and various 'shows' were put on. I'm sure I don't need to explain more here, I'll just let you read between the lines….

It was a complete coincidence that O'Che's was just a few metres away from The James Joyce, and just down the street from Zátiši, and there were many evenings when some of the old gang would do a bit of a tour from The Joyce, through O'Che's, and then up to Zátiši, usually stopping to exchange words with the policeman that spent most evenings parading up and down outside the entrance to the bar. I was always shocked at how unbelievably scruffy he was, even though a lot of the police were in those days. This one, though, was exceptional, with greasy ginger hair and a long ginger beard, very bad teeth and a uniform that had seen many better days and was way too big for him. He could often be seen directing people that were walking along the street to the bar, and this was a popular tourist route so there were a lot, or finding places for customers to park if they turned up in a car. Then I noticed one evening that he was taking tips from everyone and mentioned it to Gary, as, even in the Czech Republic, that seemed a bit off.

"But he's not a real policeman, darling," he responded. "He's just a drunken old bum. The regular police know about him and let him do his stuff as he's pretty much harmless. He helps me by bringing people in here and breaking up any fights that kick off."

Gary also employed a full-time stripper, which was fairly unusual, and he paid her a relatively large salary. His view was that if he wanted to make sure that all the stag-nighters went to his bar rather than anyone else's, he needed to have one of the best strippers in town available 'on tap', so to speak.

"Most strippers are unreliable. I need to know she is going to turn up and not take a better offer. And the better she is, the more the other bars will try to persuade her to go to work with them," he explained.

Adela, the stripper he ended up employing, was very pretty, but, during the day, when she worked behind the bar and was dressed in jeans and a sweater, you would never guess that she would turn into the sex goddess that the stag-nighters saw from late evening onwards.

Adela was very professional and took her job seriously enough that, even if Gary wasn't around, she would make sure the 'show went on', irrespective of what else was happening, which was often a lot. I remember one particularly hilarious evening when the music system had broken down and Adela was stressed that she wouldn't be able to do her show without music to dance to and was flapping about wondering what she could do as it was such a busy night.

It just so happened that earlier that evening there had been an event at the British Embassy, and they had brought a Scottish piper over from the UK to play the bagpipes. Once he had done his stuff there, he had headed down to O'Che's for a drink, before returning to his hotel nearby. Adela, seeing a solution, had gone over to him, and asked if he knew how to play whatever her favourite songs were at that time and, when he confirmed that he could, she quickly got up on the table, the bagpipes started, and off she went with her usual stripping routine. I'm not sure what was funnier, the bagpiper playing the music (and managing to keep a straight face), Adela trying to look sensual as she pranced around to the bagpipes' droning, or the look on the stagnighters' faces as they watched what they thought was her normal routine. *Fantastic.*

I got into the habit of heading down to O'Che's most workday evenings. I would sit in the corner, often with Gary, and mull over ideas for the bar's promotion over a glass of wine, before meeting up with one or other of the old gang, or just heading straight home. Ewan would usually make an appearance at about the same time, often with Paul in tow, and while Jeremy, Jonathan and Simon were less likely to appear until much later in the evening, I could catch up on what they were all doing, as Ewan had his finger on the pulse of just about every bit of gossip that was available.

During the early years in Prague, things changed so fast it was difficult to keep up with who was doing what, who had left, who had arrived, what new shops and restaurants had opened, and so on. But sadly, as things became more developed, many of the old timers started to move on to pastures new, the perception being that once their respective companies were up and running and local employees had been installed and trained, the expats were no longer needed. That, however, was later proved to be a foolish decision, but, by then, it was too late to get the people back.

On the other hand, with all the new businesses opening up, there were still a huge number of foreigners arriving, but majority of the long-standing expats that were guaranteed to still be around were those of us that had turned up to do one job, 'spotted an opportunity', and then gone on to do our own thing; and that own thing had somehow turned into a success. For some/ many, though,

341

'their own thing' often didn't work out, and it was not long before Ewan decided to call it quits on his Eagle Property Services company.

I knew that something was up when he invited me to go for a drink in The Joyce early one evening.

"Just the two of us," he had said. And then, once we had our drinks and sat ourselves down in the corner, he hit me with the news. "I know you won't be surprised to hear that I have had enough of Eagle," he said.

I shook my head, giving him a supportive sort of smile.

"But you *may* be surprised to know that I have decided to go back to the UK."

I went pale. "What do you mean? For a holiday?"

"No. For good. You know, I have always wanted to try my hand at being a stand-up comedian."

"Well, yes," I interrupted him. "You practice it all day long!"

"Yes, well, I think that if I don't do it now, I never will. I'm going to go back and give it a shot."

I was so upset, yet another of my favourite people leaving town. But I could see that there was nothing I could say or do that would change his mind.

"When will you go? How long do we have?" I asked him, feeling as if I might cry.

"Well, soon. But we'll still see each other. Just in the UK, not Prague."

Oh God.

With yet another one of my closest friends leaving, it brought home to me just what a huge thing it had been to strike out on my own and how little I had understood the consequences of making such a big move. I suppose I never considered that my company would prove to be successful, and the implications for me if that was the case. I had only really thought that it *wouldn't be,* and assumed that once it failed, I would head back to the UK myself and go back to some sort of corporate life. I could see, now, that that was unlikely to happen for a very long time. And what a strange feeling that was.

342

What I and the rest of the 'old timers' also realised was that, as things started to become a little bit more 'normal' in the Czech Republic, so the type of people that were arriving and taking up jobs would change. The big question for all of us, then, was whether we wanted to change too.

"Hmm, that's weird.
My dad's family were in Auschwitz."

Heading Towards Another Chapter

THE WORDS 'PRAGUE SPRING' are very important in the Czech Republic. They refer to the period when communism was starting to lose its grip on Czechoslovakia back in 1968, and freedom was becoming more available to its citizens. That is, until everything was crushed by the Warsaw Pact armies arriving in the August of that year. 'Prague Spring' also refers to the world-famous classical music festival which is held at the beginning of May each year, and which fills the city with musicians, and the people wanting to watch them, in all the different concert halls for nearly a month. In the early days, when good hotels were few and far between, anyone planning to visit at that time would be advised to book somewhere to stay at least a year in advance, if they were to be sure of finding somewhere, as it was that popular.

The words 'Prague Spring' to us expats, though, were much more general, since the arrival of spring in Prague usually changed our lives from near hibernation, depression, and full-on work during the winter, to something more relaxed. I always struggled in the cold and by the end of each winter, I always had a bit of a discussion with myself as to whether I really could continue to live in the Czech Republic, despite everything I have said before. But then the spring arrived, and it always felt like a new start. That particular year, while still putting in long hours at the office, heading to the gym early in the morning, and often O'Che's in the evening, I was enjoying tennis training with Václav outside of the 'bubble', and late nights watching the world go by from the new bars and clubs that were popping up on a regular basis. As usual, I was starting to enjoy living in Prague as I went into the summer of my fourth year.

As the weather warmed up, I even pondered, occasionally, whether I was ready to kick-start my love life again, after four months or so apart from Lennart and not a peep from him all that time. I did hear from Bjørn when he passed through Prague that Lennart was living a life very similar to mine, insofar as he was throwing himself, sometimes literally, into playing as much as

345

possible, and there was no sign of any girlfriend as far as he was aware.

Having said that, I had sort of come out of my nun-like existence once all our big events were out of the way. There were a few evenings when I crossed paths with Jeremy at Radost, or some other club and, after chatting to him for hours, something we never used to do too much of in our 'earlier days', I would wonder whether we should consider heading off home together again. But it never quite worked out, and that was probably a good thing, since, mostly, I was enjoying having lots of male friends around me, without any sort of complication.

Despite all the positivity of the springtime, though, I was getting sadder by the minute as I counted down the days until Ewan would leave. As you know, it took me a long time to get over Rhys going and, since then, various other friends had upped and left, and each time I felt like they were disappearing forever. Maybe there's a part of me that finds people leaving a difficult thing to cope with anyway, and perhaps that has to do with having had a lot of people die on me in my earlier years; first my dad, then my brother, and so on. Whatever the reason, the end result is that I'm not very good at actually saying goodbye and am even worse at keeping in touch once someone has gone. So Ewan leaving, I knew, was going to be a difficult one for me.

The night before his final departure date, there was a drinks reception at the British Embassy. This was completely unrelated to Ewan, but since it was the first outdoor event of the season, everyone was planning on attending, with the general idea being that afterwards us 'hardcore' Ewan friends would continue to rampage through the city until the early hours.

For the evening, and in Ewan's honour, I had put on the hugely expensive Harrods pink dress I had bought for Jeremy's summer party the previous summer. I had only worn it once since then, and that was when I had gone to a very grand lunch at a restaurant on the main Wenceslas Square and, as I had walked up the road towards it, Ewan had jumped out at me from nowhere, grabbed the rings at the top of the zips on both the front and back of the dress and then whipped them both down. Luckily, the dress fit well enough that it didn't completely fall off me, although, it being Prague, no-one would probably have blinked an eye anyway. That said, it kind of put me off wearing it again, until now. Unfortunately, the other problem with the dress was that the sandals that went with it had low stiletto heels and, not only did they cripple my feet, they also tended to get stuck in the grass if we were going to be walking about on a lawn, which was the case at the embassy.

The embassy's garden is so big that it's possible to attend one of their events and not realise that someone else you know is also there. That evening, I decided I would plant myself right by the entrance, and then I would be sure to see everyone as they arrived. Being the embassy, too, it meant everyone turned up more or less on the dot of 6.00 pm, partly so as not to offend the ambassador, but also to make sure they guzzled as many of the special gin and tonics that these events were known for as possible before they ran out. Within half an hour or so, therefore, there was a huge group of us standing there, with Ewan right in the centre of it all. Even the ambassador came over to wish him well; they hadn't always seen eye to eye, Ewan having once been found behind one of the hedges with a member of the embassy staff, doing something 'un-diplomatic', but still, he was a long-term member of the British community, so deserved a proper farewell.

By 8.00 pm, when we were all due to be slung out, there must have been about 40 people gathered and ready to head off into town to continue their farewells. Ewan led the way as we walked back into the embassy reception area and started to file down the stairs. Everyone, that is, except me. Indeed, by this time, I could barely walk in my shoes and was pondering whether I should try to grab a cab and meet everyone at the first port of call, The Joyce.

"I'll see you downstairs," I shouted down to Ewan from the top of the stairs, and then hobbled towards the lift, where the doors were just closing. Just as I got there, the doors opened again.

"Are you going down?" said the man standing there. He was dressed in a very smart navy suit and a white shirt and had black curly hair and the bluest eyes that twinkled in that slightly naughty way us women can rarely resist. His comment made me giggle.

"I am indeed," I said and stepped in.

"Have you been at the party?" he asked, which made me wonder if he was a bit nervous, since it was unlikely I had been anywhere else, unless he thought I was an over-dressed maid or something.

"Yes."

"I never saw you," he responded. "Let me give you my card."

Of course, it was better to have a card than a name, as was standard in Prague. I glanced at it. "Jan Mandanovič, Advokat," I read out loud. "That sounds like a Yugoslavian name." I knew that because my mum always had a thing about Yugoslavian men (and some of the old tennis players, in particular, all of who we used to refer to as 'something-or-other-vitch').

"You're clever. My grandfather was a Serb. But I was born and brought up in the Czech Republic. My mother is a Czech Jew. You may have heard of her as she is one of the few remaining Holocaust survivors."

"Hmm, that's weird. My dad's family were in Auschwitz." I reckoned I'd never said that to someone as a 'pick-up line' before.

Then the lift stopped at the ground floor and we kind of stared at each other.

"Well," he said. "It was nice meeting you. I hope we can see each other again one day."

"Me too," I echoed.

I walked outside. Ewan was pacing about waiting for me as the crowd had already started heading off towards The Joyce.

"Come on!" he said. "Get a move on."

"I'm sorry, Ewan. Do you mind if I don't come? I hate goodbyes, as you know."

"I don't mind," he said, smiling. He knew me well. "It won't be goodbye anyway, as you well know. But you could meet the man of your dreams tonight as there are going to be so many new people out and about."

"I think I just did," I responded.

348

THE END

TO BE CONTINUED

350

About the Author

THE REAL Jo is not so different from the one in the book, although she is now a lot older and, in some respects, wiser. While she no longer employs anyone, Jo still owns the agency JWA, which nowadays exists as a vehicle for various projects, including some marketing consultancy, a few investments, and various different sports projects, one or other of which may yet make her a very rich old lady.

When she is not working or travelling between her homes in Prague and Marbella, Jo can mostly be found on the tennis court, often competing in the 'seniors' league' where, she says, she is still able to give the little old ladies a good hiding. And when she is not doing *that*, she is usually mulling over ideas for her next books – one of which she aims to make into a 'steamy blockbuster'.

You can contact Jo on Jo@jwa.cz

Acknowledgements

THIS BOOK IS DEDICATED to the real Simon, Ewan, Jonathan and Jeremy, as, had it not been for them, I really wouldn't have stayed in Prague for much longer than my initial six months. And, of course, the real Uncle Clive, who, if he had been a normal boss, would have just ignored my idea of going it alone and sent me back to London to continue with a career that would have bored me to death. I'm sure you all know who you are!

More from Jo Weaver

www.jwapress.com

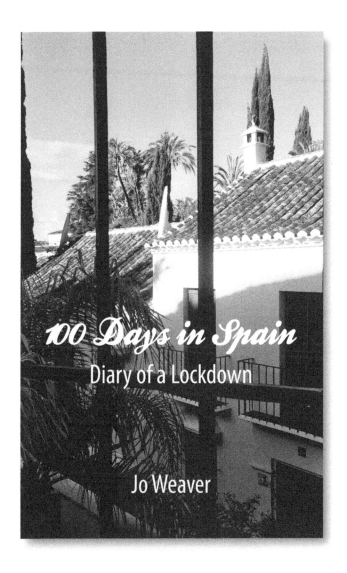

Book designed by

Made in United States
North Haven, CT
01 September 2024

56814740R00214